Virginia Woolf
Art, Education, and Internationalism

Virginia Woolf
Art, Education, and Internationalism

Edited by Diana Royer and Madelyn Detloff

Every effort has been made to trace all copyright-holders, but if any have been inadvertently overlooked, the publisher will be pleased to make the necessary arrangement at the first opportunity.

Copyright 2008 by Clemson University
ISBN 978-0-9796066-4-9

Published by Clemson University Press in Clemson, South Carolina

Editorial Assistants: Candace Wiley, Ember Smith, and Bridget Jeffs

To order copies, please visit the Clemson University Press website: www.clemson.edu/press.

Cover design by Suzanne Bellamy and Charis Chapman

Frontispiece artwork by Mihir Devare, adapted for conference program by Liz Raniere Zimmerman

Contents

Diana Royer and Madelyn Detloff • *Introduction* vi
List of Abbreviations x

Diana L. Swanson • *Imperialism and Anti-Imperialism: Leonard Woolf, M. W. Swanson, and the Role of Civil Bureaucracy* 1
Patricia Laurence • *Hours in a Chinese Library: Re-Reading Virginia Woolf, Bloomsbury, and Modernism* 8
Tracy Savoie • *Caged Tiger: Louis as Colonial Subject in Virginia Woolf's* The Waves 16
Natasha Allen • *The Critical Silence of the Other: Critique of Fascism in Virginia Woolf's* The Waves 21
Judith Allen • *Conversation as Instigation: Virginia Woolf's "Thoughts on Peace in an Air Raid"* 25
Erika Yoshida • *"The Leaning Tower": Woolf's Pedagogical Goal of the Lecture to the W.E.A. Under the Threat of the War* 33
Kimberly Engdahl Coates • *Regarding Violence: Virginia Woolf's* Three Guineas *and Contemporary Feminist Responses to War* 40
Ben O'Dell • *The Function of Filth: Waste Imagery and Cultural Identity in* Between the Acts 46
Sara Gerend • *Ghosts of Empire in Virginia Woolf's* To the Lighthouse *and Elizabeth Bowen's* The Last September 51
Richard Zumkhawala-Cook • *Tae the Lichthoose: Woolf's Scotland and the Problem of the Local* 57
Charles Andrews • *Under the Volute:* Jacob's Room, *Pacifism, and the Church of England* 64
Diane F. Gillespie • *Virginia Woolf's "Ghosts": Books, Martyrs, and Metaphors* 70
Xiaoqin Cao • *The Reception of Virginia Woolf in China* 82
Andrea Reyes • *On Patriotism and Angels: Virginia Woolf and Rosario Castellanos* 85
Julie L. Smith-Hubbard • *Falling Into the Stream: From Virginia Woolf's* The Waves *to Clarice Lispector's* Living Waters 92
Mónica G. Ayuso • *Virginia Woolf and Maria Luisa Bombal* 99
Marilyn Schwinn Smith • *A Woolfian Reversal: The Dalloway Mystique in Monica Ali's* Brick Lane 104
Lisa L. Coleman • *Roots, Woolf, and an Ethics of Desire* 110
Erica Delsandro • *Flights of Imagination: Aerial Views, Narrative Perspectives, and Global Perceptions* 117
Elisa Kay Sparks • *Bloomsbury in Bloom: Virginia Woolf and the History of British Gardens* 125
Suzanne Bellamy • *Textual Archaeology and the Death of the Writer* 131
Jane de Gay • *Virginia Woolf, Metamorphoses, and Flights from Nation* 139

Notes on Contributors 147

Introduction

by Diana Royer and Madelyn Detloff

The Seventeenth Annual Conference on Virginia Woolf focused on Art, Education, and Internationalism. One may wonder why we chose such a focus for a conference to be held in a small town in Southwest Ohio, an area of the U.S. where border crossing is far more likely to signify taking a 15 minute drive into rural Indiana or a 30 minute drive across the Ohio River into Kentucky. For starters, Miami University, the host of the conference, has, by virtue of its name, a special responsibility to recognize the internationalism implicit in the founding of such institutions on soil once occupied by Native Americans.[1] Moreover, in a small Midwestern town (where international travel is not particularly accessible to the residents unaffiliated with the university) art and education, along with military service, are the main vehicles for developing an understanding and appreciation of cultures beyond the U.S. For this reason, it behooves us, as Woolf so eloquently argued in *Three Guineas*, to assess the ideological messages that we instill in our communities through education, and to cultivate our freedom of thought through the arts. This habit of "intellectual liberty," according to Woolf, is our best defense against the destructive militarism that troubled her in the early 20th century, and that troubles many of us in the early 21st (*TG* 90).

Our goal in putting together the conference and the selected papers has been to honor Woolf's call to understand and respect the roles of Art, Education, and Internationalism in our lives. The conference provided the occasion for wide-ranging discussions of Woolf's work, life, and influence on generations to come. Art was a constant presence in Woolf's life, from the family legacy of Julia Cameron's photography, to Vanessa Bell's and Duncan Grant's painting, Roger Fry's criticism, the Omega Workshop, the Hogarth Press, and, of course, Woolf's own fiction. While *Three Guineas* and *A Room of One's Own* are probably Woolf's most famous discussions of education and systematic injustice, as many of the conference presenters noted, Woolf investigated the social ramifications of educational disparity throughout her career in a variety of genres. Woolf's life and work were permeated with hopes for international cooperation (especially through the League of Nations), and concerns about the terrible legacy of colonialism and the contemporary threat of fascism. These three themes—Art, Education, and Internationalism—generated myriad sub-themes, and thus brought a rich array of presentations to the conference.

We begin the selected papers with an essay by Diana L. Swanson on the global political vision of Leonard Woolf. Swanson's presentation also served as a local tribute to a beloved faculty member here at Miami University, Diana's father, Maynard W. (Bill) Swanson. Mary Frederickson, a professor in the History Department at Miami, introduced the panel with an eloquent description of her late colleague as "a pioneering researcher in South African urban and environmental history, within an international literary, political and ecological context. Bill Swanson was among the first Africanists to deconstruct official South African discourse to reveal the European biases that camouflaged power relationships. His unique contribution involved demonstrating the ways that science was put to work in the service of apartheid." In her essay, Swanson complicates Leonard Woolf's anti-imperialism through the lens of her father's scholarship on British bureaucratic practices in its African colonies. Leonard Woolf, she argues, identified "economic imperialism, the profit motive, and the use of the state for the economic advantage of a wealthy and politically powerful few" as the primary motivators of colonialism. To this list of powerful factors, Maynard W. Swanson adds "racist ideologies and the operations of the civil bureaucracy of colonial administrations." These important additions remind us that while Leonard Woolf's anti-imperialist thought was important and powerful, his own social location, as a British man who began his career in the Ceylon Civil Service, should be taken into consideration when contemplating the potential blind spots of his vision.

Internationalism is often a euphemism for colonial or neo-colonial ideology, especially when the flow of discourse is imagined as unidirectional (when the "West" imagines the "East" in what Edward Said calls "orientalism," for example.) It was refreshing, therefore, to hear plenary speaker Pat Laurence recount details of her meticulous study of the work of Chinese writer Ling Shuhua, a member of the Crescent Moon Group that had close connections to Bloomsbury. Laurence gives us insight into the paradigm-shifting effects of reading Woolf, Bloomsbury, and modernism from a non-European and non-Eurocentric perspective.

Tracy Savoie investigates Woolf's representation of colonial "mimicry" through the character of Louis in *The Waves*. Although Louis attempts to overcome his childhood feelings of un-belonging through economic success in adulthood, Savoie argues that his imperialist assimilation never quite succeeds. Savoie thus concludes that "Louis' continued need to mimic his colonizers even after his success at imperial commerce may well be Woolf's commentary on the inevitable failure of trying to secure one's freedom and power through the exploitation of others." Analyzing Louis's counterpart, Rhoda, Natasha Allen focuses on *The Waves* as a critique of "domestic fascism." "Rhoda's inability to adapt within the culture," Allen argues, "suggests both domestic fascism's silencing of heteroglossia and foreign imperialism's failure with regards to the colonized Other."

Judith Allen, Erika Yoshida, and Kimberly Enghdahl Coates investigate the impact of Woolf's more overt statements linking fascism and patriarchy to war. Allen analyzes the performative aspects of Woolf's essays, focusing in particular on "Thoughts on Peace in an Air Raid" in its response to and interrogation of fascism, thereby also addressing the complex relationship between the genre of the essay and the political force of fascism. Yoshida examines the pedagogical goal of Woolf's lecture (her last) to the Workers' Educational Association in Brighton on April 27, 1940, which was later published as "The Leaning Tower." Collating Woolf's speech drafts with the published essay, Yoshida explicates Woolf's strategies for reaching her working-class audience. Taking Woolf herself as an influence, Kimberly Engdahl Coates argues that contemporary feminist responses to war—by such writers as Judith Butler, Joan Didion, and Arundhati Roy—return us to *Three Guineas* as a way to recognize our failure of imagination. Woolf, Engdahl Coates argues, prompts us to behold violence in order to imagine a different future.

First looking at this pacifist alternative Woolf proposed in *Three Guineas*, Ben O'Dell turns to *Between the Acts* to explore how Woolf uses waste imagery to challenge notions of national unity. He argues that Woolf's allusions to filth (through the image of the cesspool) evoke feelings of political and bodily abjection that haunt militaristic cultures despite their efforts to cover over their "waste" of lives, resources, and international goodwill. Domestic space is analyzed differently by Sara Gerend, whose comparative reading of *To The Lighthouse* and Elizabeth Bowen's *The Last September* reveals that while the site of a country house might seem almost to eclipse World War I and the Irish rebellion, respectively, these sites are haunted not only by those who have died, but also by the altered political reality of the postwar periods. *To The Lighthouse*'s foreign setting is the focus of Richard Zumkhawala-Cook's explanation of how Woolf's elision of Scottish referents is designed to undermine the stability of nationhood, foregoing national identification for a solidarity with material conditions of gender and labor, situated primarily in the character of the Scottish housemaid Mrs. McNab.

Charles Andrews reads Woolf's appreciation for and critique of Englishness through the stable and sturdy image of St. Paul's Cathedral, a central image in *Jacob's Room*. St. Paul's, for Andrews, represents a particularly Anglican sensibility, and therefore "is simultaneously imposing and comforting, a sign of the tyrannical Church and a reassurance of Englishness." Turning to a different aspect of religiosity, Diane F. Gillespie researches Woolf's knowledge of the histories of martyrdom, revealing she had no tolerance for dogmatists, self-defined martyrs, or those who enable them, and explaining how *Three Guineas* can be read as an "anti-martyrology."

Several of the conference presentations focused on Woolf's reception outside of Europe and North America. Xiaoqin Cao offers a holistic review of Woolf studies in contemporary China, where scholars and readers have been interested in Woolf's work since the early 1930's. Suzanne Bellamy generously offered more insights from her archival work on Nuri Mass's thesis on Woolf, considering how news of Woolf's suicide affected Mass's reading of *Between the Acts*. A cluster of scholars presented groundbreaking papers on Woolf's influence on Latin American writers. Andrea Reyes traces the shared outlook of Woolf and Rosario Castellanos, the Mexican writer who shares Woolf's portrayal of social contradictions and defiance of patriotism and class privilege. Julie Smith-Hubbard delineates the influence of Woolf's *The Waves* on Clarice Lispector's *ecriture feminine* (women's writing) in her novel *Agua Viva* (*The Stream of Life* or *Living Waters*). Concentrating on the early fiction of María Luisa Bombal, Mónica Ayuso traces the aesthetic and thematic similarities of Bombal's work to Woolf's. Returning to post-imperial England, Marilyn Schwinn Smith looks at the figure of Mr. Dalloway in Monica Ali's *Brick Lane*, set in London's East End Bangladeshi enclave.

Aesthetics and technique are taken up by several scholars. Lisa L. Coleman links Woolf's essay "The Patron and the Crocus" to *The Waves* and *Jacob's Room* to outline how Woolf encourages readers to recognize their aesthetically inspired sense of subjectivity and ethical desires. The altered perspective Woolf offers in her essay "Flying Over London" presents Erica Delsandro with the opportunity to note how Woolf promotes imagination as the means to counter patriarchy's imperialist gaze and to re-envison one's identity. Woolf's connection to gardens is the concern of Elisa Kay Sparks, who draws on her recently published *Bloomsbury's Gardens* to explain how the history of British gardens appears in Woolf's fiction. Plenary speaker Jane de Gay concentrates on how the trope of metamorphosis—in particular, metamorphoses by which humans transform into birds, animals, trees, and stones—is key in Woolf's rejection of nation and nationalism, her "embracing" of transnational cultures, and her exploration of the past.

Finally, we would like to acknowledge the limitations of this volume. It is simply impossible to convey a full sense of the warmth, community, and exhilarating expressions of "intellectual liberty" that we witnessed at the conference. That is why so many of us make the trek annually to attend the conference. We owe particular thanks to all of the participants at the conference, and want to make special mention of our honored guest, Cecil Woolf, whose graceful and witty tribute to his uncle, Leonard Woolf, moved many of us to tears. Of course, such a grand event as the conference would not have been possible without the tireless work of our volunteers and the Marcum Center staff, and we are eternally grateful to the "Woolf Pack" for being so splendid. So much of the conference experience is irreproducible, and this fact, along with the fine quality of all of the essays submitted for this volume, made our job of selecting the essays here extremely difficult. Ultimately, we defaulted to a preference for new voices, and representation from as wide a selection of scholars from around the world as possible. We know that the community of Woolf readers eagerly anticipates the Eighteenth Annual Conference on Virginia Woolf, to be held at the University of Denver in June 2008.

Lastly, we would like to express our deep appreciation to Wayne Chapman and his staff at Clemson University Digital Press for guiding us so expertly (and patiently!) through the editing and publication of this volume.

Notes

1. Miami University takes its name from the people now known as the Sovereign Miami Tribe of Oklahoma. The Miami people lived in the region now known as the Miami Valley until their relocation, first to Kansas in 1840 and then to Oklahoma in 1867. Miami University acknowledges its special relationship to the Miami people through the collaborative Myaamia Project, described at http://www.myaamiaproject.org.

Works Cited

The Myaamia Project. 2007. 28 Apr. 2008. <http://www.myaamiaproject.org/>.
Said, Edward. *Orientalism*. New York: Vintage, 1979.
Woolf, Virginia. *Three Guineas*. New York: Harcourt Brace and Company, 1938.

Virginia Woolf
Standard Abbreviations
(as established by *The Woolf Studies Annual*)

AHH	*A Haunted House*
AROO	*A Room of One's Own*
BP	*Books and Portraits*
BTA	*Between the Acts*
CDB	*The Captain's Death Bed and Other Essays*
CE	*Collected Essays* (ed. Leonard Woolf, 4 vols.: *CE1, CE2, CE3, CE4*)
CR1	*The Common Reader*
CR2	*The Common Reader, Second Series*
CSF	*The Complete Shorter Fiction* (ed. Susan Dick)
D	*The Diary of Virginia Woolf* (5 vols.: *D1, D2, D3, D4, D5*)
DM	*The Death of the Moth and Other Essays*
E	*The Essays of Virginia Woolf* (ed. Andrew McNeillie, 6 vols.: *E1, E2, E3, E4, E5, E6*)
F	*Flush*
FR	*Freshwater*
GR	*Granite and Rainbow: Essays*
HPGN	*Hyde Park Gate News* (ed. Gill Lowe)
JR	*Jacob's Room*
JRHD	*Jacob's Room: The Holograph Draft* (ed. Edward L. Bishop)
L	*The Letters of Virginia Woolf* (ed. Nigel Nicolson and Joanne Trautmann, 6 vols.: *L1, L2, L3, L4, L5, L6*)
M	*The Moment and Other Essays*
MEL	*Melymbrosia*
MOB	*Moments of Being*
MT	*Monday or Tuesday*
MD	*Mrs. Dalloway*
ND	*Night and Day*
O	*Orlando*
PA	*A Passionate Apprentice*
RF	*Roger Fry*
TG	*Three Guineas*
TTL	*To the Lighthouse*
TW	*The Waves*
TY	*The Years*
VO	*The Voyage Out*
WF	*Women and Fiction: The Manuscript Versions of* A Room of One's Own (ed. S. P. Rosenbaum)

Imperialism and Anti-Imperialism:
Leonard Woolf, M. W. Swanson, and the Role of Civil Bureaucracy

by Diana L. Swanson

My father gave me my first lessons—an "unpaid-for" education (*TG* 6)—about the realities of social injustice and institutionalized oppression through bringing the family with him on his research trips to South Africa and through explaining the apartheid system to me. I vividly remember the shock I felt when he told me that in South Africa 10% of the population owned 90% of the land and that this White 10% controlled the Bantu (Black African), Coloured (mixed race), and Indian 90%. I also remember passionately explaining this injustice to some of my third-grade classmates in the lunchroom. My father also talked about the campaigns and endeavors of Black South Africans as various as A. W. G. Champion and Nelson Mandela. I attribute to my father my own passion for justice, my anger at the domestic and international imperialism of my own country, and my fervent belief that we are responsible for one another and that democratic action can create change for the better. I trace back to my father my belief that scholarship and teaching matter because ideas matter to the way individuals, communities, and nations treat each other and because ideas matter to the quality of life we build together. The location of the 2007 Conference on Virginia Woolf offers the opportunity to return, in a more scholarly way, to these early lessons and see what light they can shed on the Woolfs', particularly Leonard's, understanding of imperialism. My late father, Maynard W. Swanson, was professor of African history at Miami University and this paper is one way I can honor the lessons he taught me. In this paper, I interrogate the nature of Leonard Woolf's anti-imperialism in light of my father's research on the ideology and the bureaucratic practices of British colonial administration, particularly with regard to racial policy.

Now I am going to turn from the daughter into the scholar; in the rest of the paper, I will stop talking about "my father" and refer to "Swanson."

Leonard Woolf's firsthand experience of imperialism was in the Ceylon Civil Service from 1904 to 1911. Later, Woolf also turned his scholarship and political thought toward Africa in such works as *Empire and Commerce in Africa* (1920) and *The League and Abyssinia* (1936). M. W. Swanson's work focuses on British colonies in southern Africa, specifically the Cape and Natal Colonies, as well as the development of racial policy once the colonies became the Union of South Africa. In this paper, I will focus on Woolf's *Empire and Commerce in Africa* and his comments on his experience in the Ceylon Civil Service in his autobiography *Growing* (1961). *Empire and Commerce* was written in the immediate aftermath of WWI and during the creation and beginning of the League of Nations. It was commissioned by Sidney Webb and the Fabian Society and intended to be informative and advisory to the Labour Party and to government and citizens generally. Swanson's research focuses primarily on the late 19th century through 1920, the time period that Woolf discusses in *Empire and Commerce*. He came to his subject through the study of British colonial history while pursuing a Ph.D. in history. He did his research in the U.S., England, and South Africa in the context of the African nationalist movements of the '50s and '60s and the domestic and international movements that targeted South Africa's apartheid regime in the '70s and '80s. He had the opportunity to meet Black, Indian, and White South Africans who were or had been involved in this complex history. Thus while his work was published in scholarly journals, it was written and read in the light of current events.[1]

The different historical contexts in which Woolf and Swanson worked shaped their perspectives and conclusions in significant ways. Woolf focused on the actions of the European powers in Africa and a significant part of his focus was on the forces that led to world war and how to prevent future war. Swanson focused not only on British initiatives and actions but also on the actions and aspirations of African and Indian people in southern Africa; thus his analysis includes the agency of the subjugated and had implications for contemporary Marxist versus liberal debates about the best way forward in Africa. What Woolf and Swanson had in common, however, was their allegiance to Enlightenment values of reason and disinterestedness and their suspicion of dogmatic ideologies.

Woolf and Swanson both see imperialist policies as motivated by economic interests and by ideologies. However, Woolf identifies the controlling ideology as the European belief that the primary role of government is to further commercial development and the material interests of the nation; the problem in Africa was what he called "economic imperialism." Swanson, on the other hand, argues that racist ideologies and anxieties played key roles in the development of laws and practices that exploited and segregated the indigenous African peoples. Swanson also makes a significant argument for the independent role of the civil bureaucracy itself in the development of racial policy in the British colonies. Does Swanson's argument that "official, governmental, and administrative classes generated more pressure than did business or commercial interests for systematic social controls" shed light on Woolf's experience as a colonial administrator in Sri Lanka[2] and on his subsequent political writings on imperialism (Swanson, "'Asiatic Menace'" 401)? How do we evaluate, for example, Woolf's use of the term "non-adult races" for Black African peoples and his proposal for European trusteeship over all of Africa (*Empire and Commerce*)? I ask these questions not to devalue Woolf's anti-imperialist convictions but to investigate the content and implications of Woolf's practical education in imperialism during his service in the British imperial bureaucracy and his subsequent anti-imperialism.

Woolf developed a theory of international relations and economics based on what we today would call social constructionism. He maintained that beliefs are the most important factor governing the behavior of individuals and nations. In the introductory chapter to *Empire and Commerce*, Woolf states that "man's past was caused by what men desired and believed: the future will be caused by what we desire and believe [. . .]. Policy is determined by our beliefs and our ideals: it represents our view of what we want the State to be, and what we want the State to do in the world of States. Thus the State is what we want it to be and believe it to be, and there is here no logic of facts, but a logic of beliefs and desires" (9). He goes on to assert that

> there is no statesman or writer in any European country to-day who would contest the political axiom that the power of the State can be and should be used upon the world outside the State for the economic purposes of the world within the State. It is almost impossible to visualize the total effect which the acceptance of this axiom in the last sixty years has had upon the world. It has turned whole nations into

armies, and industry and commerce into weapons of economic war. It has caused more bloodshed than ever religion or dynasties caused in an equal number of years, when gods and kings, rather than commerce, were the "greatest of political interests." It was the chief cause of the war which we have just been fighting [. . .]. It has proved infinitely stronger than the other two great currents in nineteenth-century history, democracy and nationalism, for everywhere in Europe[,] democratic have yielded to economic ideals, and nationalism, wherever it has appeared, has applied itself most violently to economic ends [. . .]. [It] has converted the whole of Africa and Asia into mere appendages of the European State, and the history of those two continents, the lives which men live in Nigeria or Abyssinia, in India and Siam and China, are largely determined by the conviction of Europeans that "commerce is the greatest of European political interests." (10)

In *Empire and Commerce*, Woolf details events, policy decisions, and financial statistics to show that this fundamental belief in economic imperialism shaped the behavior, opinions, and policies of European government officials, financiers, explorers, merchants, and farmers in Africa.

According to Woolf, the effects of imperialism on Europeans was bad and on Africans devastating. European treasure and lives were spent to produce profits for the few at the cost of the many. In British East Africa, for example, "a few hundred Englishmen, capitalists and planters, who directly exploit the territories by the purchase of land and mining rights and the flotation of joint-stock companies, have made—and sometimes lost—money. But trade, industry, and labour, generally, have reaped no advantages" (334). The native Africans were disenfranchised politically, robbed of their land, and forced into a kind of slave labor to support British farming, mining, and trade.

Swanson would agree with Woolf that the ideology of economic imperialism, the profit motive, and the use of the state for the economic advantage of a wealthy and politically powerful few were important causes of imperialism in Africa. However, Swanson would add at least two other factors as significant in the development of policies that exploited African peoples and created and maintained European dominance: racist ideologies and the operations of the civil bureaucracy of colonial administrations.

In "Urban Origins of Separate Development," Swanson points out that the first municipal charters in the British colonies of southern Africa "embodied democratic conceptions of society and popular government" and "their terms of application were universal," with the male adult franchise based on property, not color (33). However, "when increasing numbers of non-Europeans began to exercise the freedom of the towns and to demonstrate the egalitarian implications of the basic laws, neither colonists nor their governments were prepared to or wanted to accept these consequences" (33). As early as the 1820s in some areas and the 1840s in others, there was a "climate of increasing tension, colour consciousness, distrust and fear" (33). By the 1870s, in the growing city of Durban on the east coast of southern Africa, the "white rulers felt challenged to cope with the increasing numbers of strangers who seemed to threaten the standards and even the existence of civic life" (34). Thus, Swanson says, "between 1870 and colonial self-government in the 1890s, the conceptions of an 'Asiatic Menace' and the native 'Social Pest', added to longer-standing fears of native rebellion, took definitive shape in European minds and found expression in the beginnings of systematic policies—separation, locations, a pass system and other restrictions" (34). Before what Woolf says is the high point of economic imperialism, the 1890s through the teens, Europeans' perceptions of cultural differences and the supposed moral and intellectual inferiority of darker races were already putting in place systems of racial segregation, labour exploitation, expropriation of land to European ownership, and exclusion of non-Europeans from participation in governance. Belief in the supposed "natural" racial superiority of White Europeans was a major foundation stone of these policies. According to Swanson, by 1900 in Natal, "everywhere the notion of race as a politico-social, biological and psychological entity was being accorded the currency of scientific respectability" (38). The application of this notion in Natal, for example, "came to fruition in the work of a Durban merchant, scholar, and legislator, Maurice S. Evans. 'Is it possible', he asked, for a white race 'whose race aspiration is the utmost economic development of the country . . . to live with a black one, to whom the aspirations of the white do not appeal, and yet so adjust the life of each that both shall be content . . .?'" (38). Thus the ideology of White racial and cultural superiority meets the ideology of economic imperialism. What Swanson's research points out here is that the way in which economic imperialism was put into practice was significantly shaped by the racial ideology already in place. The proposal Maurice Evans offered was for the Whites to "so guide them [the 'natives'] that they may have all reasonable opportunity for developing their race life along the best lines [. . .]; not necessarily following the line of evolution of the white man, but the one their race genius suggests. And that we [. . .] shall also have an opportunity of development, and be not subject as a race to deteriorating tendencies" (qtd. in Swanson, "Urban Origins" 38). Note the assumption on Evans's part that the "race genius" and destiny of the Africans would be separate and of a lower status than that of Europeans, that the Europeans knew what the "line of evolution" should be for the Africans, and that it was the responsibility of the Europeans to guide the Africans. This ideology underlay British imperialist policies in regard to the native inhabitants of Africa.

Swanson also differs from Woolf by showing that civil bureaucracy itself played a significant role in creating imperialist policies and exploitation. In several articles, including "'The Durban System': Roots of Urban Apartheid in Colonial Natal," "'The Sanitation Syndrome': Bubonic Plague and Urban Native Policy in the Cape Colony, 1900-1909," and "'The Asiatic Menace': Creating Segregation in Durban, 1870-1900," Swanson argues that "official, governmental, and administrative classes generated more pressure than did business or commercial interests for systematic social controls leading to the creation of the legal and administrative structures of urban segregation. It is, at the very least, possible that in these phenomena [. . .] we can see the state, as such, generating 'autonomous initiatives' and 'pursuing its own strategies and goals' independently of other societal actors" ("'Asiatic Menace'" 401). In the context of racist fears, economic rivalries between individuals and groups, and epidemics attendant on rapid urban growth, "problems and crises, and the anxieties arising from them, were useful to public authorities ambitious for greater activity and control [. . .]. Administrative officials and politicians [. . .] were the greatest source of racial formulations in the institutional responses of colonial society" (421). Administrators used fears about both moral and physical contamination, including public health, to justify segregation, expropriation of land, and pass laws. They also used paternalistic ideas about protecting Black Africans from moral degradation to justify urban and rural reserves and other restrictions on where Africans could live and work.

That the governmental and administrative classes played an important and independent role in the development of racist policies and exploitation suggests that Woolf, in his analysis of empire and commerce in Africa, neglected to consider the role of his former civil service colleagues and missed an important element that created and maintained imperialism. Woolf does say that officials in the Foreign Office and colonial administrations were susceptible to political pressure from the financiers interested in profiting from adventures in Africa. However, he does not identify civil servants' own desires for control and for greater spheres of action, nor their own racism, as part of the process of imperialism. This omission on his part may have its roots in his own experiences in colonial administration and his belief in what he calls "law and order." In discussing his experiences in the Ceylon Civil Service in his autobiography *Growing*, Woolf says, "I am all and always on the side of law and order, and my time in Ceylon, where I was on the Government side of the fence, strengthened me in this attitude, simply because without law and order, strictly enforced, life for everyone must become poor, nasty, brutish, and short" (79). Both Woolf himself and his biographer Victoria Glendinning record that Leonard's strictness in the application of laws and regulations became legendary in Ceylon. Woolf points out as a positive feature of British rule in Ceylon that it was accomplished through bureaucracy, not force: "There was a great deal to be said against our rule of Ceylon, which, of course was 'bleak imperialism' [. . .]. One of the good things about it, however, was the extraordinary absence of the use of force in everyday life and government" (92). Woolf does not seem to realize here that force need not be physical to be force. While he reports his growing unease with and ambivalence about participating in what he increasingly perceived as an arrogant and tyrannical British imperialist government (157, 133-36, 111-14, 224, 236), he admits that he felt "the temptation of power and position" (224). He also records his sense of satisfaction in settling disputes and improving the efficiency of government offices and of local industries such as salt harvesting: "My vanity was flattered because it seemed to me that, as time went on, in many ways the people seemed to trust me more and came to me to settle their disputes and solve their difficulties. It was in this kind of work that I became most deeply absorbed" (236).

Woolf's solution to the abuse and exploitation of the African peoples was the institution of a system of international trusteeship over and in the interests of what he called "the non-adult races" of Africa: "An essential part of [the] solution would be the substitution of the idea of trusteeship for that of ownership and exploitation. The white man must cease to seek his own economic interests in Africa, and must become the trustee for the interests of Africans" (*Empire and Commerce* 364). Woolf makes clear that the success of international trusteeship would depend on Europeans changing their beliefs about their purpose in Africa by abandoning the ideology of economic imperialism. He argued for international governance of Africa through the League of Nations and "systematic education of the natives with a view to training them (a) to take a part in, and eventually to control, the Government of the country, and (b) to make the best use of their land and its mineral and other resources" (362). It seems to me that, well intentioned though this proposal was, it is the proposal of a person who believes that the great faults and abuses of the British government of Ceylon lay more in the attitudes of the men running the Ceylon Civil Service than the system itself. It is the solution of the strict, efficient, but eminently fair administrator whom the people trusted to solve their difficulties. Once again, it was the responsibility of the British to guide and protect the imperial subject races. To give Woolf credit, he did assume that the peoples of

Africa were as capable of education as any other groups of people around the world—a great difference between him and most colonial administrators; however, he assumed that what Africans would learn would come out of Europe rather than Africa. He assumed, as did the colonial administrators in southern Africa, that European forms of government, industry, and trade were superior, that the cultures of Africa were less developed than those of Europe, and that the indigenous peoples needed protection. As Peter Wilson remarks in his book *The International Theory of Leonard Woolf*, Woolf "made no attempt to examine in detail the social structures, habits, myths, and customs of specific African communities. [. . .] He tended, instead, to see them as uniformly undeveloped and 'backward.' This amounts to nothing less than acceptance of the easy nineteenth-century assumption that African societies occupied an earlier stage in a simple, linear process of social evolution" (135).

Because of this assumption about African societies, Woolf overlooked or did not look for the evidence that Swanson uses to show that "significant numbers of Africans were poised by the 1880s to enter fully into the colonial economy and achieve a take-off into modernity. Their progress was vitiated, not by their ability to adapt, but by deliberate policy which trapped them in the reactionary Code of Native Law" ("'The Fate of the Natives'" 61). Swanson's research suggests that, by the beginning of Woolf's era of "economic imperialism"—the 1880s—what kept many Africans, at least in southern Africa, from achieving economic success and equal participation in creating what could have been a multiracial, multiethnic southern African culture and economy was the regulation and restrictions of the colonial laws and bureaucracy which were based in paternalism and racism. Woolf's proposal to end imperialism in Africa depended on the civil bureaucracy that was a foundation stone of British imperialism itself. Leonard Woolf's anti-imperialism was paternalistic and Eurocentric despite his dedication to the cause of democratic self-government in Africa and his admirable degree of self-awareness and self-critique.

This conclusion needs to be tempered. I know that what I have neglected in this paper are the significant strengths of Leonard Woolf's work on imperialism and anti-imperialism. I suspect that in turn I have been too uncritical of my father's research. But I hope that you have found something informative and useful in the juxtaposition of the ideas of these two men who each did their work with the best intentions of serving the interests of justice and truth and, like all of us, had their limitations and blind spots.

Notes

1. The case study chapters in Woolf's book discuss French, German, and British possessions, but not those in southern Africa. Swanson's work focuses for the most part on southern Africa. Nevertheless, I think their general conclusions can legitimately be compared given the significant similarities among Kenya, Uganda, Natal, and the Cape in terms of British policy on native political, social, economic, and land rights. In analyzing Woolf's book, I focus mainly on what he has to say about British possessions in southeast Africa.
2. When I refer to the country, I use the current name (Sri Lanka). When I refer to Woolf's employment there, I use the name of the government agency employing him at the time (Ceylon Civil Service).

Works Cited

Glendinning, Victoria. *Leonard Woolf: A Biography*. NY: Free Press, 2006.
Swanson, M. W. "'The Asiatic Menace': Creating Segregation in Durban, 1870-1900." *International Journal of African Historical Studies* 16.3 (1983): 401-421.

—. "'The Durban System': Roots of Urban Apartheid in Colonial Natal." *African Studies* 35.3 & 4 (1976): 159-176.
—. "'The Fate of the Natives': Black Durban and African Ideology." *Natalia* 14 (1984): 59-68.
—. "'The Sanitation Syndrome': Bubonic Plague and Urban Native Policy in the Cape Colony, 1900-1909." *Journal of African History* 18.3 (1977): 387-410.
—. "Urban Origins of Separate Development." *Race* 10.1 (1968): 31-40.
Wilson, Peter. *The International Theory of Leonard Woolf: A Study in Twentieth-Century Idealism*. New York: Palgrave MacMillan, 2003.
Woolf, Leonard. *Empire and Commerce in Africa: A Study in Economic Imperialism*. 1920. New York: Howard Fertig, 1968.
—. *Growing: An Autobiography of the Years 1904-1911*. New York: Harvest/Harcourt Brace Jovanovich, 1961.
Woolf, Virginia. *Three Guineas*. New York: Harcourt Brace and Company, 1938

Hours in a Chinese Library:
Re-Reading Virginia Woolf, Bloomsbury, and Modernism

by Patricia Laurence

Avant-garde artists in mainland China often speak of the need to "wake sleeping books" since the Cultural Revolution. After Mao Zedong's demise in 1976, Western literature—no longer demonized by Marxist critics—was reintroduced into China. Since then, historians and literary critics in both nations work in archives seeking to wake the historical and literary connections that existed between China and the West in the Republican Period, 1911 through the 1940s. This period of *modernism* or *mo-deng* was a dynamic era of cultural and aesthetic openness and encounter between England and mainland China. It is during this period that Chinese culture grew in the imagination of Bloomsbury: the Chinese landscapes in the translations of Tang poetry of Arthur Waley; landscape paintings on scrolls at the first International Chinese Exhibition of Art in Burlington House, London, in 1937; blue and white willow pattern dishes in every British cupboard; anglo-chinois designs influencing English gardens; the Chinese pagoda in Kew Gardens; objets d'art; ceramics and the fashion for Chinese dresses in the Liberty Department Store: all became part of an aesthetic dialectic with Bloomsbury and constitutive of British modernism, as well as a developing international modernism.

Lily Briscoe's "Chinese eyes," Woolf's glancing reference to an English artist in *To the Lighthouse*, signifies not the imperial gaze for profit traditionally associated with English trade, but, metaphorically, the incorporation of the Chinese aesthetic into an English artist (*TTL* 42). The different vision implied by "Chinese eyes" is also conferred by Woolf upon Elizabeth Dalloway. Such eyes conjure a sense of foreignness and mystery, but as unmarried *new* women, Lily and Elizabeth (as well as the South American women in *The Voyage Out* (discussed today by Monica Ayuso) are only sketched by Woolf. They are undeveloped and unknown because Woolf philosophically, culturally and aesthetically keeps open the question of what being a *woman* and, particularly, a *foreign woman*, means:

> What is a woman? I assure you I don't know; I do not believe that you know; I do not believe that anybody can know until she has expressed herself in all the arts and professions open to human skill. (*AROO* 131)

What interests Woolf about foreign authors as she observes the Greeks and the Russians is the "foreign tongue," the "angle of vision," the "accent," the "stamp," and the "emphasis laid upon unexpected places" in their writing (*CR1* 157). She does not pretend to cultural knowing, and it is a curious paradox in Woolf and other modernist authors such as Henry James that they enjoy and relish *not knowing* because it gives them a space to imagine and create. It is these spaces that international scholars in Woolf studies interpret.

Roger Fry also entered this international space in 1916, urging the British to be open to "a new mass of aesthetic experience" in the East. He warned:

We can no longer hide behind the Elgin marbles and refuse to look at the art of China, India, Java and Ceylon. We have no longer any system of aesthetics that can rule out, a priori, even the most fantastic and unreal artistic form. They must be judged in themselves and by their own standards. ("Oriental Art" 794)

Such a stance resists viewing the language and structure of British or European modernism as *enabling* other modern or postmodern cultures to articulate and imagine new literary or artistic forms, a position recently argued in relation to Caribbean literature by Simon Gikandi in *Modernism/Modernity*.

In my hours in a Chinese library, I read about the literary friendship between Virginia Woolf and Ling Shuhua—a Chinese writer of short stories; essays; and an autobiography, *Ancient Melodies*, written in English, as well as an artist and collector. I read about the cultural crossings between Bloomsbury and the Crescent Moon group, a literary community in China that thrived around 1925-1927. I followed, as Woolf does in her essay "Hours in a Library," the "uncharted ways in search of new forms for our new sensations" (*GR* 30), moving away in spirit from her father's more ponderous literary impressions in his *Hours in a Library* volumes.

My exploration began after my discovery of some letters between Ling Shuhua and various members of Bloomsbury that led to research in mainland China, mainly Shanghai and Wuhan, where I traced the conversation between Bloomsbury and the Crescent Moon Group. Anti-imperialist discourse was strong in Republican China: a period historically bracketed by two movements, the establishment of the Republic of China by Sun Yat Sen in 1911, and the establishment of the PRC under Mao Zedong in 1949. Anti-Marxism was rife in England and America also. Yet writers in these groups met, wrote or imagined one another as in Benedict Anderson's "imagined communities." Chinese and British individuals and groups took shape in daily thinking and reading, travel, markets, institutions and the arts, each culture doing the dreamwork that scholars now articulate and develop. In my research, I join a group of other Woolf scholars who have made similar international journeys out of Bloomsbury: Jessica Berman to India; Mary Ann Caws, Sarah Bird Wright and Helen Southworth to France; Melba Cuddy Keene to China; Monica Ayuso and Andrea Reyes into Latin cultures along with Susan Stanford Friedman, Emily Dalgarno, Bonnie Kime Scott, Sonita Sarker, and Urmila Seshagiri, among others.

I will begin, then, with my hours in a Chinese library. After days of walking around Shanghai, one of the most exciting cities in China with the fast rhythms of New York City, I applied to read in a particular library whose name was translated for me as the *no-name* library: a repository for Republican period magazines and newspapers, or *pre-liberation* (meaning pre-Mao) writings, as they were still labeled in 1995. Working through the prism of British modernism and post-modernism, I lived through and discovered in this research not only the ideology hidden in Western practices, but China's ideological walls as well: walls that were constructed to hide aspects of the Republican period, a time of East-West openness and connection. In order to enter the no name library as a foreign expert, I needed two letters of introduction, one provided by Professor Qu Shi-jing, known to many as Frank Chu, one of our Woolf specialists in Shanghai. When I finally entered the dimly lit archives two days later, I propped up my computer, thinking wildly—only one week more for research in Shanghai. Glancing around, I observed that neighboring scholars at long wooden tables—male, older and venerable-looking—were in more contemplative mood and had only small notebooks in which they would occasionally jot a note in neat characters. From time to time, they would stop reading, gaze, sip tea from a thermos, perhaps nap for a few minutes or go out on a small balcony for chi-gong. In the meantime, my mind clouded with suggestions, I filled out request slips for journals and waited. After half an hour, a small woman returned with a pile of periodicals, each bundle tied neatly with a string. She dusted what seemed a pagoda-shaped tower of periodicals, creating billows of dust. She had awakened the sleeping books for an American scholar.

It was in *no-name* library, and, later, the modern Shanghai Public Library and the Wuhan University Library with energetic scholars and a different ambiance, that I traveled along uncharted ways re-reading Woolf, Bloomsbury and modernism. I discovered a literary space between England and China where personal and literary relations flourished in spite of sometimes conflicting political and economic ideologies. It was then that I decided that a theoretically or ideologically driven post-colonial argument would not capture the complexity of the historical and literary relationships that I wanted to represent in my work. It was then that I decided that I would write an affective history, the biography of a group, to chart the inner spaces of community and nation to create a new space in literary criticism. Increasingly, the discourse of globalism shaped by economic and political interests and vocabulary neglects to study how the transnational knowledge is transmitted and what the results of these transnational contacts are. For example, I. A. Richards traveled to China in 1927, 1929-1930, and 1936-1938, introducing "practical criticism," influencing a whole generation of Chinese critics, as well as developing a simplified method of teaching English, Basic English, in China. He is shown below with his wife, Dorothy, and a group of educators on a trip to China (Figure 1).

In addition, Chinese writer and translator Xiao Qian, influenced by his study with

Figure 1. I. A. Richards with his wife, Dorothy, and a delegation of Chinese educators.

Figure 2. Xiao Qian.

E.M. Forster and Dadie Rylands at King's College in the 1940s, returned to China to translate James Joyce's *Ulysses* into Chinese with his wife, Wen Jieruo, in the 1990s. He is pictured below in British knickers aspiring at one point in his youth to be an "English gentleman" (Figure 2).

In my talk today, I hope to bring attention to how the writers, artists and their arts migrated and changed literatures and cultures along the way in the 1920s-1930s. What happens when we travel with Virginia Woolf and British modernism? What stays the same and what changes? The perspective we adopt should not be focused only on Woolf in a new context and the kind of knowledge we acquire, but also on how we change as well, one of the themes of the Sixteenth Annual Virginia Woolf Conference. How are we different as teachers, creators of curriculum, scholars, writers, literary critics, anthologists, speakers and cultural mediators?

Behind my talk today, then, is the specter of my own changes in my journey out of American and British libraries into Chinese libraries to explore the fascinating literary, cultural and political world of Republican China. It led me to travel to difficult and beautiful places to explore the possibilities of research in a different cultural and political space in order to register in my own experience—on my own pulses—the postmodern and postcolonial debates on identity, culture, nation and globalism. It has made me less glib.

As Eudora Welty says of *place* in fiction, I say of literary criticism: "Place…is the named, identified, concrete, exact and exacting, and therefore credible, gathering spot of all that's been felt…. Place in history partakes of feeling, as feeling about History partakes of Place" (*Place in Fiction* 6).

To illustrate, let me sketch another place, a bridge upon which Virginia Woolf and the Chinese writer, Ling Shuhua, stand (Figures 3 and 4). In their sixteen-month correspondence, March 1938-July 1939, they connect the developing aesthetic and feminist beliefs and practices of women in different countries. The conversation began on a friendship scroll that Ling Shuhua had given to her good friend, Xu Zhimo, a flamboyant poet of repute who visited Cambridge, 1920-1922. She urged him to enlist British writers and intellectuals to write or draw on the scroll, and it remains a concrete marker of the relations between Bloomsbury and China, initiated sixteen years before Ling corresponded

Figure 3. Virginia Woolf by Man Ray

with Woolf. And it inaugurates Ling Shuhua as a "Chinese Bloomsburian" (as Arthur Waley said), a new international star in the Bloomsbury constellation.

The letters between Ling Shuhua and Virginia Woolf illuminate the "inner domain[s]" of community that Partha Chatterjee discusses (912). Ling and Woolf connect as women and writers writing from a site of change and war: the British under the threat of World War II and engagement in the Spanish Civil War, and the Chinese in the midst of the Sino-Japanese War and the civil war between the Nationalists and the Communists. Two discourses, then, marginal to mainstream discourse in China and England that emerge in these letters are inscribed in the evolving narration of nation: women struggling to claim their feelings and subjectivity eclipsed during a time of war under a narrative of nation; women writing against the pro-war trend in their own countries, deconstructing the official stories of nations at war. They counter stereotypes of *feudal, colonial, imperialist, Marxist* or *capitalist* thinking, creating new kinds of narration threaded from the individual voices of women writers.

When I came upon their letters in British and Chinese libraries, Ling's words overlaying red traces of grasshoppers and bees on delicate rice paper, I discovered that Woolf had sent Ling copies of *A Room of One's Own*, *The Years* and *The Waves*, as Julian Bell, then teaching in China and involved with Ling, had requested. "One day," Ling wrote, "I happened to come across and read Virginia Woolf's *A Room of One's Own*, and I was quite carried away by her writing, so suddenly I decided to write and see if she were in my situation, what she would do." There is a lyric quality in these words written in 1938, shortly after the death of Julian Bell in the Spanish Civil War. Ling, having been the lover of Julian when he was teaching at Wuhan University, was distraught. Woolf urged her to work: "think how you could fix your mind upon something worth doing in itself. I have not read any of your writing but Julian often wrote to me about it. He said too that you have lived a most interesting life" (15 April 1938).

Shuhua's autobiography, as can be observed in the illustration below (Figure 5), embodied the sisters' arts: both the writing of Virginia and the painting of Vanessa.

Shuhua was encouraged by Woolf in letters to write an autobiography in English, and she sent Woolf one chapter at a time for commentary. *Ancient Melodies* was later published through

Figure 4. Ling Shuhua

*guanx*i (the social network) of Bloomsbury: Virginia Woolf and Julian Bell had encouraged it; Vita Sackville West wrote an introduction, and Leonard Woolf published it at the Hogarth Press in 1954. Her autobiography centered on her early years, leaving out her turbulent affair with Julian Bell: she was the wife of the dean of the School of Arts and Letters at National Wuhan University, and he had hired Julian for his teaching position in 1935 (Figure 6).

Nevertheless, few women in China had ever ventured to write in the unfamiliar genre. In her autobiography, she revealed the culture of concubines—their friendships and their jealousies—her mother being the fourth concubine of the mayor of Peking. Ling's transition from a large, complex feudal family to becoming a *new woman* in China was surprising and rapid. Disappointed with

Figure 5. Cover Illustration

the treatment of women in her father's court, Ling was one of the first modern Chinese women writers to attempt to represent the inner life of women.

Ling also expressed "the miserable mind feeling" about war that Woolf represented in *Three Guineas*. Though living through geographical displacements and political turbulence, writing about the personal dislocations of war was considered a luxury in the context of China's national needs. Every aspect of personal life was under attack. Woolf and Ling sensed the monstrous, depersonalizing effects of the war machine that threatened to silence the writer's personal voice in a world dominated, as Woolf would say, by the loudspeaker voice of the government, the radio and the newspapers.

Their conversation both observes and dissolves national boundaries and enables British modernism and feminism to expand into an international space. The loss of the

Figure 6. The triangle: Julian Bell; Chen Yuan, Ling's husband; and Ling Shuhua.

personal writing voice was one of Woolf's greatest fears, yet her letters dramatize the value of personal, cross-cultural conversation in which one artist may answer the needs of another who is oppressed by conditions in her own country. Woolf was the daughter of an educated man; Ling, the daughter of a mandarin and his fourth concubine. Woolf provided Ling with another cultural and sexual standard to place beside her own as she traveled through war zones from Wuhan to Sichuan with her daughter in 1938, often in a state of nervous tension. Ling wrote of her *refugee's fate* in the midst of a brutal war—cities and people ravaged by the advancing Japanese, the bombings, the death, the sickness, famine, and dislocation—that was still remote to Woolf. Ling wrote of *ruined houses* in China, reminding us of Woolf's descriptions of the photos of the "dead bodies and ruined houses that the Spanish government sent almost weekly" (*TG* 68). Woolf's letters to Ling were encouraging—*don't despair*—and her focus upon her writing enabled Ling to sustain her efforts psychologically during the displacements and terrors of the war.

But observe another place, a bridge that joins critics of different cultures. Ling had been encouraged to write her autobiography in English and had earlier prepared her short stories for an English audience with Julian Bell's support. One critic asserts, however, that Woolf's "subtle Eurocentric attitude" led Ling to write in English (Shumei 216). Woolf had written that Ling should "keep the charm of the unlikeness" and "the Chinese flavour" and not to worry about grammar (28 Feb. 1939). This was viewed by the critic as Ling "exoticizing herself in the gaze of the West." Woolf is placed in a Procrustean bed of postcolonial hegemony:

> The unspoken presumption behind Woolf's suggestions seems to be a hierarchical conception of language and audience, that English, the language in which she herself wrote, is the authentic, if not superior language for creative endeavors, and that the Western audience is the one worth writing for. (Shumei 216)

The facts are, however, that Ling was drawn to the English language and culture as was her husband, Chen Yuan, a historian and literary editor, who had studied at the London School of Economics for ten years and worked with H.G. Wells. Ling learned English and Japanese in school, was in an Anglophone community in Beijing and then Wuhan. Though some critics would have it otherwise, English language, literature and culture was a part of her complicated identity as a cosmopolitan Chinese artist who deeply identified with the nation of China, but whose imagination freely connected with different people in different parts of the world—long before she met Julian Bell or corresponded with Virginia Woolf.

Woolf does not adopt the tone, stance or vocabulary of *domination* or *subordination* in her letters, terms of relationship that Gayatri Spivak, a post-colonial critic, has defined as the norm in East-West relations. Ling and Woolf's relationship and others like it challenge Spivak's position that "the subaltern cannot speak" (Spivak 308). Their relationship—in letters only, as they never met—was constituted differently. Their correspondence generated not imperial gestures but relationship as they both realized their structural place as privileged and educated women and writers in their society during a time of war. They transformed paradigms as Isak Dinesen and Olive Schreiner do in Sue Horton's account of remarkable women writers who re-inscribe modernism and colonialism with different meanings than the men who have largely created such systems. Granted, Woolf was the established writer, eighteen years Ling's senior: the noted *asymmetry* is more a function of their relationship as mentor and novice. Woolf was drawn to mentoring young women writers when she was an established writer. Their letters reveal the way in which we imagine and create ourselves and one another.

The Crescent Moon group in Beijing with which Ling was associated was often labeled *decadent* because it was branded as *Western-identified, apolitical, liberal, capitalist, imperialist, anti-utilitarian, Nationalist-identified (not Communist)* and favoring *art for art's sake*. Literature and politics are inextricably intertwined in China, and the personal identity of critics and the nations into which they are born or to which they travel are always in formation—including my own as I traveled to China. Nevertheless, as Jane de Gay has said, "the female figure often survives the nation that has excluded her to sing through the years," as do Woolf and Ling.

As teachers, critics and travelers, we are cultural protagonists in a position of personal and critical flux, and vulnerability, at times, as we understand and sometimes misunderstand other cultures. Yet these cross-cultural imaginative, intellectual and actual journeys must be bravely taken if the term *globalism* is not to ring hollow. As Woolf reminds us:

> Literature is no one's private ground; literature is common ground. It is not cut up into nations, there are no wars there. Let us trespass freely and fearless find our own way for ourselves. (*M* 154)

Note

Figures 1, 2, 3, and 6 are reproduced by permission of the Master and Fellows of Magdalene College, Cambridge University, England. Figure 4 is reproduced with permission from Mr. Xu Zhenbang, Archivist, Wuhan University Library.

Works Cited

Anderson, Benedict. *Imagined Communities: Reflections on the Origin and Spread of Nationalism*. London: Verso, 1983.
Chatterjee, Partha. *The Nation and its Fragments: Colonial and Post-Colonial Histories*. Princeton: Princeton University Press, 1993.
de Gay, Jane. "Virginia Woolf, Metamorphoses and Flights from Nation." Virginia Woolf: Art Education, and Internationalism: Selected Paper from the Seventeenth Anual Conference on Virgiia Woolf. Clemson: Clemson University Digital Press, 2008, 139-146.
Fry, Roger. "Oriental Art." *Living Age* (26 March 1910): 793-802.
Gikandi, Simon. "Preface, Modernism in the World." *Modernism/Modernity* 13:3 (2006): 419-24.
Laurence, Patricia. *Lily Briscoes' Chinese Eyes: Bloomsbury, Modernism and China*. Columbia: University of South Carolina Press, 2003.
Ling Shuhua. *Ancient Melodies*. NY: Universe Books, 1988.
Shumei, Shi. *The Lure of the Moderns: Writing Modernism in Semi-Colonial China, 1917-1937*. Berkeley: University of California Press, 2001.
Spivak, Gayatri. "Can the Subaltern Speak?" *Marxism and the Interpretation of Culture*. Ed. Nelson and Greenberg. Chicago: University of Illinois Press, 1988. 271-313.
Woolf, Virginia. *Common Reader*, First Series. New York: Harcourt Brace Jovanovich, 1925.
—. *Granite and Rainbow*. 1928. New York: Harcourt Brace Jovanovich, 1968.
—. Letters to Ling Shuhua. Monk's House Papers, Sussex University, Brighton, England.
—. *The Moment and Other Essays*. New York: Harcourt Brace Jovanoich, 1974.
—. *A Room of One's Own*. 1929. New York: Harcourt Brace Jovanovich, 1957.
—. *To the Lighthouse*. New York: Harcourt Brace Jovanovich, 1927.

Caged Tiger:
Louis as Colonial Subject in Virginia Woolf's The Waves

by Tracy Savoie

By the time Virginia Woolf published *The Waves* in 1931, a new wave of British empire had rolled in. The settler colonies, including Australia and Canada, were now Dominions, which meant that they were "autonomous colonies within the British Empire" (Darwin 69). It was due to the instability of the ever-expanding Victorian empire that the Dominions were created and an "imperialism of free trade" came to replace the "Second British Empire" (71). The Dominions, according to John Darwin, came to be regarded as essential to maintaining "the principle of Imperial unity" (67).[1] Given this historical context, I read Louis as a figure who complicates the relationship between colonized and colonizer; he is a colonized subject, an Australian, turned colonizer who ushers in an empire of commerce. Throughout the novel, Louis imitates Englishness, including the English pronunciation of words, English manners and traditions, and even, finally, British imperialism. If we understand Louis' imitation of Englishness through Homi K. Bhabha's "Of Mimicry and Man," though, we can see that Louis' imitation not only reveres but also mocks colonial authority. His imitation denaturalizes Englishness and exposes the instability of colonial discourse and of the empire itself. Though Louis' homeland of Australia is emblematic of the fact that the sun never sets on the British Empire, the sun does in fact set in the novel. I read Louis' mimicry as Woolf's commentary on the inevitable fall of the newest wave of empire.

In Homi BhaBha's "Of Mimicry and Man," he reads Lacan's assessment of mimicry as camouflage[2] in the context of colonialism, in that the colonial subject is asked to mimic the colonizers but that the effect of that mimicry is to always differentiate the colonial subject as an Other. Bhabha states, "[...]colonial mimicry is the desire for a reformed, recognizable Other, *as a subject of a difference that is almost the same, but not quite*" (122). Mimicry is built "around an *ambivalence*" in that for it "to be effective mimicry must continually produce its slippage, its excess, its difference" (122). The colonizers want the colonized to take on their tastes and mannerisms but not to admit the colonized to the circle of privilege which they alone occupy. In constantly creating this "difference," though, Bhabha notes the effect that it has on "the authority of colonial discourse" in that the hypocrisy of that discourse is exposed.[3] One of Bhabha's examples is Charles Grant's[4] recommendation that rather than fully convert the Indians to Christianity, for fear that the Indians would want their liberty, that there should be a "partial reform" which would have them imitate "English manners" and make them desire English protection. In making such a suggestion, Bhabha notes that Grant "mocks his moral project" (124). Hence, the mimicry which colonial discourse requires becomes a mockery of its authority. While the effect of mimicry is to create what Bhabha calls a "partial presence" of the colonized, it also produces "a partial vision of the colonizer's presence; a gaze of otherness" (126). Mimicry reverses the gaze so that the watchers become the watched. Essentially, the "gaze of otherness" denaturalizes subjecthood so that the colonizers become aware that their identity, too, is performative.

With Bhabha's conception of colonial mimicry in mind, then, I argue that Louis' mimicry of the mannerisms of Bernard and the "boasting boys'" Englishness not only creates in himself a "partial presence," for he is never accepted as English, but also mocks English manners and the value placed on ceremony and discipline. Within the context of *The Waves*, Louis is the only colonial voice, and as Urmila Seshagiri describes him, "Louis [...] is also white, but hails from Australia and is therefore branded as the racial and cultural other of the English characters" (62). Bhabha's assertion that "to be Anglicized is emphatically not to be English" (125) seems to apply to Louis.[5] Also, the fact that the perceptible difference between Louis and his peers is not due to his skin color or even language but his accent, may provide an example of what Bhabha calls "*almost the same, but not quite*" (122). Louis focuses on imitating the English pronunciation of words since it is his Australian accent which marks him as un-English. In the classroom Louis thinks, "I will not conjugate the verb [...] until Bernard has said it. My father is a banker in Brisbane and I speak with an Australian accent. I will wait and copy Bernard. He is English. They are all English" (12). Though we should be careful not to conflate cultural status and class, the two are certainly tied in Louis's case. Louis cannot be one of the English elite because of his accent and because his father is a banker, while Neville and Bernard's fathers are "gentlemen." He, therefore, attempts to imitate them knowing that though he desires to be one of them, he never will be; he does not possess one of the boasting boys' names which "are the same always" (47). Louis' mimicry of the others exemplifies the "slippage" of colonial mimicry in that he imitates the others because he desires to be English, but it is, at least partially, his imitation which causes him to be ridiculed. Louis states, "Jinny and Susan, Bernard and Neville bind themselves into a thong with which to lash me. They laugh at my neatness, at my Australian accent. I will now try to imitate Bernard softly lisping Latin" (12). In trying to imitate Bernard and the others Louis is marked as an outsider; however, in laughing at his "neatness" and his love of order later in the novel, they mock their own rituals. It is through Louis' love of English rituals that Bernard detects his own dislike of them. He describes Louis as having "greater respect of these old ceremonies than I do" (209). Louis becomes a caricature of the disciplined male ceremonies and desire for order, demonstrating to the others their ridiculousness; it is ceremonies like these which Woolf denounces later in *Three Guineas* because they equate male status with the violence of war, creating a reverence for war and empire amongst both men and women.

Louis' imitation of the others makes his reception and return of their gaze apparent. As Bhabha states, colonial mimicry creates a "partial presence" or partial representation of the Other, but also reflects "a partial vision of the colonizer's presence; a gaze of otherness" (126). At a restaurant, Louis says to himself, "I am an average Englishman; I am an average clerk, yet I look at the little men at the next table to be sure that I do what they do" (66). Throughout his observation of these men and the people passing by the window, Louis states, "Yes; I will reduce you to order" (67). This statement foreshadows the order which he will manically seek throughout the novel and echoes the desire of empire to impose order on its subjects. We might also see this statement as meaning that he is searching for an order, a pattern in their gestures which he can imitate. He desires the order of empire, but because he is not included within the "ordinary," he is able to see that it is in fact disorderly. Louis states,

I watch it expand, contract; and then expand again. Yet I am not included. If I speak, imitating their accent, they prick their ears, waiting for me to speak again, in order that they may place me—if I come from Canada or Australia, I, who desire above all things to be taken to the arms with love, an alien, external. I, who would wish to feel close over me the protective waves of the ordinary, catch with the tail of my eye some far horizon; am aware of hats bobbing up and down in perpetual disorder. (67)

The order amounts to disorder, to a constant flux, which, as Bhabha states, the colonial discourse must continue in order to maintain itself; it must produce its "slippage" (122). Within the "protective waves of the ordinary" is the constant expanding and contracting of those waves which must occur if the "ordinary" is to continue to elude Louis and other white colonial subjects from "Canada or Australia." While wishing to be included within the ordinary he "catch[es] with the tail of [his] eye some far horizon." I read this "far horizon" as implying his home of Australia which will keep him from "passing" (a word that is used several times in this paragraph) for an Englishman.[6]

Such exclusion creates resentment in Louis and allows him to see the workings of the colonial discourse that the others both compel and ridicule his mimicry. When at the gathering to celebrate Percival's departure to India, he thinks, "But while I admire Susan and Percival, I hate the others, because it is for them that I do these antics, smoothing my hair, concealing my accent" (92). I read this hatred as a hatred of the colonial discourse which makes him a "partial presence," and read within that hatred a, if subconscious, desire for the empire's disintegration. Jane Marcus, on the other hand, interprets Louis as being mostly complicit with Empire. She states that "[a]s a former colonial subject, Louis is most afraid of the dissolution of empire. He hears the great beast of revolution stamping on the shore" (156). While I agree with Marcus' assessment that the beast is that of revolution, the fact that he at times identifies himself as this beast suggests that he may both fear and desire revolution. After proclaiming his hatred for the others, Louis states, "I am the little ape who chatters over a nut, and you are the dowdy women with shiny bags of stale buns; I am also the caged tiger, and you are the keepers with red-hot bars" (92). Louis identifies himself as a "chained beast stamping" (which he mentions in the same paragraph) by calling himself a "caged tiger." His rage is restrained, however, because of the gaze of his "keepers" who he fears will laugh at him.[7] At this point, Louis pours his rage into his poetry, though after the death of Percival he tries to right these wrongs through empire.

Though Louis takes over Percival's role as the next leader of the empire, as Bernard states, "His ascendancy was resented, as Percival's was adored" (180). Despite Louis' success in helping to, as he states, "spread [. . .] commerce where there was chaos in parts of the world" (122), Louis is still not accepted as a full member of the group. He is accepted as a successful businessman but not as the moral leader that Bernard believes Percival was meant to be. This difference, of course, signifies the change in types of empire but also indicates that his status as colonial subject denies him the role of hero. Again, Louis' mimicry becomes a mockery of the colonial discourse in that even through imitating Percival he still is not English. Instead, he and Rhoda refer to themselves as "conspirators," since they remain outside the circle (166).[8] The word "conspirator" is interesting in that it indicates a kind of rebellion on his part. It seems that Louis sees his rise as a commercial imperialist as a way to "erase old defilements" including "[his] accent; beatings and other tortures; the boasting boys" (122). Some of the caged tiger remains within Louis even in his domineering, imperialist role. Of course, as he helps himself (and the empire), he harms others. Louis states, "[…] youth coming up from the river in white flannels, carrying cushions, is to me black with the shadows of dungeons and the tortures and infamies practiced by man upon man" (161). With this comment, Louis recalls his boyhood during which he suffered such tortures. He indicates his own guilt, too, at partaking in the "infamies practiced by man upon man" with his mention of the material goods "white flannels" and "cushions," considering that most of the material would have been imported by his merchant ships. I believe that it is because Louis is an ex-colonial subject himself and because he remains an outsider that the critiques of colonial discourse which we saw from him earlier in the novel continue even when he is participating in and constructing that discourse himself. He hints at the inevitable failure of his project to create order when he states, "[…] if we blink or look aside, or turn back to finger what Plato said or remember Napoleon and his conquests, we inflict on the world the injury of some obliquity" (122). The word "obliquity" here can mean to obscure the sun, perhaps meaning that to lose purpose and acknowledge the ending that history foretells is to lose the empire.

As Kathy Phillips states, *The Waves* "criticiz[es] the Empire in that it focuses on a psychological cause for dominating others: the desire on the part of a person who has been made to feel inferior to find even lowlier victims" (153). Louis seems to be caught within a system where the only way that he might escape his cage, and gain some respect, is through empire. Woolf explains women's relation to empire in this way in *Three Guineas*: "[…] she would undertake any task however menial, exercise any fascination however fatal that enable her escape. Thus consciously she desired 'our splendid Empire'" (39). Of course, there are significant gender differences in how men and women relate to empire. Louis has more resources than a woman would and so has the power to control a portion of the empire while a woman would not.[9] Woolf's statement still seems to apply to Louis, though, in that he desires escape from his cage through "our splendid Empire" as well. *The Waves* demonstrates the futility of such a project, however, for we come to question if Louis does ever in fact break free. In ushering in the new empire, he mimics his colonizers and yet remains a "partial presence" due to the "slippage" of colonial discourse; in signing "I, I, and again I" on his letters from around the world, he still fails to construct a self (124). Louis' continued need to mimic his colonizers even after his success at imperial commerce may well be Woolf's commentary on the inevitable failure of trying to secure one's freedom and power through the exploitation of others, and therefore an indictment of the colonial discourse which encourages the cycle of imperialism.

Notes

1. Darwin explains that many British imperialists regarded "their continued adhesion to the principle of Imperial unity as worth almost any constitutional concession" (67).
2. Bhabha quotes from Lacan's "The line and the light," *Of the Gaze*: "'Mimicry reveals something in so far as it is distinct from what might be called an itself that is behind. The effect of mimicry is camouflage.... It is not a question of harmonizing with the background, but against a mottled background, of becoming mottled—exactly like the technique of camouflage practised in human warfare'" (121).
3. Bhabha argues that "in 'normalizing' the colonial state of subject, the dream of post-Enlightenment civility alienates its own language of liberty" (123).
4. From "Observations on the state of society among the Asiatic subjects of Great Britain" (1792).

5. It should be noted that Bhabha's focus in "Of Mimicry and Man" seems to be on colonized subjects' whose skin color differentiates them from their white oppressors, rather than on white colonial subjects.
6. Though Louis uses the word "passing" to mean that the people are walking by, I believe that the meaning of trying to make others believe that you are of another nationality or race could apply here.
7. Louis states, "[…] I am fiercer and stronger than you are, yet the apparition that appears above ground after ages of non-entity will be spent in terror lest you should laugh at me, in veerings with the wind against the soot storms, in efforts to make a steel ring of clear poetry that shall connect the gulls and women with bad teeth" (92).
8. Bernard also refers to the two of them as conspirators when he states, "Louis and Rhoda, the conspirators, the spies at the table, who take notes…" (205).
9. For a discussion of the differences in how Louis and Rhoda use empire, see Kathy Phillips' *Virginia Woolf Against Empire*.

Works Cited

Bhabha, Homi K. "Of Mimicry and Man: The Ambivalence of Colonial Discourse." *The Location of Culture*. New York: Routledge, 1994. 121-131.

Darwin, John. "A Third British Empire? The Dominion Idea in Imperial Politics." *The Oxford History of the British Empire: The Twentieth Century*. Vol. IV. New York: Oxford University Press, 1999. 64-87.

Marcus, Jane. "Britannia Rules *The Waves*." *Decolonizing Tradition*. Ed. Karen R. Lawrence. Chicago: University of Illinois Press, 1992. 136-162.

Phillips, Kathy J. "Securing the Circle: The Education of an Empire-Builder." *Virginia Woolf Against Empire*. Knoxville: University of Tennessee Press, 1994. 153-183.

Seshagiri, Urmila. "Orienting Virginia Woolf: Race, Aesthetics, and Politics in *To the Lighthouse*." *Modern Fiction Studies* 50 (2004): 58-84.

Woolf, Virginia. *Three Guineas*. New York: Harcourt Brace Jovanovich, 1938.

—. *The Waves*. Annotated Edition. Mark Hussey. New York: Harcourt, 2006.

The Critical Silence of the Other:
Critique of Fascism in Virgina Woolf's *The Waves*

by Natasha Allen

In Virginia Woolf's *The Waves* societal roles are explored through six lives and six voices, none, as Molly Hite notes, privileged with "authorial sanction" (lxi). In the final section of the novel, there is but one voice, Bernard's, and all others are silent. Of the five, four are silenced, but one has willingly relinquished her voice. I would like to discuss Rhoda. It is Rhoda who arrives at the precocious realization as a child that she is "outside the loop" (13), and who harbors a "hopeless desire to be Susan, to be Jinny" (17) that she must cast off at night as she casts off her frock and chemise. It is Rhoda whom Bernard identifies, along with Louis, as one of the "authentics" (83). It is also Rhoda who commits suicide, and who, long before her death, says of herself, "I faint, I fail" (40). However, I would like to suggest that Rhoda triumphs in the fact that it is she whose voice Bernard is powerless to silence in his closing, dominating soliloquy. In her suicidal leap, Rhoda chooses to silence herself.

By the time we reach Bernard's soliloquy, we have read the narrative of Percival the hero, imperialist solver and resolver, have contemplated Louis' chained stamping beast and Rhoda's "islands where the parrots chatter" (11), and have heard Jinny speak of those who make the day, "some by going to the Law Courts; others to the city; others to the nursery; others by marching and forming fours" (127). By such clues we may rightly glean that this is a story of culture and imperialism, dominance and restraint. Seven years after writing *The Waves*, Woolf would write in her feminist polemic *Three Guineas* of the example which can be taken from the "Fascist States" of what *not* to be, noting, "the 'attitudes,' the false and unreal positions taken by the human form in England as well as in Germany, are due to the limelight which paralyses the free action of the human faculties and inhibits the human power to change and create new wholes much as a strong headlamp paralyses the little creatures who run out of the darkness into its beams" (114). We might detect hints of such limelight within *The Waves* not only in the rituals of, as Patricia Cramer notes, "partings for school, graduation ceremonies, religious sermons, the mating rituals at dance parties, and school reunions" (449), but also in Rhoda's later condemnation of cultural mores when she says of those around her: "What dissolution of the soul you demanded in order to get through one day, what lies, bowings, scrapings, fluency and servility!" (149). Woolf outlines domestic fascism for the purpose of critiquing its permeation within English society, and places Rhoda before the dominant gaze, in view of the "nameless [...] immaculate people, watching [her] from behind bushes" (30) to establish her anti-imperialist assessment.

Gabrielle McIntire observes that Woolf accomplishes a critique of fascism within *The Waves* on the subtle level of metaphor and analogy, and notes: "While Woolf never actually names fascism in the novel, the ways in which she represents the group's ambivalent awe for a quasi-mystical confraternity, the characters' alternating fascination and abhorrence for order and authority, the group's hero-worship of Percival [...] all point to a sustained meditation on the nearness of fascist rhetoric and sentiment to the politics and rhetoric of everyday English life" (30). What I suggest is that Rhoda's is, in effect, a counter-narrative to Percival's that enables Woolf's successful critique of fascism, and that Rhoda's character, in the role of Other, challenges both Percival's patriarchal imperialist narrative and Bernard's privileging of it.

One of the initial facts we are given about Rhoda, by way of Louis, is that she "has no father" (12). As a result, Rhoda has no patriarchal ties to the dominant culture. Louis' refrained lament that his father is "a banker in Brisbane" (12), that he is not the son of a gentleman as are Bernard and Neville, underscores the flux that Rhoda finds herself in merely through the absence of her father. If patriarchy determines one's position in a male-dominated culture, then absence of a father equates with absence of position. Her statement that she has "no face" (22) can be read as an acknowledgement of her Otherness. As a child, Rhoda rocks her brown basin filled with water in which white petals sail as ships, and says, "Some will founder. Some will dash themselves against the cliffs. One sails alone. That is my ship" (11). She imagines her ship finding distant icy caverns and tropical islands, her Otherness privileging her to ride above the masses to distant lands that the assimilated masses, in sinking and succumbing to the rituals and traditions of dominant culture in the process of relinquishing their individuality, are unable to reach. Later, though she still locates herself outside of society, Rhoda no longer imagines herself confidently navigating her way beyond its dominating culture, rather she bitterly foretells how she is "to be cast up and down among these men and women, with their twitching faces, with their lying tongues, like a cork on a rough sea" (77). In his final soliloquy, Bernard suggests that Rhoda killed herself in order to find the place she sought, what he refers to as "some pillar in the desert" (208). In this way her suicide can be read as the ultimate act of successful resistance, allowing her to travel to her "marble columns and pools on the other side of the world where the swallow dips her wings" (76).

Part of her Otherness involves her inability to coalesce her culture's smaller components to discern the larger ideas they represent. In one analogous example, she is faced with a mathematical problem as a child and admits she sees "only figures," that she has "no answer," saying, "The figures mean nothing now. Meaning is gone" (13). Similarly, she cannot summate the individual moments she experiences to form a life entire, and says: "I cannot make one moment merge in the next. To me they are all violent, all separate [. . .]. I have no end in view. I do not know how to run minute to minute and hour to hour, solving them by some natural force until they make the whole and indivisible mass that you call life" (94). Perhaps more crippling, she cannot get past individual cultural rituals to develop an appreciation for the larger culture. Like an outsider, an alien, each social rite is unfamiliar to her and uncomfortable to perform, though at some point in her life she has "taught [her] body to do a certain trick" (163). Still, she remains faceless.

If Rhoda stands outside of society in the role of Other, then directly opposite stands Percival. Cramer notes of him: "As the center of the group, Percival embodies the imperialist values binding the group together and the social institutions he represents" (448). Bernard's narrative of Percival in India applying the "standards of the West" (98) can be juxtaposed against Rhoda's description of her fear of social interaction as a tiger who leaps, pursuing her (75). Her choice of a tiger, an animal indigenous to Asia, invites such a contrast. Her analogy locates within English society the "savagery" and violence which the others situate within Asia. As Percival is portrayed as civilizing Indian culture, in an interesting contrast, Rhoda concurrently identifies herself as prey to English society. As the others practice their formalities over dinner, it is Rhoda and Louis who note that their rituals are "like the dance of savages" (101), further lessening the divide between civilized English society and the lands subjected to colonization. Still, Rhoda, too, finds comfort in Percival's presence. She suggests that within what Jinny calls the "globe whose walls are made of Percival" (105) are "Forests and far countries on the other side of the world [...] seas and jungles; the howlings of jackals and moonlight falling upon some high peak where the eagle soars" (105). The phrase "other side of the world" echoes the site of her before-stated longing and situates the fruition of her desired escape within Percival. Just as Rhoda identified and feared savagery within English society, so, too, she placed within Percival her hope for the establishment of order within that society. As a result, his death signals both her loss of hope and her gain of clarity, as she says in a passage defining her ambivalence, "I am alone in a hostile world. The human face is hideous. This is to my liking. I want publicity and violence and to be dashed like a stone on the rocks [...]. I am sick of prettiness; I am sick of privacy. I ride rough waters and shall sink with no one to save me" (115). The death of Percival arrests her ability to believe in the dominant culture and its capacity to bring order, to right the cart, to solve the problem. Not only is she outside of this culture, she finds that this culture is outside of itself; beneath its semblance of order lies hostility, filth, and savagery.

In his famous essay "On Cannibals," Michel de Montaigne notes of the tendency of imperialist culture to devalue behavioral deviation, "Indeed, we seem to have no other standard of truth and reason than the opinions and customs of our own country. There at home is always the perfect religion, the perfect legal system—the perfect and most accomplished way of doing everything." Rhoda's inability to adapt within the culture suggests both domestic fascism's silencing of heteroglossia and foreign imperialism's failure with regards to the colonized Other, and strengthens Woolf's critique of fascism by subverting its supporting ideas. Citing Bakhtin's discourse on monologism and his definition of "philosophical monologism" as an "attempt to squeeze the artist's demonstrated plurality of consciousness into the systematically monologic framework of a single worldview," McIntire suggests, "It is precisely this type of monologism that Woolf's novel seems to take as one of its principal thematic and narratological concerns" (31). McIntire sees the force of Woolf's critique occurring most particularly in the final section of the novel, where, as she notes, "Bernard's voice quite literally 'takes over' the narration" (31). However, while accurately locating a critical component of Woolf's critique in Bernard's speaking, I would suggest that a more significant challenge to monologism lies in Rhoda's deliberate silence. Her silence becomes a speaking silence, testifying to the voicelessness of the Other. Unlike Jinny, Louis, Neville, and Susan, Rhoda has not allowed Bernard to wrest her right to define, to "sum up" her life, away from her. Rather, in the novel's final section, it is evident that Rhoda has chosen of her own accord to move beyond the text, to leap, to fly to a place she once described to the others as seeing "between [their] shoulders, over [their] heads, to a landscape [...] to a hollow where the many-backed steep hills come down like birds' wings folded" (100), where she is freed from obscurity at last.

Works Cited

Cramer, Patricia. "Jane Harrison and Lesbian Plots: The Absent Lover in Virginia Woolf's *The Waves*." *Studies in the Novel* 37.4 (2005): 433-63.
de Montaigne, Michel. "Michel de Montaigne: On Cannibals." Trans. Paul Brians. Resources for the Study of World Civilization. 23 Dec. 1998. Washington State Universty. 8 June 2007 <http://www.wsu.edu/~wldciv/world_civ_reader/ world_civ_reader_2/montaigne.html>.
Hite, Molly. Introduction. *The Waves*. By Virginia Woolf. New York: Harcourt, 2006. xxxv-lxvii.
McIntire, Gabrielle. "Heteroglossia, Monologism, and Fascism: Bernard Reads *The Waves*." *Narrative* 13.1(2005): 29-45.
Woolf, Virginia. *The Waves*. Annotated and with an Introduction by Molly Hite. New York: Harcourt, 2006.
—. *A Room of One's Own – Three Guineas*. New York: Harcourt, 1992.

Conversation as Instigation:
Virginia Woolf's "Thoughts on Peace in an Air Raid"

by Judith Allen

Speech belongs half to the speaker, half to the listener. The latter must prepare to receive it according to the motion it takes. As among tennis players, the receiver moves and makes ready according to the motion of the striker and the nature of the stroke.

"Of Experience" Michel de Montaigne (III: 13 834)

Since Michel de Montaigne advocates writing as one speaks, my epigraph presents his view of the dynamics of both verbal and written communication, a view Virginia Woolf shares and enacts in the complex conversational modes of so many of her own essays.[1] Montaigne's tennis analogy enables his readers to visualize these complex interactions, participate in them, and ultimately, become the co-creators of his texts. In this process, readers are strategically moved to various places on the court, to experience and interpret the text from that position—and then reposition themselves accordingly.[2] We all have our own extremely complicated conversations with Woolf's texts, and in subsequent readings—and there are many—we inevitably have different conversations, in new contexts, and discover new versions. And significantly, as Woolf's narrator informs us in "Notes on an Elizabethan Play," the literature we read "will not suffer itself to be read passively, but takes us and reads us" (*CR1* 48).

In Woolf's "The Modern Essay," Woolf's narrator discusses this conversational mode and finds that re-reading the essayists of the past is to "sit down with them and talk"; she compares the relationship between the book and its reader to friendship, "for one is not finished with it because you have read it, anymore than friendship is ended because it is time to part" (217). Carl H. Klaus, looking back over his thirty-seven year relationship with Virginia Woolf's "The Modern Essay"—a period including multiple readings, each interrupted by a varying number of years away from it—communicates to his own readers his continuing desire "to meet it again and again," and "finding it altered upon each visit." In the process he also admits to "finding [himself] altered each time as well" (Klaus 33). As Woolf states: "Even things in a book-case change if they are alive; we find ourselves waiting to meet them again and again; we find them altered" *(CR1* 217-18).

Seeking to engage her readers while simultaneously avoiding an authoritative stance in her writings, Woolf's conversational mode—which she experimented with in her 1920 and 1923 essays, "A Talk About Memoirs" and "Mr. Conrad: A Conversation" (*E 3* 180, 376)—finds its way, in ever increasing complexity, into many essays: "Montaigne," *A Room of One's Own,* "On Not Knowing Greek," "How Should One Read a Book?," *Three Guineas* and "Thoughts on Peace in an Air Raid." These essays enact an intricate dialogic involving a multitude of voices that enable Woolf's narrators—in their interactions with these voices—to display many contradictory perspectives. Her narrators engage in a performance that functions to unsettle and awaken her readers, and in a Brechtian sense, to "defamiliarize" cultural institutions heretofore accepted as "natural," but are simply constructs.[3] My paper will focus on Woolf's 1940 essay, "Thoughts on Peace in an Air Raid," as it interrogates and responds to the fascism so pervasive in both the public and private spheres of her life. Through the lens of both Michel de Montaigne and Mikhail Bakhtin, I will explore Woolf's inclusion of varied voices, multiple conversations, and conflicting viewpoints within this essay; ultimately, I will show the significance of the readers' struggles with these manifold voices—as they search for their own voices—in 1940s England, and in today's ever so frightening world.

For Virginia Woolf, the "essay" fights a battle similar to her own, for it also stands outside, resisting stasis and rigid definition, and takes its place beside women and other marginalized figures in order to critique the conventions and ceremonies of those in power. The essay's hybrid nature, its openness, its freedom, all serve to resist the purity, totality, and certainty of patriarchal/fascist modes of expression. The essay's crucial interaction with its readers—as well as the many conversations embedded within it—serves to perpetuate the indeterminacy of its potential meanings. This aspect of the essay is not surprising given its origins in letters and dialogues. Montaigne also fills his essays with other voices, with quotations—re-contextualizing them within his essays—offering conflicting ideas, and thus not making judgments for his readers. In Woolf's "How Should One Read a Book?" her narrator advises that readers "take no advice…and "come to your own conclusions" (258).

Conversations do not simply resist an authoritarian stance—but function to move readers in a multitude of directions, expose them to differing perspectives, and, using Montaigne's tennis analogy—place the ball in their court. The reader's task is increasingly difficult, but more rewarding. Bakhtin comments on authoritative discourse, and sounds very much like Woolf as he speaks of "its inertia, its semantic finiteness, its calcification" (*Dialogic* 343); in "Craftsmanship," Woolf's narrator conjures up the death of words if we "pin words down to one meaning," for "words do not live in dictionaries, they live in the mind" (*DM* 206, 205). The actual struggle with the language and ideas of others—the conversation—is significant. Bakhtin calls attention to "the importance of struggling with the discourse of others," and explores "its influence in the history of an individual's coming to ideological consciousness" (*Dialogic* 348). This is evident in the dialogic aspect of the Montaignean essay, and I will argue, the Woolfian essay, for both include a multitude of voices and create a situation not unlike our everyday discourse with others; we are, after all, constantly interpreting speech, conversation, tone of voice, actions, and our own expectations, and as Bakhtin asserts:

> We can go so far as to say that in real life people talk most of all about what others talk about—they transmit, recall, weigh, and pass judgment on other people's words, opinions, assertions, information; people are upset by others' words, or agree with them, contest them….At every step one meets a "quotation" or a "reference" to something that a particular person said…to one's own previous words, to a newspaper….Thus talk goes on about speaking people and their words everywhere. (*Dialogic* 338-39)

The problematic nature of these activities—interpreting and quoting other voices—was also conveyed by Montaigne to his readers in the 1580s: "It is more of a job to interpret the interpretations than to interpret the things, and there are more books about books than about any other subject: we do nothing but write glosses about each other. The world is swarming with commentaries; of authors there is great scarcity" (III: 13 818). Both Montaigne and Woolf struggle with other voices—as their readers struggle—to make language their own, to find their own voice. No voice of certainty prevails. "Thoughts on Peace in an Air Raid" clearly presents this challenge to its readers.

Woolf includes a multitude of voices in "Thoughts on Peace"—narrators, quotations from loudspeakers and politicians, William Blake, Sir Thomas Browne, newspapers, radio, Lady Astor, and a young Englishman who fought in the last war; additionally, her narrator calls attention to those internalized voices within the young airman now up in the sky. Driven by those voices within himself—"ancient instincts, instincts fostered and cherished by education and tradition" (246), these voices are also clearly internalized and echoed by the women in this text. Woolf's thinking about the issue of instinct during this period—a time she was reading several of Freud's works[4]—is expressed in her diary entry in December 9, 1939: "If we're all instinct, the unconscious, what's all this about civilization, the whole man, freedom, &c?"(*D5* 250). In her letter to Shena, Lady Simon, on Jan. 22, 1940, Woolf asks questions about "removing men's disabilities" and whether we can "change sex characteristics?" She also questions whether "the women's movement [is] a remarkable experiment in that transformation? Mustn't our next task be the emancipation of man? How can we alter the crest and spur of the fighting cock?" (*L 6* 379). Questioning the responsibility for war—while taking responsibility for transforming men's attitudes towards war—Woolf's narrator foregrounds the binary thinking of that time; men had responsibility for war, and women were responsible for peace.

According to Woolf's diary entries, the air raid warnings began in Sept. 1939, and by August 1940, the time Woolf was writing this essay, she wrote in her diary: "Yesterday... there was a roar. Right on top of us they came. I looked at the plane, like a minnow at a roaring shark..." (*D5* 312). "Now we are in the war. England is being attacked. I got this feeling for the first time yesterday. The feeling of pressure, danger horror" (*D5 313*). "A bomb dropped so close I cursed Leonard for slamming the window." " I try to imagine how one's killed by a bomb. I've got it fairly vivid—the sensation: but cant see anything but suffocating nonentity following after"(*D5* 326). "Thoughts on Peace," like these diary entries, evokes the horrifying sounds of war, sounds that interrupt "thinking about peace":

> The Germans were over this house last night and the night before that. Here they are again. It is a queer experience, lying in dark and listening to the zoom of a hornet, which may at any moment sting you to death. It is a sound that interrupts cool and consecutive thinking about peace. Yet it is a sound—far more than prayers and anthems—that should compel one to think about peace. (243)

In a letter to Shena, Lady Simon, Woolf reflects on writing "Thoughts": "what the Americans want of me is views on peace—well these spring from views on war" (*L 6* 379). As Woolf's title indicates, "peace" is spoken of in the context of "war," of "bombing," for they are inseparable. Given the polarized view of gender at the time, women would be expected to limit their writings to "peace."

In preparation for writing "Thoughts on Peace in an Air Raid," Virginia Woolf recorded the following passage in her Reading Notebook of 1939-1940: "For now the male has also [...] his attributes in Hitler, & is fighting against them. Is this the first time a sex has turned against its own specific qualities? Compare with the woman [sic] movement" (Silver 116-117). Woolf also compiled a list of authors and phrases, and included the word, "cerebration," which translates as "thinking" or simply refers to the mind or the brain. A significant dairy entry May 15, 1940 also finds its way into the essay: "This idea struck me: the army is the body: I am the brain. Thinking is my fighting" (D5 285). Here Woolf links mind with body, and equates thinking with fighting, thus transforming "cerebration" into a weapon. These Reading Notes, along with Woolf's letters and diary entries from this period, raise many questions that permeate this essay—questions regarding the construction of gender, instinct versus reason and responsibility, and the power of language to transform our world. In "Thoughts on Peace in an Air Raid," Woolf utilizes certain narrative and rhetorical strategies for the purpose of enabling her readers to revise their views, to see the complicity of those women within the text, and perhaps see their own complicity. Statements are made, questioned, qualified, sometimes re-qualified, and then restated in a new way. As readers, we also witness this complex process of thinking.

With the word "cerebration" on her mind, Woolf's title announces her focus on "thinking," as the narrator's use of "we" and "us" engage her readers in this process. The language is metaphoric, as the sounds of the "hornet "and the "saw"—the animate and inanimate that sting and cut—stand in for the sounds of planes carrying bombs. The zoom of the hornet moves to the mind as the sawing heard overhead moves to the brain. The weapon, the bomb, in the guise of the hornet and the saw, are being transferred to the mind or the brain, as the words "think," "mind," "mental," and "brain" pervade the text. The weapons, now part of the mind, have been transformed into language.

Edward Bishop has examined Woolf's use of metaphors in her essays to show how "they are used deliberately to disturb the reader's unquestioned assumptions," and to involve those readers in Woolf's exploration of "the complex relation between language, phenomenal reality, and thought" ("Metaphor" 573). The reader is made aware of "the heuristic function of language," with "words testing their connections with things" (579). As Bishop suggests, "metaphor is by definition unsettling, effecting as it does a transfer from one realm to another" (579), as well as calling attention to language itself. The "zoom of a hornet," a metaphor for the bomber overhead, interrupts thinking about peace. Waiting for the bombs to drop in "Thoughts on Peace," "all thinking stopped" and "all feeling, save one dull dread, ceased" (247). The emotions of fear and hate are linked to sterility and infertility, and only the demise of these emotions will bring the return of life, of creativity. Like the Beadle's interruption of the intellectual curiosity, the imaginings, and the desires of one of the narrators in *A Room of One's Own*, the sterility and lack of fertility present here is expressed in terms of gender politics.

With the fascists' conception of the strict polarization of gender—the militaristic and the maternal—the construction of gender is a key question in this essay. Men are fighters, and women are at home, weaponless. But these women have the potential to fight—if they "fight with the mind" (244). Transferred from sky to mind, the hornet ends its journey as language, as words on the page of *The Times*; and these words, voiced by a woman writer, ironically express the following: "Women have not a word to say in politics," for "all the idea-makers who are in a position to make ideas effective are men." "There are no women in the Cabinet; nor in any *responsible* post." The issue of women's responsibility is now foregrounded, for "that is a thought that damps thinking and encourages *irresponsibility*. Why not bury the head in the pillow, plug the ears, and cease this futile activity of idea-making?" (244 my emphasis). Weapons and words have been connected; so for women to be weaponless is also to be without a voice, without a language for political purposes. The power to make change has been with men, but a woman's words on a page of *The Times*, in conversation with the narrator about "responsible" government positions and the "responsibility" of women to "think" positively, may begin to undermine that singular power source.

The narrator, in dialogue with the woman's voice in *The Times*, explores the issue of women's resistance: "Are we not stressing our disability because our ability exposes us perhaps to abuse, perhaps to contempt?" Calling for "thinking against the current," thinking against the ideas put forth by loudspeakers and politicians, she risks contempt by calling attention to their propaganda: "every day they tell us that we are a free people, fighting to defend freedom" (244). Calling for women to "puncture gas-bags and discover seeds of truth," she rejects their statement: "It is not true that we are free"; we are "both prisoners" tonight—he "boxed in his machine with a gun handy" and "we lying in the dark with a gas mask handy" (245). Implicit in this pronouncement of their shared imprisonment is the state of denial in those who use the loudspeaker, and in those women who have been silently complicit with them. But she has broken that silence, and others may follow.

As the hornet entered the mind of a woman writing in *The Times*, "another sound begins sawing its way in the brain. 'Women of ability'—it was Lady Astor speaking in *The Times* this morning—'are held down because of a subconscious Hitlerism in the hearts of men.'" (245). The goal is to make the subconscious conscious, "to drag [it] up into consciousness…," for this Hitlerism is "the desire for aggression; the desire to dominate and enslave" (245). The weapon is the process, the dredging up, the ability to expose these underlying feelings. And what the narrator has exposed, has "made visible," appears in the next few sentences; we are suddenly in the presence of prostitutes, of "painted women: dressed-up women; women with crimson lips and crimson fingernails" (245). After "showing" the enslavement, the narrator suggests that "if we could free ourselves from slavery we should free men from tyranny. Hitlers are bred by slaves" (245). But separating the "public" women from the "domesticated" women does not change the fact that both are commodified, both are enslaved.

She now includes the voice of a young Englishman who fought in the last war. The quotation of the young Englishman, referred to as "another mind-hornet in the chambers of the brain," once again conveys what must be fought: "'To fight against a real enemy, to earn undying honour and glory by shooting total strangers, and to come home with my breast covered with medals and decorations, that was the summit of my hope.…It was for this that my whole training, everything.…'" (246). This was not simply the hornet as weapon, as previously noted, but a combined "mind-hornet," suggesting that the weapon is already part of the young Englishman's mind; this "mind-hornet" is not simply the bomb, but represents—as his statement shows—the internalization of certain ideas and values that constitute a very familiar construction of masculinity. Questions arise about his "instincts," and how they relate to the maternal "instinct"? Can "we switch off the maternal instinct at the command of a table full of politicians?" (246). In 1941, Woolf again addressed this issue in a letter to Shena, Lady Simon: "No, I dont [sic] see whats [to] be done about war. Its manliness; and manliness breeds womanliness—both so hateful" (*L* 6 464).

Woolf's familiarity with fascists' writings on gender polarization is evident in *Three Guineas*, as well as her *Reading Notebooks*. From her reading of Hilary Newitt's *Women Must Choose* (1937),[5] as well as the writings of Hitler and Mussolini, she found that war and maternity were frequently equated with one another. Hitler's 1934 speech, which Woolf would have found in Newitt, states: "That which man sacrifices in the struggles of his people, woman sacrifices in the struggles to preserve the single cells of this people" (Newitt 40). Mussolini made similar statements regarding the "nature" of men and women: "War is to man what maternity is to the woman. I do not believe in perpetual peace; not only do I not believe in it, but I find it depressing" (Finer 175). Woolf's narrator attempts to deconstruct this so-called "natural" division of the sexes as she mimics the words of the Englishman who loved fighting: "The maternal instinct is a woman's glory. It was for this that my whole life has been dedicated, my education, training, everything...." (247). Exposing the patriarchal desires that women have internalized and made their own, her narrator speaks—as the narrator of *Three Guineas* did—of the "refusal to bear children," of "other openings for [women's] creative power." But most important at this point is the narrator's repetition of "we must" in connection with women being responsible for freeing men of "their fighting instinct," and bringing him "out of his prison into the open air," for "making happiness" and "freeing him from the machine" (247). This action by women would seem to free the young Englishmen, until the narrator thinks of the young Germans and Italians who will remain slaves; and what do the women reading these words think of their own slavery? "We must," in this context, must be stricken from women's vocabulary.

At this crucial point, another voice intrudes to join the interchange. Now we hear a captured enemy soldier speak of how happy he is that "'the fight is over!'" The reader is shown an enemy soldier who hates fighting, takes tea with the families of his former enemies, and clearly desires peace; but the need to substitute something for "the loss of his glory and his gun" is acknowledged. Freeing man from the machine may transform that sterility; now "the seed may be fertile" (248). Bakhtin speaks of "the alien voices that enter into the struggle for influence within an individual's consciousness" and that "a conversation with an internally persuasive word that one has begun to resist may continue, but it takes on another character: it is questioned...to expose its weak sides, to get a feel for its boundaries, to experience it physically as an object" (348). Both men and the women need to become aware of these "alien voices" and need to be freed from their constrained roles, with men gaining "access to creative feelings" with "new openings for their creative power" (248, 247). But women are not solely responsible for that task. Woolf's complicated dialogic strategies are utilized to move her readers out of their complacency and complicity. In their struggle to find their own voices, readers become aware of opposing voices, and as Montaigne asserts: "When someone opposes me, he arouses my attention, not my anger" (III 8 705). The conversational mode is an awakening and enables critical thinking, "thinking against the current."

When Woolf's narrator speaks of "other tables" beside "the officer tables and conference tables" and the importance of "thinking against the current," we can think of the very few today who are courageous enough to sit at those "other" tables, to be that "other," that "outsider," to speak out, to resist, to potentially risk your life. And what if taking this action—in the equivocal words of Woolf's narrator—"exposes us perhaps to abuse, perhaps to contempt?" Today we can think of the "Dixie Chicks," the blacklisting, the death threats, the burning of their CDs, and of Ayaan Hirsi Ali, the woman from Somalia who moved to the Netherlands, wrote a film called *Submission, Part I*, about defiance—about Muslim women who shift from total submission to God to a dialogue—a conversation—with their deity. She made the film with Theo van Gogh, who was murdered because of the film. Hirsi Ali remains under a death threat, but continues to speak out, with bodyguards in attendance.

It is difficult to acknowledge that Woolf prepared this essay for an American Symposium *on current matters concerning women in 1940* (my emphasis). As we re-read "Thoughts on Peace in an Air Raid" in 2007, we find a current that "flows fast and furious"…"in a spate of words from the loudspeakers and the politicians," that "whirls a young airman up into the sky" (244). Today, we read about bombing deaths on a daily basis—in countries too numerous to mention—as we are bombarded with "sound bites," strategic "leaks," and fear-inspiring language from varied media outlets—unfortunately echoing the American government's political agenda. Efforts to constrain freedom, to stifle dissent, are fast becoming the norm. The necessary "conversations" are silenced—with propaganda once again winning the day. As we re-read Woolf today, we find that her comments on topics such as "patriotism" and "those prostituted fact-purveyors"—our newspapers—clearly resonate with the political situations we confront on a daily basis. This is a difficult essay to read at this time, but there is no more important time to read it once again—for the silencing of women's voices is still with us.

Notes

1. For a discussion of the many links between Virginia Woolf and Michel de Montaigne, see Judith Allen, "Those Soul-Mates: Virginia Woolf and Michel de Montaigne," *Virginia Woolf: Themes and Variations*, ed. Vara Neverow-Turk and Mark Hussey, Pace University Press, 1993, 190-99.
2. See Cathleen Bauschatz's article on Montaigne's reading theory: "Montaigne's Conception of Reading in the Context of Renaissance Poetics and Modern Criticism, *The Reader in the Text*, ed. Susan R. Suleiman and Inge Crosman, Princeton University Press, 1980. 264-291.
3. See Frederic Jameson's *The Prison-House of Language* (58) and Edward L. Bishop's "The Subject in *Jacob's Room*," and "Metaphor and the Subversive Process of Virginia Woolf's Essays."
4. Hogarth Press published translations of Sigmund Freud's works beginning in1924. While writing "Thoughts on Peace in an Air Raid," Woolf was reading several of Freud's works, including *Moses and Monotheism* (1939), *Civilisation, War and Death: Selections from Three Works by Sigmund Freud* (1939), edited by John Rickman that included Freud's 1932 letter to Albert Einstein, "Why War?"; and *Group Psychology and the Analysis of the Ego* (1922).
5. Newitt's work documents the position of women under fascism in Germany, Italy, and Austria, and exposes the careful training of these women to make them an integral part of the machinery of the State. Hitler's 1934 speech, as quoted by Newitt, states: "Man and woman must therefore mutually value and respect each other when they see that each performs the task which Nature and Providence have ordained" (*Women Must Choose* 40-41). For a discussion of the egg as "a trope of the fascist discourse on gender roles," see Elizabeth Abel, *Virginia Woolf and the Fictions of Psychoanalysis* (160n# 25).

Works Cited

Bakhtin, M. M. *The Dialogic Imagination: Four Essays*. Austin: University of Texas Press, 1981.
Bishop, Edward L. "The Subject in *Jacob's Room*." *Modern Fiction Studies* Vol. 38. 1 (Spring 1992): 147-175.
—. "Metaphor and the Subversive Process of Virginia Woolf's Essays." *Style* Vol. 21. 4 (Winter 1987): 573-88.
Finer, Herman. *Mussolini's Italy*. London: Gollancz, 1935.
Jameson, Frederic. *The Prison House of Language*. Princeton: Princeton University Press, 1972.
Klaus, Carl. "On Virginia Woolf on the Essay." *The Iowa Review* 20 (1990): 28-34.
Montaigne, Michel de. *The Complete Essays of Montaigne*. Trans. Donald M. Frome. Stanford: Stanford Univer-

sity Press, 1965.
Newitt, Hilary. *Women Must Choose*. London: Gollancz Ltd., 1937.
Silver, Brenda R. *Virginia Woolf's Reading Notebooks*. Princeton: Princeton University Press, 1983.
Woolf, Virginia. *A Room of One's Own*. London: Harcourt, 1929.
—. *The Common Reader: First Series*. Ed. Andrew McNeillie. New York: Harcourt, 1984.
—. *The Second Common Reader*. Ed. Andrew McNeillie. New York: Harcourt, 1986.
—. *The Dairy of Virginia Woolf*. 5 vols. Ed. Anne Olivier Bell and Andrew McNeillie. London: Harcourt, 1977-1984.
—. *The Death of the Moth and Other Essays*. New York: Harcourt, 1970. 243-48.
—. *The Letters of Virginia Woolf*. 6 vols. Ed. Nigel Nicolson and Joanne Trautmann. New York: Harcourt, 1975-1980.

"THE LEANING TOWER": WOOLF'S PEDAGOGICAL GOAL OF THE LECTURE TO THE W. E. A. UNDER THE THREAT OF THE WAR

by Erika Yoshida

Considering her fame, Virginia Woolf only gave a small number of lectures in her lifetime. Hermione Lee indicates that she "did not give public lectures ...or give interviews" "with rare exceptions" (16). One of the reasons she avoided giving such lectures may have been her skepticism about lecture styles. In *Three Guineas*, Woolf decries the uselessness of English literary lectures (*TG* 35, 141-2). Yet, while preparing for a lecture in 1927 at the English Club in Oxford University, she writes in her diary that "writing for an audience always stirs me"(*D3* 135). As Melba Cuddy-Keane points out, Woolf thought that there was a good lecture style, whereby audiences could acquire ways of thinking for themselves, not through a didactic, authoritarian speech, but by dialogic, improvised lectures, as Roger Fry demonstrated (106-8). Thus, the existence of an actual audience was stimulating for her, while avoiding didactic, authoritarian speech in her lectures seems to have always been a great concern.

As Beth Rigel Daugherty discusses in "Virginia Woolf Teaching/Virginia Woolf Learning," Woolf's early experience of teaching at Morley College, an institute for working people, not only motivated her to educate "the common reader" about literature in her essays, but also taught her the way by which she could best teach working-class people (62). Confronted with the situation of working-class people, who had to leave school at fourteen years old and did not necessarily have "access to a library" (63), Virginia Stephen (at that time) acquired her own teaching style in which she "identifies with her students" by finding some condition in common, and thus "uses conversation rather than lectures"(65).

In "The Leaning Tower," which was originally a lecture to working-class students, Woolf seems to have applied this teaching style when she faced a large working-class audience at the Workers' Educational Association (the WEA). The variant texts for the lecture and the publication seem to show some differences in her points of emphasis according to each audience, that is, the original working-class audience and the subsequent intellectual readership.

In this paper, I will observe how Woolf attempted to solve the problem of the traditional lecture, which was by necessity didactic. Daugherty's study, "Readin', Writin', and Revisin': Virginia Woolf's 'How Should One Read a Book?'" demonstrates how fruitful it is to study Woolf's revision of texts for different audiences. I would like to collate the two different texts to examine the extent to which Woolf's consciousness of different audiences is reflected in each particular text, and to show how Woolf's pedagogical goal for each audience was different.

Woolf gave a lecture to the WEA in Brighton on April 27, 1940 about "modern trends" (*L6* 394) of literature. The lecture was intended to be read on March 2, but was postponed until April 27, 1940 because of a bout of influenza. The lecture was published by the Hogarth Press in *Folios of New Writing* in autumn of the same year.[1] There are also four typescripts in the Berg collection (M96, M97, M98, and M99). They all have no date, so it is difficult to specify which is the speech draft. However, since only one of the typescripts (*M96*) has a preface apologizing for the postponement, this typescript may be the one closest to the actual lecture draft. So, in this paper I will use M96 as the draft of the speech. The texts which appeared in *Folios of New Writing* and the later essay collection entitled *The Moment and Other Essays* are almost identical, so I will use the text in *The Moment* as the published version.

Woolf's lecture audience was composed of working-class men and women, most of whom were adult students of the WEA. The WEA was founded in 1903 by Albert Mansbridge, with a group of Trade Unionists and Co-operators, assisted by the Universities (Tawney, Introduction 5). It succeeded the Mechanics' Institutes, the Working Men's College, and the University Extension movement, and was "more successful than any of them in bringing higher education to working people"(Rose 265). One of the purposes of the WEA was to create a demand for education among working-class people, who had not been aware of the need for education (Tawney, "Education" 4). And since the 1930s, the WEA had been working not only for adult education but also for the reconstruction of the public educational system.

Since there seems to be few records of her actual lecture, we should describe the WEA students and tutors, who might have come in contact with Woolf. Woolf's lecture was organized by the South-Eastern District of the WEA. It organized several types of classes including tutorial classes of three years, one-year classes, terminal classes, and single lectures. The students included not only manual workers but clerks, teachers, and civil servants. The number of women students was a little larger than that of men in 1940 (WEA Annual Report 1940-1 3-4).

Although the need for one-day lectures was great because the organization of formal longer-term classes was difficult during the war period, the number of one-day lectures seems to have been small. For example, the Brighton branch, the largest one in the District, held only one single lecture in 1938-9 (WEA Annual Report 1938-9 6). After 1939, the South-Eastern District of the WEA omitted records of single lectures, so we can only surmise how big the attending audience of Woolf's lecture was in 1940. Woolf writes in her letter to Vita Sackville-West that her audience was about two hundred (*L6* 394), but it may be an exaggerated number considering that the students at the Brighton branch numbered about 130 and the recorded number of attendees at other lectures was generally smaller.[2]

Cuddy-Keane indicates that Woolf's connection with the WEA was through G. D. H. Cole, who served as national Vice-President of the WEA until 1938 (92). In addition to Cole, the Woolfs knew John Bradfield, tutor organizer of East Sussex (*D5* 239). Leonard seems to have been involved in launching the Lewes branch of the WEA in 1936 (*D4* 344). He also gave two serial lectures on the League of Nations at Eastbourne to about fifty students in 1937 (WEA Annual Report 1937 17).

It seems that Woolf appreciated some leaders of the WEA. In 1939, when she got depressed, she tried to recover her sense of reality by reading R. H. Tawney's "solid" book (*D5* 235). R. H. Tawney contributed to forming a firm basis for tutorial classes as WEA president from 1928 to 1944. He writes in his presidential address that the intention of the tutorial classes are "not merely meetings where the tutor conveys information to an acquiescent audience, but alert and critical groups, in which education takes place through the free interchange of ideas in an atmosphere of fellowship and co-operative effort"("Education" 6). Cuddy-Keane suggests that the WEA's "pedagogical goal" and method of education were similar to Woolf's thoughts on working-class education (89).

Woolf's lecture followed such educational ideals, and she expected her audience to argue with her not as passive learners but as coequals who shared the same problem. As Cuddy-Keane argues, this is demonstrated in Woolf's use of the pronoun "we" (96-99). Woolf describes the writers of previous generations as those who lived in a stable "tower of middle-class birth and expensive education" (*M* 114), supported by a clear separation of social classes. However, in a time when the old hierarchy is being "rooted up" (*M* 114), Woolf asks the audience to imagine how uncomfortable writers in the 1930s feel in a leaning tower, and she argues that:

> Anger; pity; scapegoat beating; excuse finding—these are all very natural tendencies; if we were in their position we should tend to do the same. But we are not in their position; we have not had eleven years of expensive education. We have only been climbing an imaginary tower. We can cease to imagine. We can come down. (*M* 115)

By finding common ground between herself and her audience members, Woolf tries to stand in their position. That is, Woolf and the working-class people share the lack of expensive education, though they belong to different classes.

In spite of her efforts, however, the responses from the audience discouraged her. The lukewarm response may no doubt be ascribed to a large audience and the formal setting, unlike the small and intimate classroom at Morley College. Even if the students were accustomed to tutorial classes of small discussion groups of thirty to have "free and fair discussion" (Stocks 45), the formal lecture with such a big audience would necessarily make students passive and silent.

Another reason seems to have been the audience's incomprehension of Woolf's metaphorical style of speech and the conservatism of their taste in literature. Woolf cites poems to explain the features of "the Leaning Tower writers'" writings, but according to a WEA investigation of its students in London in 1939, the number of literature students reading poetry (compared to drama or biography) for pleasure was very small (WEA 7). The investigation also showed that the most popular fiction writer read by both literature students and others was Galsworthy. Virginia Woolf was mentioned by only six students, and E. M. Forster by three among the 436 students who replied to a questionnaire (10). In the early twentieth century, as Jonathan Rose points out, "the literary education of most working-class pupils stopped in the mid-nineteenth century" (127). Most of them had little chance to get to know contemporary writings. The library system discouraged them from borrowing a book by an author they had never read. And when they did have the opportunity to read modern literature, some students rejected it because they could not appreciate its abstractness and felt uneasy at the atmosphere of middle-class culture they found in it (Rose 138-9).

This speech did not appear to evoke discussion among the WEA audience, but, as might be expected, it created a sensation among the 1930s writers, who had been labelled as "Leaning Tower writers" by Woolf.[3] Her hesitation to publish the lecture was due to her anticipation of their responses, though John Lehmann insistently persuaded her to publish it. She accepted Lehmann's request unwillingly on the condition that she could bring herself to revise it (*L6* 408). Thus, the question of how she rewrote her article for the readers of *Folios of New Writing* remains.

Folios of New Writing, appearing between 1940 and 1941, was a successor to *New Writing*, which John Lehmann had edited since 1936. Lehmann's intention was to make the magazine an international outlet for young authors and new talents. The readership was considered to be intelligent, including working-class people who were sensitive to modern trends in literature and were not satisfied with Victorian or classic literature. W. H. Auden, Cecil Day Lewis, and Louis MacNeice were frequent contributors to Lehmann's magazines. Woolf's revision, however, was not aimed at diluting her criticism of the younger writers.

Let me survey first the parts where Woolf's expectation for working-class audience is shown clearly. In the first paragraph of the speech draft, which was deleted when she rewrote for publication, she advises her audience not to trust her views on her contemporary writers completely:

> But before beginning this excursion, here is a word of warning. Do not expect your lectuerer [sic] this afternoon to tell you the truth .... Ask him to look at that object through another pair of eyes—and that is what you do when you ask him to speak of the work of other living writers, and he is bound to [g]et it wrong—out of focus, out of proportion. The reason is that he is still seeing the objec[t] through his own eyes. That is why the opinions o[f] living writers are almost always worthless .... So when we come to speak of living writers, you must see with your own eyes; for I am only able to see with mine. (*M*96 1)

From the very outset, Woolf encourages her audience to change their passive attitude. This shows Woolf's challenge to the lecture mode. She tries to relinquish the authority inherent in her voice by showing her audience that her view is no more than a partial one. She urges her audience to listen to her lecture critically and judge what she says by themselves. Furthermore, Woolf's preface functions to enable her audience to practice thinking by themselves on the occasion of the lecture itself.

One of Woolf's attempts to evade a didactic mode in her lecture is also recognized in her choice of words. Woolf analyzes a poem written by Louis MacNeice, whom she calls a "leaning tower writer," and she argues that the writers who began writing around 1925 had been exposed to political and social upheavals, and that they were strongly conscious of their privileged middle-class-birth and expensive education. Due to these influences, some tendencies in their work emerge. In the draft and published texts, she explains these tendencies in a slightly different way. The italics show the substantially different parts. Please note that in the speech she referred only to "the political strain":

> Yet they feel, as Mr MacNeice has said, that they must help to bring about that society in which every one is equal and free. That explains *the political strain* in their work. Even when they talk of love they talk of love as a duty rather than as a pleasure. It is the duty of the bourgeois class to love the proletariat class; and thus to break down the barreiers[sic] between classes. That explains why their love poetry is such strange love poetry. (*M*96, 26; emphasis is mine)

> Yet as Mr. MacNeice bears witness, *they feel compelled to preach, if not by their liv-*

ing, at least by their writing, the creation of a society in which every one is equal and every one is free. It explains *the pedagogic, the didactic, the loud speaker strain* that dominates their poetry. *They must teach; they must preach.* Everything is a duty—even love. (*M* 118; emphasis is mine)

After these passages, Woolf cites poems by Day Lewis and Wordsworth to make a comparison. She declares that the leaning tower writers' poetry is "oratory, not poetry" (*M* 119), because their poetry needs to be listened to "in company," while that of Wordsworth can be heard "in solitude" (*M* 119). This leads to her essential belief that good literature should satisfy the "I," not "the 'we' of public bodies" (*E4* 223). In the speech draft, as she does not refer to "the pedagogic, the didactic, the loud speaker strain," the logical connection between "political strain" and the artistic value seems to be weaker. The reason she did not refer to the pedagogical strain, I might suggest, is that Woolf deliberately evaded taking up the didactic aspects in the poetry of the leaning tower writers in order to avoid criticism by the audience that she herself was giving a didactic lecture at that moment. Woolf meticulously constructed her speech so as to be stylistically consistent with her arguments.

On the other hand, in the published text, Woolf seems to present her artistic thoughts more freely, for there is neither the platform nor the unequal relationship between lecturer and audience. There, her statements on the writers' mind are more analytical and her use of words, such as "surface" and "inner," are more frequent, so that the contrasts between the conscious and the unconscious mind stand out. Frequent repetitions of her views on writing show her serious concern about contemporary literature and writers. Thus, in the published text, whose audience should include writers of the next generation, she seems to express her thoughts more didactically than in the speech.

The alterations made in the last part of the essay not only demonstrate her intention to be allied with her audience, but also seem to reveal her fundamental thoughts on education. When Woolf surveys the history of literature, she admits that there is a relationship between literature and education, and points out that almost all good writing has been produced by "a man who has learnt his art by about eleven years of education" (*M* 112). However, she adds that "a writer's education is so much less definite than other educations. Reading, listening, talking, travel, leisure—many different things it seems are mixed together" (*M* 112). She never admits that education of itself has produced good writing. Woolf cites a parent's expectation of uniting two educational systems, the old traditional public school and the new village school. Woolf appears to sympathize with the parent's thoughts on schools. Actually, however, Woolf's own opinion about both institutions remains obscure.

Her final assertion is that the library helps "bridge the gulf between the two worlds": the old and the new (*M* 124). She declares "we have got to teach ourselves to understand literature" by reading (*M* 124). It is noteworthy here that Woolf discounts the necessity of institutional education. In the following extracts, Woolf further intensifies her arguments, especially in the published text:

> …if literature is going to go on after the war …and it is going to go on … it will be because we, *the common readers and the common writers* have taught ourselves, by our own efforts, how to read and how to write. (*M* 96, 33; second and third ellipses are in original.)

It is thus that English literature will survive this war and cross the gulf—if *commoners and outsiders* like ourselves make that country our own country, if we teach ourselves how to read and to write, how to preserve, and how to create. (*M* 125) (For both passages, emphasis is mine.)

The most remarkable alteration here is the change from "the common readers and the common writers" to "commoners and outsiders." In the former, she tries to equate readers and writers through the use of the same adjective "common." By the juxtaposition of "we," "the common readers," and "the common writers," Woolf narrows the distance which separates the reader from the writer. This juxtaposition acts to change the fixed relationship between the writer and the reader into a more dynamic one, and also diminishes the distance separating the upper-middle-class lecturer Woolf from the working-class audience. By doing this, she encourages the audience to become writers as well as readers, and to play an important role in sustaining English literature.

On the other hand, the expression, "commoners and outsiders," seems more political. It emphasizes the opposition between the privileged educated class and the rest of the society. The statement "commoners and outsiders like ourselves make that country our own country" might have been taken as a comment on the prevailing educational system, and not just a thought on literature. If this statement had been directed to the WEA audience, it might have aroused opposition. In the published text, Woolf tries to ally herself with "outsiders," the reading audience who feel excluded from the traditional educational system; whereas, when speaking to the WEA, Woolf omitted her attempt to ally herself with "outsiders." Woolf's emphasis on active roles played by "outsiders" might have led her audience to mistakenly conclude that she was casting doubts on the value of education. We can only guess, but this change was made perhaps on the grounds that, during the 1930s and '40s, the WEA was actively involved in promoting a system of equal education. Probably she did not want to discourage their efforts, and was thus careful not to include any comments which could have been seen to slight the value of education.

It was important for Woolf in the published text, however, to ensure her position as an outsider, without any academic background, in order to demonstrate the advantage of self-teaching, which she herself had practiced as a professional writer. This statement might encourage the novice writer who deplores not having had the opportunity of higher education. Woolf suggests that literature could be better improved by autodidactic reading and by the participation of working-class writers and readers in literature, irrespective of institutional education. In the published text rewritten for *Folios*' readers, Woolf seems to stress her independent attitude as an outsider and her belief that self-teaching through reading excels school education in creating good English literature, a belief which she had attested through her long career as a novelist and essayist.

The difference of audience for each text greatly affected her writing in the point of emphasis, leading to her choice of different expressions and words in each text. In 1940, as the war situation got worse and worse, she wrote, "No audience. No echo. That's part of one's death" (*D5* 293). Lack of an audience means the loss of the sources of her inspiration and corporeal objects from which Woolf formed her narrative and constructed good relationships. Whereas Woolf's imaginary audience, the common reader, had no doubt been a fertile source of her creative inspiration, in those horrible war years, her artistic imagination, at times, might have yearned for tangible audience.

Notes

1. John Lehmann, who had launched the magazine in 1936, brought it to the Hogarth Press when he became its partner in 1938. *New Writing* was a "twice-yearly miscellany in book form of contemporary imaginative writing from England and abroad," and the *Folios of New Writing* was an alternative to it during World War II. (*D5* 118, footnote).
2. The average number of attendees of single lectures at the Brighton branch was around thirty and even the most popular lecture attracted only 100 students between 1938 and 1939 (WEA Annual Report 1938 16; 1938-9 19).
3. In the next *Folios of New Writing* issued after her death, Lehman published their response in "The Leaning Tower: Replies," *Folios of New Writing*. Spring (1941). Cuddy-Keane studies them in *Virginia Woolf: The Intellectual & Public Sphere* (101-6).

Works Cited

Cuddy-Keane, Melba. *Virginia Woolf. The Intellectual and the Public Sphere*. Cambridge: Cambridge University Press, 2003.
Daugherty, Beth Rigel. "Virginia Woolf Teaching/Virginia Woolf Learning: Morley College and the Common Reader." *New Essays on Virginia Woolf*. Ed. Helen Wussow. Dallas: Contemporary Research Press, 1992: 31-40.
—. "'Reading', Writin', and Revisin': Virginia Woolf's 'How Should One Read a Book?'" *Virginia Woolf and the Essay*. Ed. Beth Carole Rosenberg and Jeanne Dubino. New York: St. Martin's, 1997. 159-75.
Lee, Hermione. *Virginia Woolf*. New York: Random House, 1997.
Rose, Jonathan. *The Intellectual life of the British Working Classes*. New Haven, London: Yale University Press, 2001.
Stocks, Mary. *The Workers' Educational Association: The First Fifty Years*. London: George Allen & Unwin Ltd., 1953.
Tawney, R. H. "The Education of the Citizen: being the Presidential Address of R. H. Tawney: the 2nd Annual conference of the Workers' Educational Association". Ed. A. S. General Secretary. Firth and Green. E. Organising Secretary. York: The Workers' Educational Association, London, 1932.
—. Introduction. *The Story of the Workers' Educational Association From 1903 to 1924*. By T. W. Price. London: Labour Publishing Company, 1924. 5-9.
Woolf, Virginia. *Three Guineas*. Ed. Naomi Black. Oxford: Blackwell, 2001.
—. "The Leaning Tower." *The Moment and Other Essays*. 1947. Ed. Leonard Woolf. London: Hogarth, 1981. 105-25.
—. "The Leaning Tower." *Folios of New Writing* (Autumn 1940): 11-33.
—. "The Leaning Tower."("Some Modern Tendencies"), Ts. New York Public Library: Berg Collection. *The Virginia Woolf Manuscripts from the Henry W. and Albert A. Berg Collection at the New York Public Library*. Woodbridge: Research Publications International (1994) : reel 11. M96, 97, 98, 99.
—. *The Diary of Virginia Woolf*. Ed. Anne Olivier Bell and Andrew McNeillie. Vols. 3, 4 and 5. New York: Harcourt, 1980, 1983, 1984.
—. *The Essays of Virginia Woolf*. Ed. Andrew McNeillie. Vol. 4. London: Hogarth, 1994.
—. *The Letters of Virginia Woolf*. Ed. Nigel Nicolson and Joanne Trautmann. Vol. 6. New York: Harcourt, 1980.
The Workers' Educational Association, South-Eastern District. *WEA District Annual Report*. Chatham, 1937, 1938, 1938-9, 1940-1.
The Workers' Educational Association, London District. *The Leisure of the Adult Students: A Sample Investigation in London*. London, 1937.

Regarding Violence: Virginia Woolf's *Three Guineas* and Contemporary Feminist Responses to War

by Kimberly Engdahl Coates

Galvanized by reading Spanish Civil War pamphlets and by viewing photographs of children lacerated by Franco's bombs, Virginia Woolf wrote *Three Guineas* in an effort to understand war's precipitating causes and perhaps in hopes of finding an antidote to its future inevitability. As Naomi Black, in *Virginia Woolf as Feminist*, and more recently Jane Marcus, in her introduction to the newly annotated edition of *Three Guineas*, have reminded us, Woolf's manifesto against war was of preeminent importance to the "foundational debates of Second Wave feminism in the United States, Britain, Europe, and abroad" (Marcus xxxvi). As Marcus notes, new feminist scholars and activists of the 1970s and 1980s referred to Woolf's polemic continuously as they confronted many of the same issues themselves: women and citizenship, gender and identity, the economics of motherhood, patriotism and pacifism (xxxvii).

The new edition of *Three Guineas*, edited by Mark Hussey, has been released into a contemporary world that bears uncanny similarities to the one Woolf found herself struggling to apprehend in her final years. The horrors of the Spanish Civil War, which Woolf had experienced indirectly, gave way to her direct experience of the Blitz. Today, as a recent article in *The New York Times* (1/14/07) by Helene Cooper suggests, the "best we can hope for" regarding the war in Iraq might be a repeat of the Spanish Civil War, a contained, if horribly bloody conflict, that did not extend beyond Spain's borders to engulf the continent. "Probably," Cooper sardonically remarks in a parenthetical aside, "because the continent was busy getting engulfed in World War II, but let's not be too technical" (Sec 4: 14). Cooper leaves the reader uncomfortably aware that the war in Iraq, however contained it might appear from our privileged position here in the United States, may be the spark in a much larger, much less manageable conflagration.

As Woolf's time was, so is ours one in which the powerful have emptied words of meaning and have replaced truth with politically expedient lies: violence has come to mean liberty, dictatorship is supposedly democracy, and militancy masquerades as diplomacy. Once again, we daughters are left wondering if the best investment of our time and money might not be rags, petrol, and matches so as to "burn the house to the ground" (*TG* 42). However, like their foremother, today's feminists are choosing a "mental fight": brandishing words rather than fire in an effort to blaze through the current stupefying haze of hegemonic grammar. This afternoon, I will argue that contemporary feminist responses to our current wars return us once again to Virginia Woolf's seminal text but this time in hopes that we might recognize the utter failure of our imaginations. In *Three Guineas*, Woolf reminds us, writes the late Susan Sontag in *Regarding the Pain of Others*, that our "failure is one of imagination, of empathy: we have failed to hold [war's] reality in mind" (8). To "imagine," we must be able to "see" differently, for a "failure of the imagination" is first and foremost, as Arundhati Roy defines it, "the inability to see the world in terms other than those the establishment has set out for [us]" (50). But in order to "see" differently, we have to "behold" what is before us long enough to "feel" its impact; it is only then, that we may in turn "think" differently—and "think," as Woolf ardently instructs us, "we must" (*TG* 77). In what follows, I contend that whether implicitly, like Arundhati Roy and Judith Butler, or explicitly like Susan Sontag, contemporary feminists invoke Virginia Woolf's *Three Guineas* as a text which can teach us how to regard violence so that we might linger with our grief long enough to imagine, and thus to think, an alternative future.

Woolf's influence on recent feminists who are speaking out against war, imperialism, and globalization has much to do with grief and the power it has, as we work through it, to radically alter our perspective. In using the phrase "working through," I am specifically invoking the distinction Dominick LaCapra, in his book *Writing History, Writing Trauma*, draws between "working through" grief that is born of traumatic loss vs. "acting out" that grief, terms he borrows directly from Freudian psychoanalysis but rearticulates with historical analysis and a socio-cultural political critique. For LaCapra, "acting out" refers to the tendency that victims of trauma have to become compulsively caught up in a repetition of the traumatic event and its symptoms. While "acting out," argues La Capra, can be a necessary process and even a condition for "working through" a grief born of loss, the individual, or in some cases the society, may never transcend the force of that repetition compulsion and thus will more than likely remain incapable of ethically responsible behavior. By contrast, "working through," which LaCapra insists exists not in diametric opposition to "acting out" but rather in a dialogic relation to it, operates as a "counterveiling force" (71). The person or society "working through" grief attempts to get enough critical distance on the traumatic event to distinguish "now" from "then." In other words, "working through" enables a reconceptualization of socio-political issues and action that then in turn allows for systemic revision. According to LaCapra, it is only by "working through" a traumatic loss that one acquires the possibility of being an ethical and political agent for change. It is very important to realize, however, that LaCapra is not denying the emotional necessity of "acting out," especially for the individual trauma victim; his goal is instead to encourage conditions at a social and historical level in which "working through" never transcends the force of "acting out" and the repetition compulsion, but rather remains able to counteract and/or mitigate that force so as to generate a "different possibility, a different force field" (71).

According to Arhundhati Roy, the Indian and American governments have executed foreign policies that "act out" a response to injury and therefore only repeat an ongoing history of violence. In addition, they have denied their citizens the possibility of "working through" the grief such "acting out" continues to perpetuate. In her collection of speeches published in book form and titled *War Talk*, Roy, best known for her stunning novel *The God of Small Things*, insists that in today's world, people's grief has been manipulated and packaged: "What we are seeing now is a vulgar display of the business of grief, the commerce of grief, the pillaging of even the most private feelings for political purpose. It is a terrible, violent thing for a state to do to its people" (52). With regards to America, Roy has in mind the way the Bush administration and media, following the traumatic events of 9/11, dictated how we were to grieve: fly those American flags made in China, hail the chief with chants of "USA," watch your television to be reminded again and again of the evildoers who "hate us because we are free," and of course, go shopping! Roy indicts the Bush administration for inciting American citizens to support more violence rather than urging them to think through what kind of policies may have given rise to the 9/11 attacks or promoting conversations about shared loss and suffering. In contrast, Roy stands before her American audience and says, "What I would really love to talk to you about is loss. Grief, failure, brokenness, numbness, uncertainty, fear, the death of feeling, the death of dreaming. [...] What does loss mean to individuals? What does it mean to whole cultures, whole peoples who have learned to live with it as a constant companion?" (52). Roy proceeds to guide her audience through a prolonged meditation on shared suffering by calling their attention to other tragedies that have occurred across the world in Septembers past not, she says, as "an accusation or a provocation. But just to share the grief of history. To thin the mist a little. To say to the citizens of America, in the gentlest, most human way: Welcome to the World" (52).

Similarly Judith Butler, in her recent book *Precarious Life: The Powers of Mourning and Violence*, implores us to "tarry with grief": "Is there something to be gained from grieving?" Butler asks, "from tarrying with grief, from remaining exposed to its unbearability and not endeavoring to seek a resolution for grief through violence?" (30). In powerful and moving ways, Butler explores the possibility of a non-violent ethics rooted in our willingness to "tarry" and thus to be "undone" by each other. Grief, according to Butler, challenges our assumptions of corporeal autonomy by revealing the "thrall in which our relations with others hold us" and moves us to ask what kind of politics, what kinds of communities and international ties might be imagined and brought to fruition in an effort to "sustain precarious lives across the globe" (23). Our ability to imagine a future without violence, then, depends on our willingness to embrace the way in which we are bodily enmeshed with those not only in our immediate proximity but also across global distances.

Virginia Woolf's *Three Guineas* is also a text informed by loss and one, I would argue, which like the work of Roy and Butler, urges us to tarry with grief albeit in a much more rhetorically complex fashion. Maggie Humm has referred to *Three Guineas* as a "profoundly innovative image/text" that "breaks with the formal generic frontiers of narrative in [its] textual heterogeneity, [its] multiple boundaries and frames" (213). Humm refers to the photographs that Woolf did not include in her text—those of the dead Spanish children and ruined houses—as "photographic memories" whose feminine "affect" counters the patriarchal ideology represented by the five newspaper photos she does include in the text. I would like to expand on Humm's assertion by suggesting that the absent photographs function as "photographic memories" primarily because they bear traces of Woolf's personal loss: the death of her nephew Julian Bell, killed while driving an ambulance on the Spanish front.

Woolf first mentions receiving photographs from the Spanish government in a letter she writes to Julian Bell in November 1936 which begins: "My dearest Julian, I dreamt of you so vividly last night that I must take my typewriter and write, though its not my turn" (*L* 6 84). Towards the end of the same letter, she notes that Lord Cecil will be coming to tea, "to talk about Spain I think. [...] This morning I got a packet of photographs from Spain all of dead children, killed by bombs—a cheerful present" (85). Throughout 1937 while she is conceiving *Three Guineas*, Woolf struggles in her diary entries with Julian's decision to go to Spain to fight fascism and then ultimately tries to reconcile herself to his consequent death in July of that same year: "a complete break; almost a blank; like a blow on the head; a shriveling up" (*D* 5 104). While it stands in stark contrast to the zest she conveys as she "gallops" through to the end of *Three Guineas*, Woolf's grief over the loss of Julian, compounded by her sister Vanessa Bell's despair, lends the text its final emotive force. As she worked on revisions throughout the end of 1937 and into 1938, revisiting the photographs of Franco's victims as she did so, it is reasonable to assume that the photographs, haunting on their own, would now also serve as a painful reminder of Julian's sacrifice and violent death: "It is an unnatural death his. I can't make it fit in anywhere. Perhaps because he was killed, violently. I can do nothing with the experience yet" (*D* 5 112-113).

However, Woolf does do something with the experience; she makes it the reader's experience as well. Like Butler, Woolf is aware that our bodily beings, and the vulnerability thereof, place us beyond ourselves and implicate us in lives that are not our own, in lives both within and outside the nation's borders: "As a woman I have no country. As a woman I want no country. As a woman my country is the whole world" (*TG* 129). The absent photographs, inflected by her own loss, become the lens through which her readers, including, of course, the barrister, are to see the world before them. They function for the reader as what Brian Massumi, in "The Autonomy of Affect," has referred to as a "shock to thought": a sudden jolt that does not so much reveal truth as thrust us involuntarily into a mode of critical inquiry" (qtd. in Bennett 11). Because Woolf wants us to disengage from the hegemonic narrative and visual frames symbolized by the newspaper photographs and instead to "hold" war's reality in our mind so as to "feel it beneath our skin," she describes the Spanish photographs only once in vivid detail; thereafter they haunt the text as a refrain brought in at strategic moments to moor the reader in a concrete reality when rhetoric, even if it is her own, threatens to distract the reader's attention. Photographs, she tells us, "are not arguments addressed to the reason; they are simply statements of fact addressed to the eye" (*TG* 13). But the eye, as Woolf goes on, "is connected with the brain; the brain with the nervous system. That system sends its message in a flash through every past memory and present feeling" (*TG* 14).

This statement, which appears early on in the first letter of *Three Guineas*, actually serves as an apt structural analysis of the entire text. Lest our brains prompt us to forget what we see, Woolf shocks our nervous systems again and again with her relentless refrain. In the first letter, for example, while insinuating that of course "the emotion is too positive to suffer patient analysis" and we therefore should "concentrate on the practical suggestions which [the barrister] brings forward for our consideration," she proceeds to list those practical considerations: "to sign a letter to the newspapers; to join a certain society; to subscribe to its funds" (15). However, Woolf soon returns us to the photographs and the emotion—the horror, the grief invoked by them—that remains unappeased: "That emotion, that very positive emotion, demands something more positive than a name written on a sheet of paper; an hour spent listening to speeches; a cheque written for whatever sum we can afford—say one guinea. Some more energetic, more active method of expressing our belief that war is barbarous, [...] seems to be required"(15). Simultaneously invoking her reader's tendency to regard, then glance away, from war's disturbing reality—"but you are busy, let us return to the facts"—and highlighting the various truths hidden in such facts by asking her reader to "behold" them consistently from different angles, Woolf demands that her reader work through the emotions incited by war's atrocities so as to deconstruct the patriarchal system that has been allowed to continue fueling the war machine. What she wants most radically and most profoundly is total systemic change.

Her refusal to include the actual photographs, as scholars like Jane Marcus and Diane Gillespie have also noted, is an effort to deflect the masculine gaze away from atrocities that might only encourage the "fight instinct" and instead to redirect it through multiple descriptive vantage points all designed to coalesce in an understanding of the ideological link between patriarchy and war. If the absent photographs become the new lens through which readers are to view the "facts," those "facts" gain new emotional currency as Woolf begins developing what culminates in "another picture": "It is the figure of a man; [...] He is called in German and Italian Fuhrer or Duce (Duche); in our own language Tyrant or Dictator. And behind him lie ruined houses and dead bodies—men, women and children" (168). This other picture is reached only after Woolf places the Kodak in the daughter's hands and then positions the barrister and her readers to "behold" the world from that "queer" new angle: "Though we see the same world, we see it through different eyes. [...] Let us by way of a very elementary beginning lay before you a photograph—a crudely coloured photograph—of your world as it appears to us who see it from the threshold of the private house" (*TG* 23). Although the final photograph we are asked to look upon implicates men as the progenitors of war's destruction, Woolf will not permit we "daughters" to deny our own culpability, insisting instead, "we are ourselves that figure" (*TG* 168).

In *Three Guineas*, Woolf presents a complex visual and rhetorical argument that is invested in the hope that grief, if appropriately worked through, might have the potential to effect political and social change. Susan Sontag, in what was to be her last book, *Regarding the Pain of Others*, appreciates Woolf's insistence on this point but doubts whether the strong emotions generated by viewing shocking photographs of war's atrocities can ever be transformed into political action. Initially, Sontag holds Woolf accountable for failing to convince her that visual images have the power to prevent war. Sontag's criticisms of Woolf in this regard can be briefly summed up as follows: 1) Woolf misses the point that "photographs of the victims of war are themselves a species of rhetoric"; 2) Woolf invokes the hypothetical shared experience of looking at the Spanish photographs and then naively assumes that the shock cannot fail to unite people of good will; 3) Woolf reads the photographs as confirming a general abhorrence of war and therefore stands back from "an engagement with Spain as a country with a history. [...] For Woolf, as for many anti-war polemicists, war is generic, and the images she describes are of anonymous, generic victims" (9).

Sontag's criticisms of Woolf are very much tied up in the distinctions she herself makes between photographs and narrative: photographs, she tells us, have the capacity to move us deeply, but that emotion is fleeting whereas narrative has the capacity to elicit understanding and therefore is more likely to translate into some form of political action. "A narrative," writes Sontag, "seems likely to be more effective than an image. Partly it is a question of the length of time one is obliged to look, to feel" (122). Rather than analyzing the politically powerful interweaving of these two genres as they are exhibited in Woolf's *Three Guineas*, Sontag instead fixates on the visual, reading Woolf as if she had actually included the photographs of Franco's atrocities in her text. As a result, she fails to attend to the way Woolf quite deliberately uses each genre to its fullest advantages, asking us to embody the images as she moves us through the interstices of a narrative produced from multiple points of view. It is precisely because she understands visual images as a "species of rhetoric" that she makes invisible those photographs capable of provoking further violence—the dead bodies and ruined houses—and makes visible those which, cloaked in the guise of ordinary pomp and circumstance, persuade viewers to enlist in and to support military action. If Woolf does not explicitly engage with "Spain as a country with a history," she nevertheless powerfully dissects the ideology with which she is most familiar—British patriarchy—urging her fellow citizens to attend to the tyranny in their own backyards.

Despite her criticisms of Woolf and her ensuing ambivalence about the role the visual might play in a critique of violence, Susan Sontag ends her book by exclaiming, "Let the atrocious images haunt us. Even if they are only tokens, and cannot possibly encompass most of the reality to which they refer, they still perform a vital function" (115). Neither Woolf, Roy, Butler, nor Sontag give us a formula for turning affect into action. Butler, urging us to view our "dislocation from first world privilege" as an opportunity to "start [imagining] a world in which violence might be minimized, in which an inevitable interdependency becomes acknowledged as the basis for a global political economy," confesses to "not knowing how to theorize that interdependency" and submits that it is her humble hope that the essays in *Precarious Life* might begin the process of imagining how we can do so (xii-xiii). We cannot rid the world of violence and injustice over night, but we can refuse hegemonic strategies to contain our grief and our outrage. We can imagine, and we can struggle to articulate and live, as Woolf advises us to do in *Three Guineas*, according to "the connections that lie far deeper than the facts on the surface" (169). We can heed Woolf and refuse to repeat "their words" and follow "their methods," continuing instead to find "new words and new methods" (170). And we can hear Woolf today in Arundhati Roy's insistence that our strategy should be "not only to confront Empire, but to lay siege to it. To deprive it of oxygen. To shame it. To mock it. With our art, our music, our literature, our stubbornness, our joy, our brilliance, our sheer relentlessness—and our ability to tell our own stories" (112). We can, we must, as Woolf reminds us again in "Thoughts on Peace in an Air Raid," "fight with the mind," and we can, we must, teach others to do the same (244).

Works Cited

Bennett, Jill. *Empathic Vision: Affect, Trauma, and Contemporary Art*. Stanford: Stanford University Press, 2005.
Black, Naomi. *Virginia Woolf as Feminist*. Ithaca: Cornell University Press, 2004.
Butler, Judith. *Precarious Life: The Powers of Mourning and Violence*. London: Verso, 2004.
Cooper, Helene. "The Best We Can Hope For." *New York Times* 14 Jan. 2007, late ed., sec 4: 1+
Gillespie, Diane. " 'Her Kodak Pointed at His Head': Virginia Woolf and Photography." *The Multiple Muses of Virginia Woolf*. Ed. Diane F. Gillespie. Columbia: University of Missouri Press, 1993.
Humm, Maggie. "Memory, Photography and Modernism: Virginia Woolf's *Three Guineas*." *Modernist Women and Visual Cultures: Virginia Woolf, Vanessa Bell, Photography and Cinema*. New Jersey: Rutgers University Press, 2003. 195-216.
LaCapra, Dominick. "Trauma, Absence, Loss." *Writing History, Writing Trauma*. Baltimore: Johns Hopkins University Press, 2001. 43-85.
Marcus, Jane. "Introduction." *Three Guineas*. By Virginia Woolf. New York: Harcourt, 2006. xxxv-lxxii.
Roy, Arundhati. *War Talk*. Cambridge: South End Press, 2003.
Sontag, Susan. *Regarding the Pain of Others*. New York: Farrar, Straus, and Giroux, 2003.
Woolf, Virginia. *The Diary of Virginia Woolf*. Vol. 5. Ed. Anne Olivier Bell. New York: Harcourt Brace, 1984.
—. *The Letters of Virginia Woolf*. Vol. 6. Ed. Nigel Nicolson and Joanne Trautmann. New York: Harcourt Brace Jovanovich, 1980.
—. "Thoughts on Peace in an Air Raid." *The Death of the Moth and Other Essays*. New York: Harcourt Brace Jovanovich, 1970. 243-248.
—. *Three Guineas*. Annotated Edition. Ed. Mark Hussey. New York: Harcourt, 2006.

The Function of Filth:
Waste Imagery and Cultural Identity in *Between the Acts*

by Ben O'Dell

Virginia Woolf could be a tough critic. In a letter to Vanessa Bell dated October 24th, 1938, Woolf notes the effect war has had on contemporary literature, briefly stating that "All books are now rank with the slimy seaweed of politics; mouldy and mildewed" (*L6* 294). Her commentary illustrates the unfortunate circumstances confronting the modern novelist. To Woolf, it is clear that anxieties associated with the onset of World War II threatened to degrade contemporary art forms. Working within a climate of political instability, she indicates her belief that her peers have abandoned their natural pursuits in favor of creative projects steeped in ideology.[1] Woolf's assessment of current literary trends points towards her desire to undermine this tendency and return to a writing style free from overt reference to national politics. In this sense, her letter is common in that it displays her characteristic rejection of international aggression and suggests an artistic approach similar to her work in earlier novels like *Jacob's Room* and *To the Lighthouse*. Yet at the same time, Woolf's letter poses a number of questions when considered alongside her work in her final novel.

To what degree could Woolf write without referencing the threat of war? What would the purpose of her project be? Could Woolf assert the pacifist alternative she began in *Three Guineas* without falling victim to the qualities she associates with topical literature? As readers of *Between the Acts* know, Woolf could not avoid contemporary events.[2] The purpose of this essay is to explore how she incorporates "the slimy seaweed of politics" into her work and expand upon previous studies that have intimated the importance of waste to her final novel. In this paper, I argue that Woolf centers her project on images of filth and defilement as part of her larger effort to reexamine fixed categories of cultural identity. In my reading of the text, I suggest that Woolf's use of waste subtly challenges contemporary notions of national unity in three key ways: first, it acts as a site of resistance against military efficiency; secondly, it exposes the body's malleability; and finally, it reframes the importance of the relationship between the individual, the community, and the environment.[3]

Readers first encounter the "messiness" of Woolf's novel in the opening paragraph, when they are informed that the sewage project envisioned for the village surrounding Pointz Hall has yet to get underway. From this scene, it emerges that local authorities are currently struggling to provide residents with even the most basic of amenities. As Bartholomew Oliver sits discussing the matter with Mr. and Mrs. Haines, it becomes clear that the bureaucratic snafu is a popular topic of conversation, at least for the elderly Oliver. Yet Bart's interest in the county's plan for a cesspool is based primarily upon the site's *historic significance*. Through Woolf's narration, he describes how "From an aeroplane... you could still see, plainly marked, the scars made by the Britons; by the Romans; by the Elizabethan manor house; and by the plough, when they ploughed the hill to grow wheat in the Napoleonic wars" (*BTA* 4). To Bart, the "scars" left over from past eras of civilization reveal traces of a storied national identity. In each instance, the marks he alludes to bear some connection to English military history, either in the form of civil war or foreign invasion. Bart draws from these events in order to make sense of his identity. As with the view of Hogben's Folly, and the chapel within his home, he consistently looks towards his surroundings to construct a coherent interpretation of the world.

At all points, Bart's perceptions are infused with a sense of military achievement. Given his position as a former member of the Indian Civil Service, he sees England's ability to manipulate the land as a source of national pride. From this, one might infer that the county's decision to turn the old Roman road into a sewage pit threatens to undermine Bart's sense of order and remove generations of martial distinction. The novel quickly establishes that the community's cesspool has become an unmentionable topic for moneyed residents like Mrs. Haines. Despite the land's tie to history, its proposed use challenges the conventions of social decorum, leading residents to cast it aside as an object of scorn. When Isa enters the room later that evening, she inquires directly as to just *what* her father-in-law has said (*BTA* 4). From her tone, one can speculate that she fears he has breached the most important rule governing the family's social position. As the flamboyant Mrs. Manresa notes elsewhere in her recollection of an anecdote about a public lavatory built to celebrate the coronation of King George VI, bathroom humor is strictly off limits at Pointz Hall (*BTA* 102).

Bart's account thus illuminates a persistent tension. On the one hand, the land near Pointz Hall is described as a place of importance for its ability to chronicle the nation's history. On the other, it is treated as a site of contempt for its connection to unspeakable acts. In each instance, the cesspool looms over the novel's events, providing an impetus for future action. Nevertheless, recent scholarship has failed to address the project's significance, with some critics going so far as to dismiss the matter as "mundane" (Barnaby 312). From their perspective, Bart's stake in the land is little more than a tired historical anecdote—interesting to him, but ultimately irrelevant to everyone else. While I agree with these critics that it is important to consider the cesspool as one of the many visual markers employed in the production of historical metanarratives, I wish to further explore the intricate relationship between waste and identity.[4] From crumpled newspapers to spoiled fish, spent objects appear in countless scenes, implying a direct connection between individuals and their experience.[5]

In this sense Woolf's cesspool does more than refer to the stories characters tell themselves about the past. The novel's opening section reveals the transformation of identity through the process of abjection. In *Powers of Horror*, Julia Kristeva defines the abject as "A massive and sudden emergence of uncanniness, which, familiar as it might have been in an opaque and forgotten life, now harries me as radically separate, loathsome" (230). To Kristeva, the abject is a quality that serves a mediating function in marking distinction between social categories. In her work, she suggests that cultures use forms of abjection to separate themselves "from the threatening world of animals and animalism" (239). In addition, Kristeva sees abjection functioning within the social order to enact hierarchy in the human sphere. By removing themselves from the abject—all that is said to be corrupt, unclean, and impure—individuals raise themselves to a higher status and secure distinction. What is perhaps most interesting about the cesspool in *Between the Acts* is that it confuses this process. Woolf's decision to employ the "scars" of military conquest as a site for human waste challenges the solidity of dominant historical narratives, leaving readers to look elsewhere for stable categories. As Woolf's characters glance towards an object previously claimed as a source of pride, they are forced to reject it on the basis of ideological necessity.

Woolf extends her use of abjection beyond the military. Following the trajectory of her argument in *Three Guineas*, she asserts that the conditions of war cannot be prevented without social change. Woolf begins with the premise that we all perform. From there, she takes pains to uncover the moments where our hidden qualities shine through. At various points, the novel zooms in on its character's bodies to depict intimate physical details.[6] When Mrs. Swithin leads William Dodge to the nursery, Woolf describes the elderly widow touching "her bony forehead upon which a blue vein wriggled like a blue worm" (*BTA* 73). If this description turns stomachs, it is nevertheless indicative of Woolf's efforts to shatter romantic notions of the body through her depiction of physical imperfections. From the thick-limbed Mrs. Oliver to the delicate William Dodge, Woolf's characters are fleshed out in full. In each case, their bodies tell us something about their identity. From this, one might infer that Woolf has strayed into the realm of essentialism. Although she flirts with the prospect of cliché, she nevertheless remains committed to her belief that all characters are subject to change as a result of material circumstances.

Unfortunately, such change is rarely for the best. Woolf's bodies have a tendency to bend and break under the world's pressure. Nowhere is their deterioration more evident than in Isa's analysis of prosthetic teeth. Near the novel's beginning, Isa describes the invention of false teeth during the time of the Pharaohs. As she contemplates their medical expertise, the elderly Oliver traces the inside of his gum to note his own prosthetics. The scene ends shortly thereafter without further explanation. Yet once more, fixed categories have come into conflict. In an earlier passage, Bart returns to his youth to wage war against a group of "savages" (*BTA* 17). Armed with the tools of imperialism—a helmet & a gun—his dream sustains not only the Empire, but his sense of purpose. Bart's deterioration is readily apparent. His veins, once filled with vigor, now swell with a sickly "brownish fluid" (*BTA* 18). In denigrating his body, Woolf takes an interesting turn, alluding to Bart's physical proximity to the racialized Other both he and Isa depict. That Woolf fails to expand upon this matter is not surprising. In Woolf's novels, the subaltern rarely speak (see Spivak). Rather than dwell on issues of representation, Woolf asks *her readers* to make sense of her scattered references to imperial discourse and cultural identity. More often than not, sound conclusions are difficult to discern. Nevertheless, it is in this sense that the author confirms Kristeva's belief that, despite modernity's best efforts to "repress, dodge, or fake," the abject remains a part of our existence, signaling not only our difference, but the transformations we've endured (Kristeva 243).

In *Civilization and Its Discontents*, Freud writes that "We do not think highly of the cultural level of an English country town in Shakespeare's time when we read that there was a big dung-heap in front of his father's house in Stratford" (40). The same could perhaps be said of Pointz Hall. Woolf's characters cannot escape their filth. In an attempt to distinguish an ethic behind the author's depiction, one might suggest that Woolf cares not for appearance—that pesky "ghost of convention"—but the relationship between the individual and the material world (*BTA* 46). In other words, Woolf's subjects are defined through their connection to technologies of production and consumption. With the rise of the automobile plant and the aerodrome, mass culture has invaded Pointz Hall. The novel is littered with signs of rampant consumerism in refrigerators, gramophones, and yes, even delivery food. That these products routinely spoil and malfunction reveals their inadequacy in fulfilling cultural needs.

In leading her contemporaries to the landfill, Woolf asks a pertinent question: can anyone cleanse these characters of their impurity? Critical sentiment on this issue has varied widely, with some asserting the novel's utopian ends while others maintain a more conservative tone.[7] Woolf clearly sets up Miss La Trobe as the one figure capable of modifying her characters' actions. Yet her desire to "douche" the audience with a dose of "present time reality" fails when her avant-garde performance leaves the villagers befuddled (*BTA* 179). For all her good intentions, La Trobe's play is a waste of time. Still, the novel suggests that she will try again and, given her willingness to tackle tough issues within a hostile political climate, one imagines that her next play might be worth seeing. La Trobe accepts her relationship to the world. Standing arms "akimbo" in the village pub, she almost revels in her abjection (*BTA* 212). More than an outsider, La Trobe is entangled in her community's existence—an integral part of the whole. Ever aware of her position, she must use her experience to mock, bear witness, and recycle once more.

Notes

1. Among the works Woolf may be referring to are George Orwell's *Homage to Catalonia*, Thomas Mann's *The Coming Victory of Democracy*, Vladimir Nabokov's *Invitation to a Beheading*, Eric Ambler's *Cause for Alarm*, and Murray Constantine's *Swastika Night*—all written between 1935 and 1938.
2. In his writing on Virginia Woolf, Alex Zwerdling claims that nowhere is the author more "conscious and responsive to contemporary events" than in *Between the Acts* (302). His analysis outlines the "persistent intrusion" of public affairs in Woolf's life, leading Zwerdling to interpret the text in negative terms as "a return from civilization to barbarism" (302, 306).
3. Literary critics such as Tim Armstrong have argued elsewhere how "the conceptualization of 'waste' pervades economic and social thinking in the twentieth century," touching upon all aspects of life, including modernist fiction (58). Armstrong, while avoiding *Between the Acts* directly, nevertheless provides an interesting framework for the novel's interpretation.
4. Historical metanarrative is Hayden White's term for the literary and aesthetic devises governing the conscious process of historical construction. In *The Content of the Form*, White argues that historical events assume meaning not because they have occurred, but because they have been remembered and are capable of finding a place in a chronologically ordered sequence (20). White asserts that literary tropes figure prominently in this process, reframing historical narratives as the product of emplotment.
5. Biographically speaking, waste serves yet another function. In her writing, Hermione Lee observes that in October, 1939, the Woolfs returned to Mecklenburgh Square where, in addition to other discomforts, they encountered broken lavatories and "chamber pots in all the wrong places" (706).
6. Christine Froula notes Woolf's perspective shifts in *Virginia Woolf and the Bloomsbury Avant-Garde* when she argues that "*Between the Acts* zooms in on the acts between the acts, those unnoticed random moments that shape our real lives" (296). According to Froula, the narrator's viewpoint is paramount, as the novel's "wide-angle lens" complicates La Trobe's localized artistic vision, thereby blurring the boundary between life and art (305).
7. For a depiction of these positions see Ames and Zwerdling. Drawing from Mikhail Bakhtin's analysis of Grotesque Realism and the Carnival Spirit, Ames argues that "Woolf uses a folk celebration to assert the vital connection between cotemporary festivity and its communal roots" (405). Zwerdling, in contrast, claims the novel's pageant "fails to unite the spectators, and their comments in the intervals and after the performance only confirm their separateness," thus revealing the author's belief that "certain qualities in human beings could never be altered" (320, 327). My reading is somewhat more in line with Detloff, who contends that the novel "provides a demystifying counterdiscourse" through its use of performativity; however, I would slightly extend her argument in suggesting that the "new plot" Woolf envisions for the unacted scene in her novel's conclusion will inevitability yield traces of previous inequalities, the filth of life (407, 428).

Works Cited

Ambler, Eric. *Cause for Alarm*. 1938. New York: Knopf, 1939.
Ames, Christopher. "Carnivalesque Comedy in *Between the Acts*." *Twentieth Century Literature* 44. 4 (1998): 394-408.
Armstrong, Tim. *Modernism, Technology, and the Body*. New York: Cambridge University Press, 1998.
Bakhtin, Mikhail. *Rabelais and His World*. 1941. Trans. Helene Iswolsky. Cambridge, Mass: M.I.T. Press, 1968.
Barnaby, Edward. "Visualizing the Spectacle: Woolf's Metahistory Lesson in *Between the Acts*." *Virginia Woolf: Turning the Centuries, Selected Papers from the Ninth Annual Conference on Virginia Woolf*. Ed. Ann Ardis and Bonnie Kime Scott. New York: Pace University Press, 2000. 311-317.
Constantine, Murray. *Swastika Night*. 1937. London: V. Gollancz, 1940.
Detloff, Madelyn. "Thinking Peace Into Existence: The Spectacle of History in *Between the Acts*." *Women's Studies* 28. 4 (1999): 403-433.
Freud, Sigmund. *Civilization and Its Discontents*. Trans. James Strachey. New York: Norton, 1962.
Froula, Christine. *Virginia Woolf and the Bloomsbury Avant-Garde: War, Civilization, and Modernity*. New York: Columbia University Press, 2005.
Kristeva, Julia. "*Powers of Horror*." *The Portable Kristeva*. Trans. Leon Roudiez. Ed. Kelly Oliver. New York: Columbia University Press, 1997.
Lee, Hermione. *Virginia Woolf*. New York: Random House, 1996.
Mann, Thomas. *The Coming Victory of Democracy*. New York: Knopf, 1938.
Nabokov, Vladimir. *Invitation to a Beheading*. 1935-1936. Trans. Dmitri Nabokov in collaboration with the author. New York: Putnam, 1979.
Orwell, George. *Homage to Catalonia*. London: Secker and Warburg, 1938.
Spivak, Gayatri Chakravorty. "Can the Subaltern Speak?" *Marxism and the Interpretation of Culture*. Ed. Cary Nelson and Lawrence Grossberg. Urbana: University of Illinois Press, 1988. 271-313
White, Hayden. *The Content of the Form: Narrative Discourse and Historical Representation*. Baltimore: The Johns Hopkins University Press, 1987.
Woolf, Virginia. *Between the Acts*. 1941. New York: Harcourt, Brace, Jovanovich, 1969.
—. *The Letters of Virginia Woolf*. Ed. Nigel Nicolson and Joanne Trautmann. 6 vols. New York: Harcourt, Brace, Jovanovich, 1975-1980.
Zwerdling, Alex. *Virginia Woolf and the Real World*. Berkley: University of California Press, 1986.

Ghosts of Empire in Virginia Woolf's *To the Lighthouse* and Elizabeth Bowen's *The Last September*

by Sara Gerend

In Virginia Woolf's *To the Lighthouse* (1927) and Elizabeth Bowen's *The Last September* (1929), the spaces of an English and an Anglo-Irish country house dominate the narratives to the point of seeming to eclipse more significant outside political events. In Woolf's "Time Passes" section, the empty rooms of the Ramsays' vacation home take center stage while the ravages of World War I and the sudden deaths of three family members appear as bracketed asides. In Bowen's novel, the static focus on the "Big House," Danielstown, strives to shut out the realities of the Irish troubles occurring just beyond the demesne. In both novels, the narratives at times, in the words of Maud Ellmann, "[cocoon themselves] in the sense that many events occur off stage as in a Greek tragedy" (65). However, if, as Jon Hegglund has argued, the "home" in early twentieth-century Britain was "the quintessential icon of the nation," Woolf and Bowen's insistent foregrounding of domestic spaces holds important imperial implications (Hegglund 398). Specifically, as I will argue, both authors' home spaces are haunted, not merely by individuals who have died, but by transformations in the British empire in the post-World-War-One period. While in Woolf's *To the Lighthouse* ghosts of empire emerge within the island homeland to signal the fading of imperial might, in Bowen's *The Last September* empire's ghosts arise as the living colonized Irish rebels who reflect back on the members of the Anglo-Irish ascendancy a sense of their own near extinction.[1] In both novels spirits appear to speak for a changed political reality and a loss of British imperial power.

Focusing on the interior monologues of a host of characters staying at the Ramsays' summer vacation home in the Isle of Skye, *To the Lighthouse* first appears far removed from the politics of empire in early twentieth-century Britain. Yet despite Woolf's primary intentions for the novel to stress "all character, <u>not</u> a view of the world" (qtd. in Lee 469), I am particularly drawn to those moments in the novel where the thickly foregrounded politics of family and domestic life flicker with suggestions about the larger imperial world Woolf attempts to marginalize. Even in a novel, not explicitly about "the world," I believe Woolf's spectral form in part three highlights the changed reality of Britain after the war. For instance, unlike sections one and two that focus solely on the Ramsays' home, "The Lighthouse" contrasts Mr. Ramsays' "great expedition" by sea to the haunting appearance of Mrs. Ramsays' ghost inside the island—a space which is taken as a metaphor for the nation (*TTL* 193). While critics such as Winifred Holtby have rightly identified Woolf's novel as "'a ghost story' aimed at burying the phantom of the dead mother" (qtd. in Clewell 197), *To the Lighthouse* is a ghost story not only or merely about the personal/maternal, but also about the mother country. Woolf's structuring of "The Lighthouse" suggests that in the post-war world, one needs to think beyond the confines of the island nation home and probe Britain's relationship to its activities beyond its shores. In my reading, *To the Lighthouse* is also a ghost story of empire aimed at expressing and perhaps mourning Britain's changed imperial reality.

Throughout *To the Lighthouse*, Mr. Ramsays' post-war sea voyage resembles a pre-war imperial journey. From the beginning, the narrator calls the boat trip an "expedition" or a crusade with a definite purpose, rather than a mere pleasure cruise (193). Moreover, at the start of the excursion, Mr. Ramsay emerges as a "king" with "the appearance of a leader" (140, 146). As the head of state and ship, Mr. Ramsay is viewed by his crew members Cam and James as an oppressive ruler who subjects his people to a state of silence. James glows with hatred at his father's "tyranny, despotism…making people do what they did not want to do, cutting off their right to speak. How could any of them say, but I won't, when he said, come to the lighthouse" (*TTL* 173). Mr. Ramsays' subjects see him as a captain ruling by force, rather than by consensus.

Indeed, the father's coercive manner echoes, though in a reduced form, Britain's naval strength as it was viewed by other imperial nations before the Great War. In *The Spectre of British Navalism* (1915), Julian Corbett argues that before World War I, Germany saw Britain's "naval predominance" as a tyrannical "force" that denied "the world the freedom of the sea" (4). For Germany, the "specter of British navalism" hinders the nautical rights of other nations and arises as a form of imperial despotism (Corbett 4, 3). In Corbett's essay, Germany's view of the haunting "menace" of Britain's navy resonates with the children's image of the despotic nature of their captain, hinting that Mr. Ramsays' sea voyage resembles a journey of empire.

Yet the specter of Britain's pre-war naval force is not the only apparition that emerges in conjunction with Mr. Ramsays' excursion. During the expedition to the lighthouse, Mrs. Ramsays' ghost appears on the mainland. The final section, "The Lighthouse," emphasizes the concurrent actions and spaces of the ship and the ghost, for it cuts sharply back and forth between the movements of the vessel at sea and the spectral older woman on shore. In fact, Woolf strives to achieve a feeling of "balance" between these separate spaces. Hermione Lee writes, "In the last part, moving between Lily painting her picture on the lawn, and Mr. Ramsay with his two children in the boat, [Woolf] wrestle[s]…with problems of balance…she want[s] to get the feeling of simultaneity" (471). For Woolf, the emergence of the ghostly older woman conjured by the painter Lily Briscoe coincides with the action of the imperial voyage to stress how the two images share a close affinity.

During the final section of the novel, ghosts and ships appear within the same visual space. Specters become elements of transition wedding the fragmented spheres of the voyaging ship and the British island. Ghosts appear as figures of mediation linking the children, who feel imprisoned, with the imagistic conjuring of Lily Briscoe, who thinks of and in a kind of artistic séance resuscitates the deceased Mrs. Ramsay on the lawn. At one point, for example, Cam notices the highly spectral nature of the British island from her confined perspective at sea. She "looked doggedly and sadly at the shore, wrapped in its mantle of peace, as if the people there had fallen asleep…were free to come and go like ghosts. They have no suffering there she thought" (*TTL* 160). However, when the text shifts suddenly to the haunted shore, Lily Briscoe, ironically, reaches a sharp crescendo of grief as she conjures the presence of Mrs. Ramsays' ghost. The narrative voice describes the wrenching scene:

> Oh Mrs. Ramsay. [Lily] called out silently to that essence which sat by the boat, that abstract one made of her, that woman in grey, as if to abuse her for having gone, and then being gone, come back again. It had seemed so safe thinking of

her....Ghost, air, nothingness, a thing that you could play with easily and safely. She had been that, and then suddenly...wrung her heart thus. (*TTL* 168)

Just as Cam contemplates the spectral shore from her confinement on the voyaging ship, Lily imagines the seemingly safe spectral "essence" of Mrs. Ramsay literally sitting beside the imperial vessel from her outlook on the island. The mainland inhabitant imagines the "abstract" and heart-wrenching ghost firmly anchored to the progress of Mr. Ramsays' vessel and expedition. Indeed, throughout the final section, the ship and the apparition appear unavoidably connected. Repeatedly as Lily remembers "that woman in grey," the progress of the boat intrudes upon her spectral imaginings. When Lily recollects the haunting image of the dead Mrs. Ramsay "putting her wreath to her forehead and going unquestioningly with her companion, a shadow, across the fields," her vision of this female shade is distinctly interrupted by "a brown spot in the middle of the bay" or "Mr. Ramsays' boat" (*TTL* 170-71). The voyaging ship literally and forcefully intersects with Lily's spectral remembrances, suggesting that the two images are inseparable.

In a recent essay Mark Gaipa reads Woolf's section "The Lighthouse" as a narrative attempt to reconcile two journeys or different ways of seeing the world. Gaipa believes that the voyages in section three, "one outward over water; the other inward, back through memory," represent Woolf's desire to unite her agnostic father's materialist beliefs with her mother's spiritual role as the Victorian "angel in the house" (Gaipa 29). On a larger cultural level, however, Gaipa also believes Woolf's dual voyages bring together the worlds of paternal matter and maternal spirit to wrestle with the Victorian crisis of religion or "the drama of conflicting spiritualist and materialist perspectives" that Woolf inherited from her parents' generation (Gaipa 8).

Yet Woolf's wedding of matter and spirit extends, I believe, beyond both the personal and cultural layers to lay bare an image of the post-war nation that can no longer equate its imperial quests overseas to a robust, living national identity. The imperial voyages abroad to hold colonies and bring back material goods now equate for Woolf in the post-war years with a spirit-filled, haunted homeland. Indeed, in the novel's central section, "Time Passes," a powerful metaphor links ships with ghosts stressing how the nation's "specter of navalism" foreshadows, *not* Britain's continued imperial strength, but its imminent decline. Soon after Andrew Ramsay dies fighting in France during WWI, the narrator announces, "there was a silent apparition of an ashen-coloured ship...come, gone; there was the purplish stain upon the bland surface of the sea as if something had boiled and bled, invisibly, beneath" (*TTL* 125). The image of the sinking spectral ship resonates with the death of the British World War I soldier. And as Janet Winston believes, the picture conjures further the subtext of Woolf's novel, "not just the events of World War I, but rather the entire institution of British imperialism, which made World War I inevitable" (46). The purple bruise-like stain left by the phantom vessel in the middle of *To the Lighthouse* reverberates with the waning of the British Empire after the war. Through the lens of imperial decline, the joint image of the imperial ship and ghostly woman at the close of Woolf's novel become a sign of Britain's post-war diminished imperial force, a fading from the nation's former glory and dominance.

"'Isn't it very ghostly?'" This is a question that many people ask when Elizabeth Bowen tells them she lives in one of Ireland's famous "Big House[s]" (Bowen, "The Big House" 195). Born in 1899 to members of the Anglo-Irish Ascendancy class, Bowen was the first female inheritor of Bowen's Court, a large country home in north Cork, in the south of Ireland. Given her family's long history of inhabiting the house (back to the time of Oliver Cromwell), Bowen is highly conscious of the way the spirits of the past thoroughly inhabit her home space. She explains, "The dead do not need to visit Bowen Court's rooms ... we had no ghosts in that house—because they already permeated them" (*Bowen's Court* 451). Although Bowen speaks here of spirits in terms of dead ancestors who saturate the domestic scene, the ghosts that emerge in her second novel, *The Last September,* are visitors who are not directly related, and who are not necessarily welcome within the Anglo-Irish homestead.

As in the final section of *To the Lighthouse*, *The Last September* is set in the post-WWI period, but the scene is in the first of Britain's colonies to become independent in the twentieth century, set during the "Irish Troubles" of 1921. In Bowen's novel while the British Black and Tans patrol the countryside in armored cars and rebel Irish people smuggle arms and ambush passers-by, the Anglo-Irish Naylors, living in the "Big House" Danielstown, go about their social engagements having visitors, hosting tea parties, and playing tennis, as though the troubles have nothing to do with them. Seemingly suspended in the house as though in another world, the Naylors live apart. "Inside [their] demesne and mansion, [in their] centripetal and rather cut-off life," the Naylors actively work to ignore the political realities surrounding them (*Bowen's Court* 125-26). Whether their desire to turn inward, away from the conflicts arises from their contradictory position "caught between warring factions" of the British who are there to protect them and of their neighbors and friends, the Irish who "champion the rebels" (Ellmann 55), or from their guilt over their inability or unwillingness to help their surrounding community, the residents at Danielstown are self-absorbed. In the words of Phyllis Lassner, they "create an artificial world whose only proclaimed inhabitants are themselves ...[and] the estate ... becomes its own island-nation" (Lassner 44).

The first mention of ghosts in *The Last September* emerges during a discussion involving the rumors that the Irish insurgents have buried guns "in the lower plantation" (29) of the estate. Lois tells her guest Mrs. Montmorency in an excited tone, "Michael Keelan swears he was going through there late, and saw men digging" (29). When Lois continues with a little too much ardor, her uncle intrudes, "'Ah, that's nonsense now ... Michael would see anything: he is known to have seen a ghost. I will not have the men talking, and at all accounts, I won't have them listened to" (29). While Lois is eager to relay the rumor, Sir Naylor wishes no one in the house to see or to hear anything about the fighting. In this passage, Lois' uncle likens witnessing the war-like activities of the rebel Irish to the likelihood of seeing a ghost. So deep runs the Naylors' desire to distance themselves from the political realities beyond the hedge, that the mere reporting of the Irish insurgents' actions is as ridiculous as acknowledging the existence of spirits.

That same evening, however, Lois encounters for herself Michael Keelan's "spirit." After the guests sit out on the porch taking in the "sinister" (38) sounds of British lorries patrolling the countryside and then retire indoors, Lois dares to dance down the estate's avenue and darts adventurously through a dark shrubbery path. While she runs partly terrified and partly thrilled through the black thicket a powerful image of Danielstown appears. Bowen writes, "The shuttered-in drawing room, the family sealed up in lamplight, secure and bright like flowers in a paperweight, were desirable sharply, worth coming out to regain" (42). As Lois bolts through the black hedge at an unsafe hour, fighting within herself conflicting emotions of fear and excitement, the house, in all its bright, island-like autonomy intrudes upon her thoughts. "Shuttered-in" and "sealed up in lamplight," she thinks of the rooms that entomb, in protection, her closest kin. Indeed, her family momentarily appears to be floating "like flowers" unnatural and unattached to any landscape, petrified, suspended, in a miniature, highly artificial, and decorative glass world. From the darkness of the hedge, the Big House of Danielstown shrinks to the microcosm of a mere "paperweight."

Immediately following this brief mental reverie, Lois comes to a crossroads. Bowen notes, "At first she did not hear the footsteps, and as she began to notice the displaced darkness thought what she dreaded was there within her—she was indeed clairvoyant, exposed to horror, going to see a ghost. Then steps smooth on the smooth earth; branches slipping against a trench coat" (42). At first Lois believes her spectral encounter is merely psychological—stemming from "within." Like Lily in *To the Lighthouse*, Lois seems clairvoyant, conjuring forth the dead through her imagination; however, she quickly discerns that the ghost she encounters is another Irish rebel: "It must be because of Ireland he was in such a hurry, down from the mountains making a short cut through their demesne" (42). The spirit Lois accidentally comes upon, however, is probably closer to home or within than she may originally want to admit. In *Bowen's Court,* Bowen writes that, "in Ulster, the Protestant Ascendancy was a living fact; in Munster, Leinster, and Connaught, it had become within the last fifty years a ghost only" (430). The mistaken ghost on the path is not, therefore, only the Irish rebel or the figure of the Irish colonial insurgency the Naylors wish to ignore, but a symbol of the reality of the waning Anglo-Irish ascendancy. Bowen's protagonist comes face-to-face with a ghost of empire that signifies the new phantom nature of the Anglo-Irish way of life. The Naylors, sealed up like the "undead" in the paperweight of Danielstown are already living an afterlife, though they do not know it (Ellmann 65, 58). Indeed, Bowen underlines this fact when she describes that Lois, hesitating momentarily in the darkness, wishes to address the spectral intruder with an encouraging remark such as "Up Dublin!," for "not to be known of seemed like the doom of extinction" (42).

At the end of *The Last September,* the fictional Danielstown is invaded and its artificial world smashed by the uninvited Irish ghosts who haunt its hedges. Bowen's description of the burning "furnace" of the house is at one point equated with the entire Irish nation, suggesting that the Ireland as the Anglo-Irish had known it would soon be forever gone: "looking from east to west the sky tall with scarlet ... the country itself was burning" (303). In reality, however, the real Bowen's Court was spared by the Irish rebels and survived until the 1960s when it was demolished. Although in one night in 1921 three neighboring houses were burnt to the ground and in the four months between December to March of 1922-1923, 192 Big Houses were destroyed by fire in the south of Ireland, Bowen's Court remained unscathed throughout the turmoil (Ellmann 55).

However, in the summer of 1922, Irish republican troops marched down the avenue of Bowen's Court, invaded, and took over the Big House. The Anglo-Irish hospitality so famous in Bowen's novel *The Last September,* extended in real life to seventy Irish republicans. While the rebels planted mines in the avenue and wired the house through the library to blow it up in case of an attack, perhaps the most memorable detail of their stay involved what the uninvited spirits did with their free time. According to Bowen, "When the men woke up, they read. They were great readers, and especially were they attracted by the works of Kipling: a complete set of these in flexible scarlet leather, with gilt elephants' heads were available" (*Bowen's Court* 442). In the midst of the Irish civil war, newly freed from centuries of oppression by their British colonizers, the fighting Irish read Rudyard Kipling, whom George Orwell has called "the prophet of British imperialism in its expansionist phase."

As fictions of a spectral modernity, both Woolf's *To the Lighthouse* and Bowen's *The Last September* use spirits of empire to highlight post-war transformations. Whether within the nation or within Britain's nearest colony, ghosts emerge not only as individuals who have died but as social and political figures who rearticulate the changed meaning of home.

Notes

1. I agree with Urmila Seshagiri who, in "Orienting Virginia Woolf," finds that "[Woolf's] critique of the Empire is self-reflexive, focused on imperialism's damage to England rather than to its subject nations" (61).

Works Cited

Bowen, Elizabeth. "The Big House." *Collected Impressions*. New York: Longmans Green, 1950. 195-202.
—. *Bowen's Court*. 1942. Cork: The Collin's Press, 1998.
—. *The Last September*. 1929. New York: Anchor Books, 2000.
Clewell, Tammy. "Consolation Refused: Virginia Woolf, the Great War, and Modernist Mourning." *Modern Fiction Studies* 50:1 (2004): 197-223.
Corbett, Julian. *The Spectre of Navalism*. London: Darling and Son Limited, 1915.
Ellmann, Maud. *Elizabeth Bowen: The Shadow Across the Page*. Edinburgh: Edinburgh University Press, 2003.
Gaipa, Mark. "An Agnostic Daughter's Apology: Materialism, Spiritualism, and Ancestry in Woolf's *To the Lighthouse*." *Journal of Modern Literature* 26:2 (2003): 1-41.
Hegglund, Jon. "Defending the Realm: Domestic Space and Mass Cultural Contamination in *Howards End* and *An Englishman's Home*." *English Literature in Transition* (1880-1920) 40:4 (1997): 398-423.
Lassner, Phyllis. "The Past is a Burning Pattern: Elizabeth Bowen's *The Last September*." Ireland. Spring (1986): 40-54.
Lee, Hermione. *Virginia Woolf*. New York: Knopf, 1998.
Orwell, George. "Essay on Rudyard Kipling." *George Orwell-Org*. 1 June 2007 <http://www.george-orwell.org/Rudyard_Kipling/0.html>.
Seshagiri, Urmila. "Orienting Virginia Woolf: Race, Aesthetics, and Politics in *To the Lighthouse*." *Modern Fiction Studies* 50:1 (2004): 58-84.
Winston, Janet. "'Something out of Harmony': *To the Lighthouse* and the Subject(s) of Empire." *Woolf Studies Annual*. Vol. 2. New York: Pace University Press, 1996.
Woolf, Virginia. *To the Lighthouse*. 1927. Hertfordshire: Wordsworth Editions, 1994.

Tae The Lichthoose:
Woolf's Scotland and the Problem of the Local

by Richard Zumkhawala-Cook

Virginia Woolf's 1927 novel *To the Lighthouse* presents the convergence of two critical, but seemingly contradictory traditions in Scottish cultural history. Set on the rocky shores of the Isle of Skye along the western edge of Scotland's mainland coast, the narrative reproduces what even in this time period would have been a well-worn cliché of Scotland as both the literal and psychic escape from English modern life and the exotic background for the main characters' personal, philosophical and aesthetic contemplations. Mr. Ramsay's petulant quest to advance from Q to R, Mr. Tansley's fumbling longing for sympathy, Mrs. Ramsay's troubled reflections on "suffering, death, the poor," and, of course, Lily's final vision, all take place in a vacation spot, or what feels to Mrs. Ramsay like "three thousand miles" away from their English lives. At the same time however, the novel's unsettling of English heroism and cultural supremacy echoes some of the Scottish nationalist rhetoric that reached its most intense fervor precisely when Woolf's novel was published. But is Scotland merely a backdrop for this critique? Does the narrative's scant acknowledgement of this socially and culturally distinct region elide the national space which it inhabits, reproducing the modernist imperialist tradition of transforming lived social spaces and their inhabitants into mere extensions of the modern metropole's consciousness? Or is Scotland and its chain of Hebridean Isles involved in, and a central aspect of, this critique? In short, this paper attempts to entertain, rather than answer, the question: why Scotland?

Despite the fact that the Scottish Book Trust announced at the 2005 Edinburgh International Book festival that *To the Lighthouse* was amongst the list of the 100 Best Scottish Books of All Time, Woolf's novel seems to ignore the literary techniques regularly employed by English and Scottish authors alike that would highlight Scotland's particularity—place names, dialect, local cultural or historical references, conventions I should mention that were certainly popular amongst many of the other books on that top 100 list. The novel is set in Scotland, but does not seem to want to be conventionally "Scottish." Virginia Woolf didn't visit Scotland until eleven years after the novel was published, claiming about the novel's Scottish setting, "I don't defend my accuracy" (qtd. in *Travels* 138). And when she did finally visit the Scotland of *To the Lighthouse*, she described in a 1938 postcard to Duncan Grant that the Isle of Skye was "Remote as Samoa; deserted; prehistoric" (qtd. in *Travels* 138). Not surprisingly, Woolf hadn't been to Samoa either.

Nonetheless, I argue that the narrative setting of Scotland functions as an effort to disrupt the stability of nation altogether, at once leaving and standing outside of England, which as a nation and culture suffers a salvo of critical blows from the novel, but also resists nationalizing Scotland itself. Prefiguring her 1938 assertion in *Three Guineas*, "as a woman I have no country. As a woman I want no country," I want to address the "why Scotland?" question by arguing that *To the Lighthouse* resists national identifications so as to highlight alternative solidarities, namely the material conditions of gender and class represented throughout the text. This occurs, I argue, primarily in the obviously Scottish surnamed local housemaid, Mrs. McNab, whose prominence in the "Time Passes" section is at once structurally associated with the devastating revelation of Mrs. Ramsay's death while also serving as the historical hinge which links the Ramsays' and Lily Briscoe's pasts to their present. The problem of the local is largely resolved through Mrs. McNab's character as the human and humanized embodiment of the Scottish working class, of domestic labor, and of regional identity, placed at the center of the narrative.

Throughout the novel, the tension between two competing versions of Scotland contributes to, if not undergirds, Mrs. Ramsay's and Lily's struggle to arrive at a fulfilling sense of self outside patriarchal definitions of civilization, representation, and work. One Scotland is as an aesthetic piece, an artifice, empty landscape, and leisure getaway, captured in Paul Rayley's parroting of his traveler's guidebook, which describes the Western Isles of Scotland as "being justly celebrated for their park-like prospects and the extent and variety of their marine curiosities" (*TTL* 75). As park-like, this Scotland is constructed as an enclosed parcel of nature protected from the inconvenient realities of social life that actual inhabitants bring with them. As a park, it is space for free movement and individual autonomy revered by Mr. Ramsay as he looks out into the distance:

> That was the country he liked best, over there; those sandhills dwindling away into darkness. One could walk all day without meeting a soul. There was not a house scarcely, not a single village for miles on end. One could worry things out alone. There were little sandy beaches where no one had been since the beginning of time. The seals sat up and looked at you. (69)

And it is in this distance where Mr. Ramsay imagines his escape: "It sometimes seemed to him that in a little house out there, along—he broke off, sighing. He had no right. The father of eight children he reminded himself" (69). His fantasy of solitude is projected onto the land itself, whose sparse population enabled by the ecological severity, it seems, endorses both his longing for a flight from family, from modern responsibility, from social connection, as well as his understanding that to "worry things out," moving from Q to R, is a process that best occurs in isolation, not having to meet a soul, what he later states is

> a desolate expedition across the icy solitudes of the Polar region [that] would have made him the leader, the guide, the counsellor, whose temper, neither sanguine nor despondent, surveys with equanimity what is to be and faces it, came to his help again. (34)

This image of imperialist mobility, where every "undeveloped" landscape is wilderness, and every region is open and available for settlement, renders the local inhabitants either a nuisance or invisible. However, amongst the borderless expanse enough of the social exists to provide that "little house" of refuge for travelers, making the citizens of the Hebrides perhaps just useful enough to offer their labor. Even further, it suggests that this relationship is necessary to human advancement, to enlightenment, and to genius. Echoing his comment that "Possibly the greatest good requires the existence of a slave class. The liftman in the Tube is an eternal necessity" (43), the moments in which Mr. Ramsay has direct interaction with the Scottish citizenry are marked by the economic and social power of his class position. As old Macalister, one of the few local characters afforded speech in the novel, narrates the death of the fisherman at the same time as he is navigating the Ramsay family to the lighthouse, his tale of tragedy is translated by Mr. Ramsay into exciting drama as loss of life is turned into local color:

> He liked that men should labor and sweat on the windy beach at night. Pitting muscle and brain against the waves and the wind; he liked men to work like that, and women to keep house, and sit beside sleeping children indoors while men were drowned out there in a storm. (164)

The perils of working mariner life are understood by Mr. Ramsay to be aestheticized portraits that he can identify with, associating the heroism of his philosophical musings with the heroism of seafaring, perhaps, but only from a distance. He can, as James and Cam notice, begin to affect a Scottish accent in speaking to Macalester, performing a kind of manly bond with the working classes, but only inasmuch as he can deny his or anyone else's relationship to the perils of poverty, oppression and death that accompany such a life. It is what makes the Sir Walter Scott Waverley novels and their clean lines of chivalry, heroism and history seem so comforting.[1] His identification with this version of Scotland and with seafaring Scottish masculinity naturalizes not only the difficult conditions of work, but also substantiates his fantasies of patriarchal gender relations, where men are working heroically amidst the harsh elements of public life and women are sitting peacefully by the hearth fire.

Within the history of representing Scotland this rendering of the far reaches of the Scottish countryside, its Highlands and its Western or Northern Isles, Mr. Ramsay's version of Scotland draws from just about every cliché about Scotland that would have been available. Only two and half decades before *To the Lighthouse* was published, the most popular fiction in Britain, called the Kailyard School, was set in Scotland, and had an enormous readership in the United States and Canada, as well as England. The idyllic portraits of Kailyard novels and short stories about a fantasy of Scotland's original national order appealed to contemporary international middle-class desires for political stability, economic liberty, obedient women, and disciplined workers (Cook, "The Home-ly" 1055). In effect these reactionary representations of the agrarian poor, working classes, immigrant Irish and Gypsy populations, and women would have made Mr. Ramsay proud. This period's nostalgia for Highland traditions also included what was called the "Celtic revival" of folk tale and folk culture collections. Titles such as the *Waifs and Strays of the Celtic Tradition* and *Popular Tales of the West Highlands* were devoted to preserving the practices of a lost society (Cook, *The Twentieth Century 51-2*). Distributed by British publishers, these volumes of bed-time prayers, addresses to the saints, seasonal hymns, carols, ryhmes, etcetera, helped to aestheticize contemporary "backwards" ways, preserving the "culture" in print while simultaneously banishing these practices into the annals of the past.

If we return to Mr. Ramsay's gaze into the distance of a largely empty landscape, we see not only an attempted resolution to his middle-class anxieties about his loss of autonomy, privilege, and mastery, but also the material evidence of the policies of British modernity. The Isle of Skye, like most all of the Highlands and Western Isles of Scotland, was decimated by the clearances throughout the 19th century, evicting 34,700 inhabitants between 1840-1883 in order to improve lands by transforming family croft farms into sheep and cattle grazing fields, or hunting and fishing grounds for city tourists (Cooper 54). Told that the region could no longer offer them employment or subsistence, farmers and their families were either forced to the cities or, as it happened on Skye in 1851 and again in 1853, those who were "peaceable, orderly, moral and hardworking" were directed by the state sanctioned Skye Emigration Society to board ships to Australia and Canada (Prebble 198-205). In this way, it is not only Ramsay's imaginative erasure of the Scottish citizenry that the novel brings to bear, but also the deliberate mechanisms of modernity that have depopulated the landscape and have made possible for the Ramsays the Island as tourist destination. Remembering Paul's guidebook, it is no wonder the region appears "park-like."

In response to these conditions, and the familiar cultural politics of representation associated with Mr. Ramsay's perspective, at the time that *To the Lighthouse* was published, nationalist fervor was gaining momentum in Scotland, and quite vibrantly from its literary leaders. The late 1920's for Scottish literature were marked by fierce socialist realist novels about the hardships of both rural and urban national life. They attempted to retrieve Scotland from sentimental "folk" stories, as did some experimental dialect poetry that revered and rivaled the willful fragmentation of the European avant-garde.[2] Not surprisingly much of this work railed against England and its imperialist brutality and cultural arrogance in the same way that we see Woolf's novel critiquing the plodding linearity, misogyny and emotional volatility of Mr. Ramsay, the patriarch and distinguished scholar, who repeatedly compares his accomplishments to "all of England." The narrative's distance from Mr. Ramsay's sensibilities are obvious and frequent, William Bankes and Lily wonder "why so brave a man in thought should be so timid in life; how strangely he was venerable and laughable at one and the same time" (45), the youthful James shows reasonable contempt for his father's irrational authoritarian severity, and Mrs. Ramsay, in one of her many moments that distinguish herself from her husband, explosively reflects in the prose that "had she said half of what he said, she would have blown her brains out by now" (69).

However, England is not merely represented as an extension of Mr. Ramsay's character and his philosophical viewpoints, but a reference point throughout the novel to excess, isolation, bad cooking, war, empire, and the failures of modernity. Mrs. Ramsay's multiple mentions of the iniquitous English dairy industry decry "Milk delivered at your door in London positively brown with dirt. It should be made illegal" (89), revealing a metropolitan system unable to prevent the contamination of its basic goods. Not unlike the work that was coming from Scottish modernist authors, the indictment of English transcendence structures the novel's narrative development, as the story stands figuratively and literally outside of England's center.

To the Lighthouse, however, is not at all interested in demonstrating the merit of Scotland's distinction, as many of Woolf's Scottish contemporaries hoped to maintain, but is similarly motivated to humanize the struggles of the Scottish locals. Certainly in contrast to Mr. Ramsay's version of Scotland, Mrs. Ramsay's sympathies for the limited prospects of the Islands, the suffering fishing industry, pervasive unemployment, and emigration support Raymond Williams' comment in *The Country and the City* that "a working country is hardly ever a landscape" (120). Mrs. Ramsay is arrested by the "terribly dangerous work" and the scars of hard labor evident on the one-armed man standing on a ladder posting a bill and in viewing the lack of infrastructure of the Hebrides, envisioning on two separate occasions a model dairy system and hospital brought to the Island. The fact that England also lacks her desired dairy system disrupts any notion that these inefficiencies and inequities are specific to the Isles of Skye, but a reality of the class system that cuts across national boundaries, recalling her mantra of the "suffering; death; the poor." Against the philosophical heroism of her husband, Mrs. Ramsay imagines herself going beyond the whinging and hand wringing of her class:

> [...] the things she saw with her own eyes, weekly, daily, here or in London, when she visited this widow, or that struggling wife in person with a bag on her arm, and a note-book and pencil [...] in the hope that thus she would cease to be a private woman whose charity was half a sop to her own indignation, half a relief to her own curiosity, and become, what with her untrained mind she greatly admired, an investigator, elucidating the social problem. (9)

Yet her understanding of universal, or at least, transnational conditions of what she calls "of rich and poor," "here [Scotland] or in London" is limited by her sense of bourgeois charity. Her well meaning, but somewhat clumsy attempt to grasp the work of tending the lighthouse leads her to patronizingly reflect on the duties as if they were a culmination of leisure activities, thus moving her to send

> [...] a pile of old magazines, and some tobacco indeed, whatever she could find lying about, not really wanted, but only littering the room, to give those poor fellows, who must be bored to death sitting all day with nothing to do but polish the lamp and trim the wick and rake about on their scrap of garden, something to amuse them. (5)

While her sympathies undoubtedly lead her to consider the hardships of manual labor, she is unable to see beyond the limitations of her class experience. Indeed one may wonder whether she is anxious about the lighthouse attendants' isolation and boredom, or that of her own family, who, being "3000 miles away" from their homes on the precipice of North Atlantic ocean, are also "sitting all day with nothing to do." Despite the evident distinction between the Scotland Mr. and Mrs. Ramsay see and experience, her conclusions render her incapable of seeing the local social environment as anything more than an extension of herself. In the end she is just another tourist.

What prevents *To the Lighthouse* itself from being a tourist and turning Scotland into a mere backdrop is its almost complete break in the "Time Passes" section from the frame of the Ramsays' social circle, focusing instead on the daily mechanisms that sustain vacation life. One might say that the narrative stays loyal to its regional setting by remaining fixed on the Scottish vacation house, rather than following the Ramsays back home, and drawing forward, at least in part, the activities and reflections of Mrs. McNab, a local domestic servant. At the same time, this shift sends the dramatic events of the Ramsays' lives—death, illness, birth, and war—radically into the narrative background: quite literally, Mrs. Ramsay's death sparsely appears as a parenthetical aside, an event and nothing more. While the narrative of the section seems to move into the realm of abstraction—where plot and character gives way to descriptions of the patterns of the seasons, the evidences of decay, and the cycles of days, nights, and tides—the description of Mrs. McNab at times is cut from the realist cloth. The language of the chapter plunges into the detailed unsentimental reality of her relationship with the Ramsays and their vacation house: her work and the physical exertion that it requires: "Mrs. McNab, tearing the veil of silence with hands that stood in the washtub, grinding it with boots that had crunched the shingle, came as directed to open all the windows of the bedroom" (130). Juxtaposed with the continuity of Mrs. McNab's 70-year presence in the region is the bodily and expressive energy she musters in maintaining both herself and the fixtures of the deteriorating home. In addition to the tearing, grinding, and crunching of the previous passage, she is also presented upon her introduction as lurching, clutching, hauling, leering, rubbing, singing, dusting, bowing, creaking, groaning, hobbling, ambling, taking up, putting down, twisting, grinning, smiling, walking, mumbling, drinking and gossiping, all of which appear in a single paragraph.

And it is this labor, her efforts, her assertions, as well as later Mrs. Bast's and her son's, and in effect the collective energy of a local community ("Oh, they said, the work" [139]) presented in detail, that rescues the house from the chaos of time. As the house is recovered from the punishing assault of decay and filth, the labor enables the return of the Ramsays' family circle, while also structurally hinging the two sections of the novel and the two eras of the English characters' lives together. In this way, Scotland functions in the novel as much more than a passive setting, much more than a landscape or interesting cultural backdrop, but a diligently and painstakingly maintained field upon which the political, emotional, and aesthetic concerns can be entertained and resolved. Both outside the narrative of "The Window" and "The Lighthouse" sections, the full scope of Scotland's labor, and its culture, are both essential to, and largely absent from, the tensions and developments of the characters in the rest of the novel. Returning to my initial question, then, why Scotland, the "Time Passes" section situates the drama of the Ramsays and the critique of English arrogance not in order to diminish its import, but to situate its limitations and socially constructed myopia. The Ramsays, Charles Tansley, Mr. Bankes, Augustus Carmichael, Paul Rayley, Minta Doyle, and Lily Briscoe in the end are shown to be tourists; the novel, however, is not.

With this in mind, while we are not exactly sure what Lily's final stroke on her canvas looks like, or where that line she draws with sudden intensity delivers her, what is certain is that it occurs in the ignorance of Mrs. McNab and her critical narrative of local working-class life. However, despite the absence of Mrs. McNab in "The Lighthouse" section, her words creep into Lily's prose. As she looks over her painting, she repeats the same "line" that Mrs. McNab delivers upon completing the recovering of the vacation house: "it was finished." Whether Lily's art is equated with labor or Mrs. McNab's labor is equated with art, the novel re-asserts the centrality of Mrs. McNab's life and efforts to modernity's visions and discoveries. But this equation does not level the social distinctions between them; Lily is still an artist on vacation, Mrs. McNab is still a maid. And remaining loyal to the historical conditions of the Isle of Skye, the English enjoy leisure time and the Scots serve them. In order to move this question out of us versus them nationalist rhetoric, however, *To the Lighthouse* goes outside England to demonstrate that there is no outside at all. The relationships of power that draw the boundaries and hierarchies which separate nations, classes, and genders also rely on an intimacy and interdependence that may be unacknowledged on the canvas, on the beach or in the parlor room, but are nevertheless fundamental to making these contexts and their meanings possible.

Notes

1. Judith Wilt notes that the narrative's specific mention of Scott's least historical novel, *The Antiquary*, problematizes not only Mr. Ramsay's understanding of Scott's oeuvre, but also the conventional reading of Scott as a voice of unambiguous history.
2. See Harvie for a discussion of inter-war nationalist discourse in Scotland. For studies of Scottish literary nationalism, see Crawford, Glen, and Corbett.

Works Cited

Cook, Richard. "The Home-ly Kailyard Nation: Nineteenth-Century Narratives of the Highland and the Myth of Merrie Auld Scotland." *ELH* 66.4 (Winter 1999): 1053-1073.

—. *The Twentieth-Century Tartan Monster: The Cultural Politics of Scottish National Identity.* Diss. Miami U, 2000.

Cooper, Derek. *Skye*. London: Routledge & Kegan Paul, 1970.

Corbett, John. *Language and Scottish Literature*. Edinburgh: Edinburgh University Press, 1998.

Crawford, Robert. *Devolving English Literature*. Oxford: Oxford University Press, 1992.

Glen, Duncan. *Hugh MacDiarmid and the Scottish Renaissance*. Edinburgh: W. & R. Chambers, 1964.

Harvie, Christopher. *Scotland and Nationalism: Scottish Society and Politics 1707 to the Present*. London: Routledge, 1998.

Prebble, John. *The Highland Clearances*. London: Penguin, 1963.

Williams, Raymond. *The Country and the City*. New York: Oxford University Press, 1973.

Wilt, Judith. "Steamboat Surfacing: Scott and English Novelists" *Nineteenth-Century Fiction*, 35.4 (March 1981): 459-486.

Woolf, Virginia. *To the Lighthouse*. New York: Harvest Books, 1989.

—. *Travels with Virginia Woolf*. Ed. Jan Morris. London: Hogarth Press, 1993.

Under the Volute:
Jacob's Room, Pacifism, and the Church of England

by Charles Andrews

Like many of her colleagues and contemporaries, Virginia Woolf opposed the culture of war and patriotic fervor of the 1920s, remarking, "We were all C. O.'s in the Great War" (qtd. in Briggs 88).[1] Her sister Vanessa Bell even expressed disdain for the commemoration on Armistice Day, saying "The waste of the whole thing strikes me as more idiotic than ever" (qtd. in Zwerdling 282). But as Alex Zwerdling has noted, Woolf's passionate anti-war stance exceeded the reactionary views of her associates: "To [Woolf], nonviolence was an article of faith rather than a discretionary tactic—the closest thing to a religion her secular skepticism permitted" (274). Regarding pacifism as a religion extends its reach beyond political position and into the realm of faith. In her fiction, Woolf's pacifism appears through representations of an Englishness thoroughly enmeshed in a culture of war that erupts within "civilized" English life. The tendency for war to emerge in her representations of social organization displays a pacifist aesthetic capable of simultaneously constructing a portrait of English culture while criticizing its military foundations.

The Church of England plays a special role in this construction and critique. The national religion contributes to the national character and provides a kind of comfort and stability while at the same time being an agent for maintaining order, disciplining citizenry, and ensuring homogeneity. As London is the center of the nation, St. Paul's Cathedral becomes for Woolf the architectural center of the city, an emblem of Anglican Christianity and British authority, and a site of frequent return in her novels. The Cathedral carries with it a range of cultural meanings both reproduced and interrogated. The edifice itself is simultaneously imposing and comforting, a sign of the tyrannical Church and a reassurance of Englishness.

Various forms of Christianity influenced and had appeal for Woolf, but the Church of England is the most prominent, particularly because of St. Paul's protrusion into the London skyline. With the variety of practices and convictions encompassed by Anglicanism and the related variety of responses to national context, Woolf's continual return to St. Paul's as the emblem for the Church of England suggests nuanced critique of British Christianity. Though "The verger with his rod" is the church's man in *Jacob's Room*, the most public Anglican voice from St. Paul's was the chapel dean, William Ralph Inge, who held the office from 1911 to 1934 and was a leading proponent of conservative politics during the interwar years (*JR* 54). Inge published a column in the *Evening Standard* from 1921 to 1946 where he expressed his views on the political agency of the Church, anti-socialism, and eugenics.[2] His cantankerous tone in these writings earned him the moniker "the gloomy dean." He professed an animosity toward secular, liberal nationalism, writing that "A 'nation' is a society united by a common error as to its origin and a common dislike and contempt for its neighbors. A popular religion is a superstition which has enslaved a philosophy" (*Pacifist* 41). And yet, as Matthew Grimely observes, Inge contradicted the Liberal Anglican tradition by asserting that "the Church's first duty was to the nation" (Grimely 149). Inge claimed in a *Times* article that the Church of England was "held together by something better than an Act of Parliament—namely, by the national character" (qtd. in Grimely 149). And he referred to his denomination as "the Church of the English nation" (qtd. in Grimely 149).

Woolf's essays and diary show that she regarded Inge as the figurehead for an especially distasteful sort of ecclesial authority. After a spat with Ethel Smyth, Woolf wrote in her diary: "she took to reading Dean Inge, she says, when she assumed from my voice—exhausted, cold & gruff—that 'all was over'" (*D4* 13).[3] In an extravagant and humorous gesture of despair, Smyth threatens to revert from Woolf's progressive feminism to Inge's authoritarian gloominess. Inge was also one of the churchmen whose work she consulted while writing *Three Guineas*, and she names him among the religious professionals whose notions of religiosity and citizenship undermine social, physical, and familial flourishing: "That bears out what so many people are saying now about the Church and the nation. Our bishops and deans seem to have no soul with which to preach and no mind with which to write. Listen to any sermon in any church; read the journalism of Dean Alington or Dean Inge in any newspaper" (*TG* 71). Inge exemplifies the reprehensible state of social discourse among national and religious leadership. And, in *A Room of One's Own* (1929), Woolf uses Inge as an exemplary antagonist to female artists: "Now what food do we feed women as artists upon?...To answer that question I had only to open the evening paper and to read that Lord Birkenhead is of opinion—but really I am not going to trouble to copy out Lord Birkenhead's opinion upon the writing of women. What Dean Inge says I will leave in peace" (53).

Woolf's critical or satirical view of the Church of England as seen through its representation in her novels should not be mistaken for a simplistic broadside attack on all Christianity. Her use of St. Paul's suggests a particular sort of Anglicanism associated with figures like Inge. Other important religious figures and sites more compatible with Woolf's values might have been chosen. The most prominent member of the Anglican Church through the inter-war period was William Temple, who served as bishop of Manchester, then bishop of York, and eventually archbishop of Canterbury.[4] Temple was one of many liberal Anglican clergy who worked toward a greater communitarian sensibility while retaining allegiance to the nation. But Woolf does not address Temple, choosing instead to focus on the physical structure of St. Paul's and by implication its gloomy dean. Despite the range of political and theological positions sustained by Anglicans, St. Paul's dean had authority and a platform for teaching his political conservatism. He was a leader who regarded static class hierarchy as essential to the well-being of both the church and the nation.

Woolf's cityscapes, especially noteworthy in *Jacob's Room* and *Mrs. Dalloway*, bring her characters together to create a unifying force and form modern, urban community. And, she probes the implications of cityscape marked by religious structures. For Woolf, the city is a nearly-natural shelter with the Anglican Church as its most prominent feature. In *Jacob's Room*, the narrator observes: "if there is such a thing as a shell secreted by man to fit man himself here we find it, on the banks of the Thames, where the great streets join and St. Paul's Cathedral, like the volute on the top of the snail shell, finishes it off" (*JR* 54). Like a shell, the city offers intricate structures "secreted" for habitation and protection. Men have built a zone of security to fit themselves, and this constructed safe-space appears to be natural, emerging from human bodies on a river-bank essential to the English landscape. Conrad concluded *Heart of Darkness* in horror that this "tranquil waterway leading to the uttermost ends of the earth…seem[s] to lead into the heart of an immense darkness" (95). Woolf suggests a deeper ambivalence. The Thames is the natural basis for the city's comforts in the domain of St. Paul's spire. But the snail image implies both natural safety and sluggishness. If London is a shell, then Londoners are snails—slow, soft, timid, ineffectual, bodies notable only for their secretion.[5] Rather than a powerful imperial center basing national status on violent capabilities, Woolf's London is withdrawn into the shelter of its "great streets" topped by St. Paul's dome. This volute which "finishes off" the London snail is emblematic of the interaction between nationalism and religion in Britain. The spire is an architectural marvel that calls attention to the religious institution, and yet its prominence in the London skyline diminishes the religious meaning as the cathedral becomes instead a sign of the secular city. Much like the Thames, St. Paul's is a landmark that becomes naturalized in the perception of English nationalism.

Jacob's Room exhibits dissonance between the multitude which forms English society and the titular character who appears separate from community. To be part of the English masses means assimilating into the array of urban structures. Jacob Flanders remains aloof, joining the tourism but gazing disaffectedly at "all these multitudes" who "have no houses. The streets belong to them; the shops; the churches; theirs the innumerable desks; the stretched office lights; the vans are theirs, and the railway slung high above the street" (*JR* 55). These elements of city life—homes, streets, churches, offices, transportation— give the sense of urban development in its modern, technological form. For the multitude of English people, habits and rituals of daily life are repeated without reflection. Jacob distinguishes himself by studying books at his fireside "at nine-thirty precisely" with the diligence of a monk (*JR* 55). Yet throughout the novel Jacob is also a representative Englishman, most notably in the way he joins the other English youth in military sacrifice. His national identity exhibits a striking ambivalence: he is attracted to the ancient foundations of English culture found in Homer, Shakespeare, and the Elizabethans rather than "Shaw and Wells and the serious sixpenny weeklies" (*JR* 28). But he also wants to forge for himself some place in the world, a world distinct from "the world of the elderly…[with] the moors and Byron; the sea and the lighthouse; the sheep's jaw with the yellow teeth in it" (28).

The dissonance between Jacob's intellectualism versus the multitude's possession of urban space, his insistence upon private interiority against their public exteriority, is the basis for Woolf's pacifist critique in the novel. The sphere of social action in London perpetuates a culture of violence that ultimately leads to Jacob's wasteful death. Nancy Knowles argues that Woolf juxtaposes violence in the "backdrop of her novels with indirect or 'structural' violence…immediately depicted in the foreground" (5). But Woolf's juxtaposition in *Jacob's Room* is between the individual, positioned like the Outsider from *Three Guineas*, and the social institutions that perpetuate violence. Affixed to the buildings are reminders of British conquest which produces the safety Londoners enjoy: "The posters are theirs too; and the news on them. A town destroyed; a race won" (*JR* 55). Like the ram's skull on the beach, Jacob's copy of Finlay's *Byzantine Empire*, and the Roman skeletons on the moor that "accept[s] everything" (*JR* 117), the posters on London buildings are subtle reminders that battle, death, and imperial power undergird all contemporary social structures and lead to the world war that will claim Jacob in its surge.

News printed on posters stuck to London walls echoes the newspapers Jacob pores over while pondering the violent essence of British identity. The current events chronicled in the *Globe* are grisly and sensational: "A strike, a murder, football, bodies found; vociferations from all parts of England simultaneously" (*JR* 84). If, as Benedict Anderson argues, newspapers are crucial to the imagined community of the nation, then the national imagination produced in the *Globe* is decidedly bloody.[6] Violent activities shape English nationalism, and the narrator associates this violence with the Anglican Church: "These events are features of our landscape. A foreigner coming to London could scarcely miss seeing St. Paul's" (84). By analogy, the prominence of St. Paul's and its attraction to the tourist for "authentic" Englishness is much like the violence that fills the country and its periodicals.

From the description of London's cityscape as a snail-shell, Woolf shifts to the Cathedral's interior where Jacob witnesses the tension between the official Church's authorization of class rigidity and the more democratizing effect of worship space. This tension between hierarchical social order and intermingling of classes through tourism is essential to the national representation of the scene, which includes all parts of English society. Functioning as a social arbiter, a church official appears to sanction the status quo: "The verger with his rod has life ironed out beneath him…For ever requiem—repose" (*JR* 54). Like the dome of St. Paul's that protrudes above the city, the church's official representative stands above the laity to authorize "the order; the discipline" (*JR* 54). Amid the "thin high sounds of voice and organ," the verger with his iron rod seems a petty tyrant, and the limitation of his reign is exposed by Old Spicer, the jute merchant whose office overlooks St. Paul's churchyard which despite his proximity and fifty-year tenure he has never entered (*JR* 54). The church is a constant presence in Old Spicer's life, but its thrall is only slight. For other English people, St. Paul's offers comfort that the verger's dictatorial presence, the frozen statuary, and the rigid hierarchy do not extinguish. Despite his exalted position, the verger shares the Cathedral with the working classes, represented by Mrs. Lidgett who

> tired with scrubbing the steps of the Prudential Society's office, which she did year in year out…took her seat beneath the great Duke's tomb…A magnificent place for an old woman to rest in, by the very side of the great Duke's bones, whose victories meant nothing to her, whose name she knows not, though she never fails to greet the little angels opposite. (*JR* 54)

Though her body is spent from labor for the upper classes, she has access to the repose shepherded by the verger and his rod. To be sure, this image of the cleaning woman soaking in religious mystery at the end of her hard-worn life bears traces of Marx's "opium of the people" (131), but this critique of the scene does not eliminate the sense of momentary equality that she finds in "thoughts of rest" and "sweet melodies" (*JR* 54). Her ignorance of national history beside the Duke of Wellington's tomb is part shortcoming and part transcendence. She is excluded from a knowledge-base that contains the narratives of English nationalism, the stories of heroes upon which the modern nation stands. But her ignorance also manages to reduce the importance of these national narratives by suggesting that the putti on Wellington's tomb are more emotionally resonant than the relic that lies inside. St. Paul's becomes in this scene a microcosm of England, infused with the national church, class tension, and public tradition. However ironic Woolf's treatment of the scene, her choosing the interior of St. Paul's as a space of heightened national resonance indicates recognition of the church's role in producing and stimulating national imagination. In this national production, Mrs.

Lidgett prefigures the Outsider Society member Woolf invented in *Three Guineas*. As Jane Marcus suggests, "female marginality could be exploited for collective political purposes," and the homely figure of Mrs. Lidgett finding momentary respite in St. Paul's, absorbing its pleasures while ignoring its perpetuation of mythical Englishness, becomes a woman in the liminal space between individuality and national assimilation (116).

Woolf's depictions of Anglicanism force us to contemplate the ways in which the national church is complicit in masculinist, patriotic war-mongering—elements deemed essential to the construction of national identity—while at the same time her critique of the institution creates a space where the individual British subject resents and resists the dominant structures. Though Woolf found much to dislike in the Anglicanism of figures like Dean Inge, the Church seems an inescapable part of her London narratives. Unavoidable and oddly compelling, domineering and identity-forming, the national religion functions in Woolf's texts as a very difficult institution.

Notes

1. Woolf's statement may be hyperbolic. Michèle Barrett notes that "Virginia Woolf's 'we,' referring to the pacifism of the Bloomsbury Group, touches on a tiny number of cases, so small that although they figure in the historical analyses of Great War pacifism, it is usually in terms of the individuals involved" (37).
2. For more on the life and works of W. R. Inge, see Grimley, pp. 7-8 and 230. Inge's journalism is found in his collected volumes *Outspoken Essays* (2 volumes, 1919-1922), *England* (1926), *Lay Thoughts of a Dean* (1926), *More Lay Thoughts of a Dean* (1931), *A Rustic Moralist* (1937), *Our Present Discontents* (1938), and *A Pacifist in Trouble* (1939).
3. In her diary, Woolf described the incident with Smyth as "one fine blaze, about Lady Rosebery's party with Ethel" (*D4* 13). The circumstances seem to be a party held in Ethel Smyth's honor to which Woolf was invited. Much to Woolf's dismay, the event devolved into an "Exhibition of insincerity and inanity" with "elderly butlers, peers, champagne and sugared cakes" (*L4* 297-8). More than just the surroundings which Woolf found disconcerting and phony, she was aghast at her discovery that "'Ethel likes this sort of thing'," a revelation of her friend's character that caused her to go "home therefore more jangled and dazed and out of touch with reality than I have been for years" (298).
4. See Grimely, p. 5 for an elaboration of Temple's clerical roles. Alan Wilkinson notes that Temple's progressive views were well-known. In 1924, the ecumenical Conference on Politics, Economics and Citizenship (COPEC) drew 1500 delegates to Birmingham, chaired by William Temple, Bishop of Manchester (Wilkinson 88). See also the published resolutions of the Lambeth Conference of 1930 at <http://www.lambethconference.org/resolutions/1930/>.
5. This image in *Jacob's Room* is not the only instance where snails find their way into Woolf's work. Henry Massingham writing in the *Nation* said that the absence of sexuality in *Night and Day* made Woolf's lovers into "four impassioned snails" (qtd. in Briggs 98). However, when Woolf herself used the image, its connotation is more positive than Massingham's usage. In her introduction to *Mrs. Dalloway*, Woolf described the writing process being much like "the snail to secrete a house for itself. And this it did without any conscious direction" (qtd. in Briggs 141).This metaphor of the snail's secretion as the artist's creation suggests that her image in *Jacob's Room* may be more than an ironic stab at Londoners and their self-made home.
6. See *Imagined Communities: Reflections on the Origin and Spread of Nationalism* (New York: Verso, 1991).

Works Cited

Barrett, Michèle. "Virginia Woolf and Pacifism." *Woolf in the Real World: Selected Papers from the Thirteenth International Conference on Virginia Woolf.* Ed. Karen V. Kukil. Clemson, SC: Clemson University Digital Press, 2005. 37-41.

Briggs, Julia. *Virginia Woolf: An Inner Life*. New York: Harcourt, 2005.

Grimley, Matthew. *Citizenship, Community, and the Church of England: Liberal Anglican Theories of the State Between the Wars*. Oxford: Oxford University Press, 2004.

Inge, William Ralph. *A Pacifist in Trouble*. 1939. Freeport, NY: Books for Libraries Press, 1971.
Marcus, Jane. "The Niece of a Nun: Virginia Woolf, Caroline Stephen, and the Cloister Imagination" *Virginia Woolf and the Languages of Patriarchy*. Bloomington: Indiana University Press, 1987.
Marx, Karl. *Critique of Hegel's 'Philosophy of Right'*. Ed. Joseph O'Malley. Cambridge: Cambridge University Press, 1970.
Wilkinson, Alan. *Dissent of Conform? War, Peace and the English Churches 1900-1945*. London: SCM, 1986.
Woolf, Virginia. *The Diary of Virginia Woolf: Volume Four, 1931-1935*. Ed. Anne Oliver Bell and Andrew McNeillie. New York: Harcourt Brace Jovanovich, 1982.
—. *Jacob's Room*. 1922. New York: Penguin, 1992.
—. *The Letters of Virginia Woolf Volume IV: 1929-1931*. Ed. Nigel Nicolson and Joanne Trautmann. New York: Harcourt Brace Jovanovich, 1978.
—. *A Room of One's Own*. 1929. New York: Harcourt Brace Jovanovich, 1981.
—. *Three Guineas*. 1938. New York: Harcourt Brace Jovanovich, 1966.
Zwerdling, Alex. *Virginia Woolf and the Real World*. Berkeley: University of California Press, 1986.

Virginia Woolf's "Ghosts": Books, Martyrs, and Metaphors[1]

by Diane F. Gillespie

Prologue: "as dull as ditch water"

"When a body dies the ghost it is said sometimes haunts." So Woolf writes in an incomplete story called "Ghosts." "But," she asks, "when a book is read, and shut up and put away, what happens to that ghost? Some haunt us almost whole;" she replies, "but the greater number fade, and [...,] as they are blown about the corridors of the brain[,] change, and mingle with other shapes, so that after some years they are scarcely recognizable" (*CSF* 335). Brenda Silver has catalogued, usefully, the reading notebooks Woolf kept, mostly to help her in writing reviews and essays. Julia Briggs notes, however, "how little we actually know of her thoughts and reading, despite the numerous surviving records she left" (378). If we use, carefully, the Woolfs' remaining books now at Washington State University, we can identify some ghosts and fill in more gaps.

I found one such gap when I reread a passage in *Orlando*. In the seventeenth century, Orlando finds herself endangered in Turkey. Some young male gypsies, appalled by the very heritage she reveres, plot to "cut her throat" (152). Woolf's narrator notes, with ironic hyperbole, how differences among cultural values "are enough to cause bloodshed and revolution. Towns have been sacked for less, and a million martyrs have suffered at the stake rather than yield an inch upon any of the points here debated. No passion is stronger in the breast of man than the desire to make others believe as he believes [....] But," Orlando's biographer concludes, "these moralities belong, and should be left to the historian, since they are as dull as ditch water" (149). What, I wondered, did Woolf know about martyrs or histories of martyrdom?

In letters and diaries, Woolf indicates only moderate interest in accounts of martyrs—actual or literary, secular or religious, contemporary or historical. She couldn't "squeeze a tear," for instance, when she read Bernard Shaw's *Saint Joan* in 1924 (*L3* 130). In the thirties, Vita Sackville-West's biography *Saint Joan of Arc* (1936) didn't move her much either (*L6* 57), and she dismissed Eliot's *Murder in the Cathedral* as a "pale New England morality murder" (*D4* 356). Yet, as younger Virginia Stephen, she had access to other, earlier published sources. These helped to develop her distaste for dogmatists who forced their beliefs on others, and for self-defined martyrs who paraded self-sacrifice for ego gratification.[2] In early novels, she deflates martyrdom, treating it as a metaphor for inflexibility, self-interest, and vanity, the very stuff, according to George Meredith, of comedy.[3] However dedicated to a cause, these so-called "martyrs" expect servitude and admiration from others they consider less valuable than themselves. From their positions in traditional power hierarchies, they create simplistic narratives of right and wrong, good and evil. Woolf also exposes people who enable self-styled martyrs, as well as unthinking people who accept the values of religious and political institutions, lazily contributing to a climate for oppression. Ultimately, her interest in ordinary minds on ordinary days, and her increasing suspicion of exclusionary systems of belief, leave little room for martyrdom, heroically defined.

I. A Holy "Ghost"

Books die when readers finish them, according to Woolf's metaphor, but their ghosts in readers' brains confer a kind of immortality that includes (for book lovers) not only words, but also frontispieces and illustrations, bookplates and inscriptions. Woolf's knowledge of martyrdom began with gifts from her two brothers, seemingly odd choices of books that later haunt her and, transformed, flit through her writing. Thoby Stephen, who had just gone up to Cambridge, first gave his seventeen-year-old sister Thomas à Kempis's *Of the Imitation of Christ* (1898). He inscribed it, "Adeline Virginia Stephen from J. T. S. Xmas 1899." The elegant volume has sinuous designs by Laurence Housman.[4] It is a style of book illustration Vanessa Bell and Roger Fry later dismissed, along with much *fin de siecle* work, as overly ornate and sentimental (Gillespie, *Sisters'* 116-18). A ghost of Housman's curvilinear engraving of the martyred Christ (see Figure 1) may have been in Woolf's mind, however, when, in *The Voyage Out*, the tourists in Santa Marina attend church and, during the service, segue from bits of the Old Testament to the "New Testament and the sad and beautiful figure of Christ" (52).

Figure 1. Laurence Housman. Frontispiece to Thomas a Kempis. *Of the Imitation of Christ* (1898).

In ironic contrast to the lush visual interest of the volume, however, are the austere admonitions of Thomas, the fifteenth-century mystical monk. Although none of them appear among Woolf's later reading notes, she may well have read, "It is vanity to seek after riches, [...] to lay oneself out for honours, and to raise oneself to a high station" (4). Is Thomas a holy "ghost" who materializes in *Three Guineas*? There Woolf's letter-writing persona exhorts women to embrace "poverty;" reject honors, and avoid competitive values (78-80). Like Thomas before her, but speaking for "daughters of educated men" (*TG* 4), she advocates an egalitarian version of the New Testament "very different from the religion now erected upon that basis" (*TG* 113).

II. "Ghosts" of Christians Past

Rona M. Fields, writing on "The Psychology and Sociology of Martyrdom," emphasizes "choice" as the operant word—not a choice to die, but rather a *"choice to live"* according to a belief, even if the consequences are death (27). For traditional Christian martyrs, death with honor was not "to go down fighting," as in warrior cultures, but to embrace "a humiliating death by torture," because it "imitated the death of Christ, and would be rewarded in the next life" (Cormack xiii). Probably the most influential present from Thoby Stephen that haunts Woolf's work is *The Book of Martyrs Containing an Account of the Sufferings and Death of the Protestants in the Reign of Queen Mary the First* by exiled religious reformer John Foxe.[5] It is a hefty volume, also absent from the later reading notebooks. Thoby's inscription reads "Adeline Virginia Stephen from J. T. Stephen P Old Court Trinity College Cambridge Sunday Nov. 18th 1900, being the day after the performance of the 'Agamemnon' of Aeschylus at Cambridge" (see Figure 2).

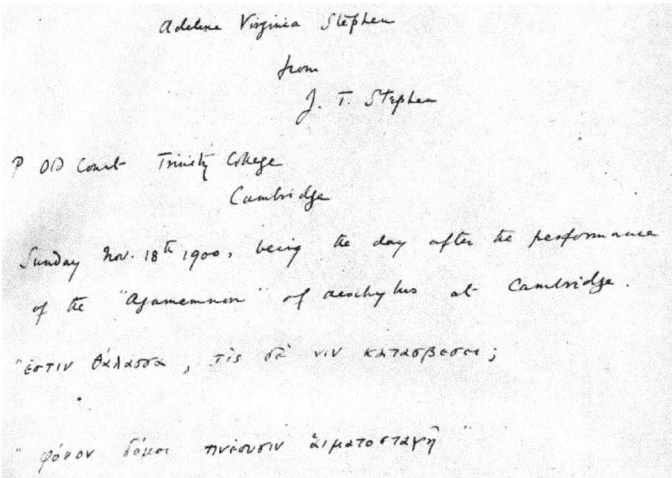

Figure 2. Thoby Stephen's inscription. John Foxe *The Book of Martyrs* (1776).

Virginia had begun her study of classical languages two years earlier, in the fall of 1898. Appropriately, Thoby copied two lines of Greek from the Aeschylus play. In Richmond Lattimore's modern translation, the first reads, "The sea is there, and who shall drain its yield?" Clytemnestra speaks, deceptively welcoming home her husband Agamemnon as he returns with Cassandra, a spoil of the Trojan War (l. 958). In the second line, Cassandra envisions the death of Agamemnon by Clytemnestra's hand. "That room within reeks with blood like a slaughter house," she cries to the uncomprehending Chorus (l. 1309).[6] Thoby's quotations imply a link between Clytemnestra and Queen Mary (dubbed "Bloody Mary"). Both wield power to destroy violently those who violate their tenets of behavior or belief.

Foxe identifies 300-some Protestants martyred during Mary's short reign (1553-58), details their trials and punishments, and provides an alphabetical index of their names and the ways they died. Over 160 black-and-white engravings, most by "G. Terry" or just "Terry," stiffly render individuals and groups of Protestant men as well as women being tortured—on the rack, by scourge, in stocks, or otherwise humiliated, before being burned. Nicholas Burton, an English merchant in Spain, for instance, was paraded to his death backwards on a horse, clothed in devil images, with his tongue forced out of his mouth by a cloven stick (see Figure 3). Although the illustrations also include beheadings, most of the images, often four to a page, are of named Protestant heretics being burnt, singly or in groups, at the stake (see Figure 4). These engravings from an earlier era, although very different in style from those in *Of the Imitation of Christ*, also try to beautify martyrdom. Framed with garlanded architectural details, portrayals of the tortured range from general and formulaic to individualized.[7] An example of the latter is the engraving of Thomas Cranmer, Archbishop of Canterbury. He was condemned for heresy, but recanted by admitting papal supremacy and accepting all Roman Catholic doctrine except transubstantiation. Still he was burned at the stake, at which time he repudiated his recantation by putting the hand that had signed it into the fire first (see Figure 5).

Figure 3. G. Terry, Sculp. "The Manner of carrying Nicholas Burton through the City of Sevill, to the Place of his Martyrdom." John Foxe *The Book of Martyrs* (1776).

Foxe and his publishers and editors did not share the modern view that "writers have no need of painters to explain what they want to say," as Henri Matisse put it (qtd. in Gillespie, *Sisters'* 118). These engravings were to make a strong impression on the illiterate (Wooden 49). Yet I would be surprised if even the literate Virginia Stephen waded through all of Foxe's long accounts of individual martyrs. The graphic illustrations more likely impressed ghosts upon her brain, not just because they are so numerous and repetitive, but because visual images tempted her to find words to probe human psyches beneath physical façades. The revelations of human history and biography prompted her

Figure 4. Terry, Sculp. Burnings of men and women at Canterbury, Colchester, and Ipswich.

Figure 5. G. Terry, Sculp. "The Martyrdom of Dr. Thomas Cranmer at Oxford." John Foxe. *The Book of Martyrs* (1776).

to imagine omissions and alternatives. Finally, this graphic visual evidence of abuses of power raised the possibility that women who move into public positions might uncritically adopt institutional values.

Take "The Procession to St. Mary's Church" where Thomas Cranmer, Archbishop of Canterbury; Hugh Latimer, Bishop of Worcester; and Nicholas Ridley, Bishop of London, disputed with divines and learned men from Oxford and Cambridge about "the sacrament" (28) (see Figure 6). Note the book burning in the inset, a visual metaphor for the martyrdom of heretical writers. Virginia Stephen's perusal of this engraving may well have culminated not only in her later support of censored authors, but also in the photos of elaborately costumed patriarchs on parade in her own dissenting book, *Three Guineas*. How, she wonders, might women now "trapesing along somewhere in the rear [....] enter the professions and yet remain civilized human beings?" (*TG* 69, 75). In his account, Foxe lists those processing along with their official positions, regalia, and retinues: "first, the quire in their surplices followed the cross; then the first-year regents and proctors; then the doctors of law, and their beadles before them; then the doctors of divinity of both universities," and so on (29). In the procession are inquisitors who doom alleged heretics. Assisting them are beadles, functionaries whose descendent mock-heroically shoos Woolf's female narrator off the lawns of Oxbridge in *A Room of One's Own* (6).

When Woolf uses martyrdom metaphorically in *The Voyage Out*, she shows how choosing to live one's beliefs may include posturing designed to garner sympathy and to inflate one's ego. Ridley Ambrose's first name echoes that of Nicholas Ridley, Bishop of London, prominent in Foxe's frontispiece.[8] In the martyrdom tradition, when there

Figure 6. Terry, Sculp. "The Procession to St. Mary's Church Cambridge." John Foxe. *The Book of Martyrs* (1776).

is no opportunity for physical death, honor resides in "ascetic or pietistic alternatives" (Cormack xv). Woolf's Ridley has not devoted his life to Protestant Christianity, but to classical Greek scholarship. Yet his self-image as an intellectual rests upon condescension towards women's activities—unless directed towards admiring or facilitating translations he laments are widely "ignored." When Ridley "emphatically" rejects, in favor of his work, the prospect of going with the women to mail letters, he looks less like "a secluded Professor" than like "a commander surveying a field of battle, or a martyr watching the flames lick his toes." "We'll leave you to your vanities," Helen Ambrose says astutely (*VO* 98). Woolf's description is, in part, a comic revision of Foxe's *Book of Martyrs* illustrations.

III. "Ghosts" of Christians Prescient

Foxe's book, I'm sure, was one source of allusions to martyrdom in *Orlando* and in Woolf's early fiction. Another was Edward Gibbon's *The History of the Decline and Fall of the Roman Empire* (1820), a gift to the new instructor at Morley College from her younger brother Adrian Stephen, in his last year at Trinity College, Cambridge. It is inscribed, simply, "Adeline Virginia Stephen from A.L.S. Jan 25th 1905," and her "AVS 1905" bookplate is pasted inside the front cover of all twelve volumes. Gibbon provides, in volume two, a history of Christian martyrdom under Roman rule, noting motives and misconceptions on both sides. Not sure which accounts to believe, he refrains from detailing the sufferings of particular Christians (489). Nor does he include engravings. Gibbon does note, ironically, that, although the Romans martyred Christians, their descendents do likewise: "from the time that Christianity was invested with the supreme power," he writes, "the governors of the church have been no less diligently employed in displaying the cruelty, than in imitating the conduct, of their Pagan adversaries" (382). Ironic summations like these, which certainly had the support of Foxe's earlier *Book of Martyrs* and other martyrologies, got Gibbon into trouble with clergymen of the eighteenth century (Aston 253).

Three decades later, in 1937 (as her reading notebooks do indicate), Woolf went back to *The Decline and Fall* and published "The Historian and 'The Gibbon'." She recognizes the scandals he caused by his attacks on "the cruelty and intolerance of superstition" (*DM* 88-89). She also realizes that irony, in his hands, "is a dangerous weapon" (*DM* 89). Still, his treatment of the hypocrisy of institutionalized Christianity anticipates a strategy Woolf very soon employs in *Three Guineas,* with similar risks. The ironic ghost of Gibbon's *Decline and Fall* stalking her brain, she suggests that representatives of England's patriarchal institutions display the same war-causing tendencies as do the continental dictators they denounce.[9]

IV. "what my mother [...] felt for Christ"

In her first two novels, Woolf adds a modern psychological complexity that Gibbon's discussion of motives anticipates. Richard Dalloway, as he appears in *The Voyage Out,* is an even better example than Ridley Ambrose. Dalloway dramatizes "the strain of public life" and thus initially appears to young Rachel Vinrace in the guise of "a battered martyr, parting every day with some of the finest gold, in the service of mankind" (*VO* 65). Clarissa Dalloway, although sometimes critical of her husband, enables his self-sacrificing image. She wonders "whether it is really good for a woman to live with a man who is morally her superior, as Richard is mine." She even invokes the ultimate martyr in Western cultural history when she supposes that she "feel[s] for him what my mother and women of her generation felt for Christ" (*VO* 52). Dalloway undercuts his moral superiority, however, with a dogmatist's inflexibility. He declares, "may I be in my grave before a woman has the right to vote in England!"(*VO* 43). He also dismisses the value of writers and artists to society (*VO* 45). In line with his wife's image of him as an imitation of Christ, he conquers trials of his commitment. So he dramatizes his lust for Rachel: "You tempt me," he says, his voice "terrifying" (*VO* 76-7). Blaming Rachel rather than himself, and oblivious to his disruptive effect on her, at dinner he "slid his eyes over her uneasily once, and never looked at her again" (*VO* 77).

Yet even artists, at whom Dalloway sneers, can pose as martyrs, sacrificing themselves to art. In *Night and Day,* Ralph Denham defines William Rodney as "one of those martyred spirits to whom literature is at once a source of divine joy and of almost intolerable irritation." He devotes himself to literature but suffers from the suspicion that he has "very little facility" (*ND* 56). Still, like Woolf's other masculine martyrs, he courts feminine support: Katharine Hilberry is to admire his obsessive metrical lines, even though she is "fairly certain that plays should not produce a sense of chill stupor in the audience" (*ND* 139-40).

Consistent with her early exposure to "Bloody Mary" and to images of women burning at the stake, Woolf's look at the psychology of martyrdom in her early novels includes women. In *The Voyage Out,* Rachel reads Gibbon,[10] and Mrs. Flushing remembers that in her youth, "We used to lie in bed and read [...] about the massacres of the Christians." In the same breath she recalls the book as having provided her with "some of the happiest hours of [her] life." (*VO* 200). For Mrs. Flushing, safe in her bed, historical accounts of suffering provided, and still do provide, vicarious pleasure. Similarly, Mrs. Milvain, Katherine Hilbery's aunt in *Night and Day*, incorporates what Woolf calls "some of the agreeable sensations of martyrdom" into her role as bearer of what she thinks are bad tidings when she tells her niece that William Rodney now loves Cassandra (*ND* 408). Women too can be fascinated by human suffering as well as enjoy their own self-sacrificial roles.

V. "relapsed tamely into [...] acquiescence"

Most people, however, are not sufficiently committed to religious or secular principles to martyr or be martyred. Again, Thoby Stephen put his sister in the way of a text, this time his own. In about 1904, the year of Leslie Stephen's death and perhaps, in part, a tribute to him, Thoby wrote and had printed an unsigned, eight-page pamphlet entitled *Compulsory Chapel: An Appeal to Undergraduates on Behalf of Religious Liberty and Intellectual Independence*. Virginia Stephen sent a copy to Madge Vaughan. It "will make you laugh, I think," she wrote (*L*1:161). Virginia apparently found the whole issue an amusing idiosyncrasy of men's higher education. Thoby points to a ruling that men who are not members of the Church of England need not go to chapel. The University assumes, however, that everyone *is* a member and therefore must be punished for nonattendance. Undergraduates go along with this injustice out of "apathy," "ignorance," and "cowardice" whereas they should be standing up, Thoby writes, for religious liberty (7).

In *The Voyage Out*, Rachel Vinrace detects a similar apathy, ignorance, and cowardice among the English congregation in Santa Marina: "One after another, vast and hard and cold, appeared to her the churches all over the world [...] filled with innumerable men and women, not seeing clearly, who finally gave up the effort to see, and relapsed tamely into praise and acquiescence" (*VO* 228). This indifference numbs church-goers and creates an environment for the potential exercise of unchallenged power represented, not by the ineffectual Mr. Bax, but by the institution he represents.

With the exception of *Orlando*, Woolf, in her later novels, no longer uses the word "martyr," although she often rings variations on the word "torture." Yet fiery images, ghosts of Foxe's martyrology, remain. Clarissa in *Mrs Dalloway*, for example, defends and enjoys her sacrifices to high society, but also suffers torments. "Why seek pinnacles and stand drenched in fire?" she wonders as she greets her party guests. "Might it consume her [...]! Burn her to cinders!" (*MD* 167). She feels like "a stake driven in at the top of her stairs" (*MD* 170). When she hears of, and vicariously experiences, Septimus's death, "her dress flamed, her body burnt" (*MD* 184).

VI. "I must create a system"...or not.

A final salvo from Thoby, who died the following year (1906), was his gift to his sister Virginia of nineteenth-century poet and essayist James Thomson's 1896 book, *Biographical and Critical Studies*. Thoby's inscription reads "A. V. Stephen from J. T. S. 'There is no God' J. Thomson," a quotation suitable to this free-thinking author (see Figure 7). In his first chapter, Thomson quotes Rabelais as saying, "'The ministers of religion are its worst enemies: he who is wise will be tied by as few dogmas as may be, but he will possess his soul in patience'" (6).

Virginia Woolf spent the rest of her life dismantling or complicating overly simple dualities and dogmas. She does not say, with William Blake's Los in *Jerusalem*, "I must Create a System, or be enslaved by another Man's" (151), a recommendation followed

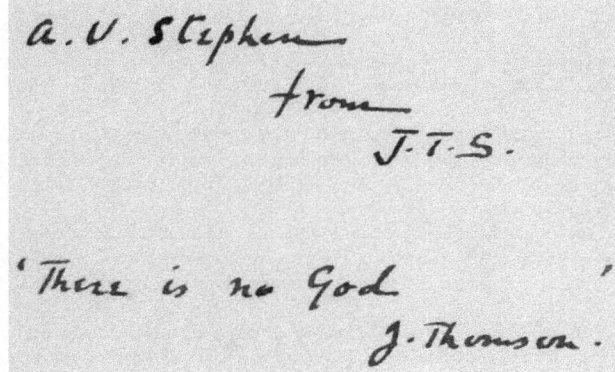

Figure 7. Thoby Stephen's inscription. James Thomson *Biographical and Critical Studies* (1896).

by male contemporaries like Yeats and Lawrence. As Herbert Marder rightly says, Woolf's "mind was supple and diverse, shunning formulas and doctrines, devising ways to include rather than shut out" (137). Woolf, Anne Fernald notes, tried to show women in particular how to be critical, and thus "liberate" their "imaginations from official memory without constructing an equally imposing replacement" (101, 110).

Yet it is tempting to read *Three Guineas*, with *A Room of One's Own* as predecessor, as feminist martyrologies, accounts of how women have been psychologically, if not physically, martyred by, and sacrificed to, the patriarchy. Indeed, Woolf, in her irritation with Affable Hawk's (Desmond MacCarthy's) dismissal of women artists in his columns in the 1920s, describes women painters, denied "paints and studios" and confined to household duties, as undergoing "a species of torture more exquisitely painful, I believe, than any that man can imagine" (*D2* 341). And, she says in *A Room of One's Own*, Florence Nightingale "shrieked aloud in her agony" at the limitations imposed upon her life and aspirations (57-8). Yet for all her anger and sympathy, Woolf shied away, not from her own experiences, or her observations of other women, or her historical and biographical research, but from "feminism" hardened into dogma.

It therefore seems at least equally accurate to read *Three Guineas* as an anti-martyrology. Woolf mocks, complicates, and rejects the traditional narrative of martyrdom that depends upon rigid adherence to dogmas and the hierarchical power to impose them on equally inflexible dissenters, or on uncomprehending victims. *Three Guineas*, as an anti-martyrology, imagines an Outsiders' Society, one with no gods, no dogmas, no proselytizing, no hierarchies, no official titles, no regalia, and certainly no martyrs. All these negatives add up, ironically, not to apathy, not to anarchy, but to something both moral and positive, a pervasive mindset, a co-existing social stratum, that consistently leavens the system by creative rather than destructive acts. *Three Guineas* suggests that separate individuals, all embracing their outsider status, can achieve and foster freedom—to live, speak, and create. If Woolf contemplates the stake, it is, as she writes in "Anon.," a "stake against oblivion." It is putting "two and two together—two pencil strokes, two written words, two bricks (notes)" (403). It is the nudging of tolerant and humane ghosts into the minds of readers of books, viewers of art, and listeners to music. Individual constructive, creative acts are enough, if not "to die for," then at least in order to live.

Notes

1. My thanks to Manuscripts, Archives and Special Collections at Washington State University, Pullman, WA, for permission to reproduce in this paper the images from books in the Leonard and Virginia Woolf Library.
2. Writing on T. S. Eliot's *Murder in the Cathedral,* Coilin Owens notes that "a true martyr" becomes "the instrument" of a belief, "no longer desir[ing] anything for himself; not even the glory of being a martyr" (17).
3. Meredith's *An Essay on Comedy and the Uses of the Comic Spirit,* among Virginia Woolf's books at Washington State University Library, contains her bookplate.
4. The illustrations were "engraved upon wood by Miss Clemence Housman," and printed at the Chiswick Press, London. Laurence Housman (1865-1959), playwright and poet, was active as a book illustrator from the 1890s. He also contributed to the notorious *Yellow Book,* for which Aubrey Beardsley was art editor (Thorpe 227, 187, 195, 198).
5. Thoby gave Virginia a large 1776 engraved edition. Foxe's *The Book of Martyrs,* as it was popularly called, had first appeared in English in 1563 as *Actes and Monuments.* The clergyman who wrote the introduction to the edition Virginia owned warns that "Popery" still burns Protestants in Spain and Portugal. When she traveled to Spain in 1905, Virginia recalled the Spanish Inquisition (*PA* 263) of the fifteenth century and the efforts of "Ferdinand and Isabella to rid Spain of heretics and unbelievers by trial and torture" (Gillespie, "The Rain" 271).
6. My thanks to Robin and Trevor Bond for identifying these lines for me.
7. The architecture is classical and, in addition to garlands of flowers, there are occasional cherubs, eagles, lambs, and crowns, all to emphasize the holiness and heroism of the martyrs as well as their eternal rewards.
8. "Ridley" is more appropriate for Woolf's character than "Geranium," an earlier draft choice (Hussey 3).
9. In this same year, two months before the appearance of *Three Guineas,* Leonard Woolf's review of G. G. Coulton's *Inquisition and Liberty* (London: William Heinemann, 1938) was published as "The Religion of the Stake" in the *New Statesman & Nation* (9 April 1938, 624). Leonard writes, "The horrible barbarities practiced by the Church in God's name have been resurrected in the greater part of Europe and are being practiced with the same methods and the same organization in the name of Fascism, National Socialism, or Communism." Although he indicts "the human species" in general, he does not go so far as Virginia to indict his own government.
10. For fuller treatments of Woolf's use of Gibbon in *The Voyage Out,* see Dane and Wittman.

Works Cited

Aeschylus. *Agamemnon. Oresteia.* Trans. Richmond Lattimore. Chicago. University of Chicago Press, 1953. 33-90.

Aston, Nigel. "A 'disorderly squadron'? A fresh look at clerical responses to The Decline and Fall." *Edward Gibbon: Bicentenary Essays.* Ed. David Womersley. Oxford: Voltaire Foundation, 1997. 253-77.

Blake, William. "Jerusalem." *The Poetry and Prose of William Blake.* Ed. David V. Erdman. New York: Doubleday, 1965. 143-256.

Briggs, Julia. *Virginia Woolf: An Inner Life.* Orlando: Harcourt, 2005.

Cormack, Margaret, ed. *Sacrificing the Self: Perspectives on Martyrdom and Religion.* Oxford University Press, 2002.

Dane, Gabrielle. "Thinking Back Through Her Fathers: Virginia Woolf and Edward Gibbon." *Virginia Woolf: Turning the Centuries: Selected Papers from the Ninth Annual Conference on Virginia Woolf.* Ed. Ann Ardis and Bonnie Kime Scott. New York: Pace University Press, 2000. 16-24.

Fernald, Anne E. "The Memory Palace of Virginia Woolf." *Virginia Woolf: Reading the Renaissance.* Ed. Sally Greene. Athens: Ohio University Press, 1999. 89-114.

Fields, Rona M. ed. *Martyrdom: The Psychology, Theology, and Politics of Self-Sacrifice.* London: Praiger, 2004.

Foxe, John. *The Book of Martyrs: Containing an Account of the Sufferings & Death of the Protestants in the Reign of Queen Mary the First.* London: H. Trapp, 1776.

Gibbon, Edward. *The History of the Decline and Fall of the Roman Empire.* 12 vols. London: T. Cadell & W. Davies, et al., 1820.

Gillespie, Diane Filby. "'The Rain in Spain': Woolf, Cervantes, Andalusia, and *The Waves.*" *Virginia Woolf: Out of Bounds: Selected Papers from the Tenth Annual Conference On Virginia Woolf.* Ed. Jessica Berman and Jane Goldman. New York: Pace University Press, 271-78.

—. *The Sisters' Arts: The Writing and Painting of Virginia Woolf and Vanessa Bell.* Syracuse, NY: Syracuse University Press, 1988, 1991.
Hussey, Mark. *Virginia Woolf: A to Z.* New York: Facts on File, 1995.
Marder, Herbert. *Feminism and Art: A Study of Virginia Woolf.* Chicago: University of Chicago Press, 1968.
Meredith, George. *An Essay on Comedy and the Uses of the Comic Spirit.* 2nd ed. Westminster: Constable, 1898.
Owens, Coilin. "A Literary Preamble." Fields, 3-21.
Silver, Brenda R. *Virginia Woolf's Reading Notebooks.* Princeton: Princeton University Press, 1983.
Stephen, Thoby. *Compulsory Chapel: an Appeal to Undergraduates on Behalf of Religious Liberty and Intellectual Independence.* Cambridge: privately printed, [1904?].
Thomson, James. *Biographical and Critical Studies.* London: Reeves & Turner, 1896.
Thorpe, James. *English Illustration in the Nineties.* New York: Hacker Art Books, 1975.
Wittman, Emily O. "The Decline and Fall of Rachel Vinrace: Reading Gibbon in Virginia Woolf's *The Voyage Out*. *Woolf and the Art of Exploration: Selected Papers from the Fifteenth International Conference on Virginia Woolf.* Ed. Helen Southworth and Elisa Kay Sparks. Clemson: Clemson University Digital Press, 2006. 160-68.
Wooden, Warren W. *John Foxe.* Boston: Twayne, 1983.
Woolf, Virginia. *The Death of the Moth and Other Essays.* Ed. Leonard Woolf. New York: Harcourt, Brace, 1942.
—*The Diary of Virginia Woolf.* Ed. Anne Olivier Bell. 5 vols. New York: Harcourt Brace Jovanovich, 1977-84.
—"Ghosts." *The Complete Shorter Fiction of Virginia Woolf.* 2nd ed. Ed. Susan Dick. San Diego: Harcourt Brace Jovanovich, 1989. 335-7.
—"The Historian and 'The Gibbon.'" (1937). *The Death of the Moth.* 82-93.
—"A Letter to a Young Poet." (1932). *The Death of the Moth.* 208-26.
—*The Letters of Virginia Woolf.* Ed. Nigel Nicolson and Joanne Trautmann. 6 vols. New York: Harcourt Brace Jovanovich, 1975-80.
—*Mrs. Dalloway.* San Diego: Harcourt Brace Jovanovich, 1981.
—*Night and Day.* New York: Harcourt Brace Jovanovich, 1948.
—*Orlando: A Biography.* New York: Harcourt Brace Jovanovich, 1956.
—*A Passionate Apprentice: The Early Journals 1897-1909.* Ed. Mitchell A. Leaska. San Diego: Harcourt Brace Jovanovich, 1990.
—*A Room of One's Own.* New York: Harcourt Brace Jovanovich, 1957.
—*Three Guineas.* New York: Harcourt, Brace and World, 1966.
—*The Voyage Out.* New York: Harcourt, Brace and World, 1948.

The Reception of Woolf in China

by Xiaoqin Cao

Research on Virginia Woolf and China has long been on the periphery of Woolf studies, even though Woolf has a deeper connection with China in her life and works than most people would imagine. As early as 1913, Woolf wrote a review on Chinese stories written by Pu Songling of the Qing Dynasty, claiming that "[t]he barriers against which we in the West beat our hands in vain are for them almost as transparent as glass" (CE2 7). In 1923, Woolf wrote another review, "The Chinese Shoe," to argue for women's conditions in the Victorian Age. She says that "the old Chinese custom of fitting the foot to the shoe was charitable compared with the mid-Victorian practice of fitting the woman to the system" (CE3 390). The issues raised by Woolf in both reviews have become a paradigm for the reception of Woolf in China. The cross-cultural literary reading between East and West and women's issues are the keynotes of Woolf's reception in China.

Woolf was first introduced into China in the 1930s. In 1932, Ye Gongchao translated "A Mark on the Wall" and made a brief comment on it. Two years later, translations of "Mr. Bennett and Mrs. Brown" and "On Russian Novels" appeared respectively in two literary journals. In the following years, Woolf was included in a book on English literary history (Gao and Lu 36). Chinese readers became further acquainted with Woolf through her nephew Julian Bell's teaching in National Wuhan University between 1935 and 1937. In his lectures, Julian Bell made *To the Lighthouse* a set book for British modernism (Laurence, *Lily Briscoe's* 54). The Chinese literary world at this time was under the influence of the May Fourth Movement, which laid "a foundation…to adapt foreign ideas and institutions creatively to the Chinese situation" (Cuddy-Keane and Li 136). Thus, in the 1930s, Chinese readers showed a range of responses to Woolf. For example, Xiao Qian "relegated Woolf to 'an ivory tower'" (Laurence, *Lily Briscoe's* 209). The stream of consciousness style was regarded as "western," "narcissistic," "bourgeois," and "weak" (54). Among women writers, however, Woolf's works were greatly admired. The Chinese woman writer and painter Ling Shuhua, for instance, was particularly interested in Woolf's writing. Woolf's novels also influenced quite a few modern writers of the 1930s, such as Xu Zhimo and Lin Huiyin, who tried to apply the technique of "stream of consciousness" in their writings (Gao and Lu 36). These writers were key members of the Crescent Moon Group in China which Patricia Laurence argues resembled the Bloomsbury Group in Britain (*Lily Briscoe's*).

The establishment of the People's Republic of China in October 1949 also brought about a change of policy in foreign literary studies. Foreign literature from different ideological points of view was strictly controlled. Woolf studies were no exception. It was only after 1979 that a new official policy emerged, liberating literary studies from serving politics directly. Thus, from the 1980s on, there was a revived interest in Woolf among Chinese scholars. Many essays and novels by Woolf were translated into Chinese. Qu Shijing, known as Frank Chu, was one of the major contributors to Woolf studies in this period. His books of introductory and critical discussion of Woolf have, for a long time, been an important reference for Chinese readers. Most of the critical discussions of Woolf "focus on Woolf's style with specific attention to details of imagery, symbolism, sentence structure, interior monologue, stream of consciousness, and the use of multiple perspective" (Cuddy-Keane and Li 140). As Melba Cuddy-Keane indicates, "what might seem in the West to be a repetition and extension of older work signals, in the East, a rapid acquisition of the nuances and possibilities of a foreign language and an intense interest in the markedly different thought patterns that a Modernist style liberates" (141).

Chinese Woolf studies began to flourish from the late 1990s. The publication of Woolf's works became increasingly systematic. Some of her novels were re-translated. Two leading publishing houses published the complete collections of Woolf's essays and novels in 2001 and 2003 (Gao and Lu 37). In 2005, Xiao Yi translated Woolf's biography by Quentin Bell, and Dai Hongzhen and Song Binghui translated Woolf's diary. The translation of S. P. Rosenbaum's book *The Bloomsbury Group: A Collection of Memoirs and Commentary* appeared in 2006. These trends of publication indicate Chinese readers' extended interest from Woolf's work to her life and cultural circle. The development of Woolf criticism among Chinese scholars, together with the publication of Woolf's works, suggests the intimate and sustained relationship that Chinese scholars have had with Woolf studies. With a continued interest in Woolf's novelistic innovations, they have also shown an interest in feminist criticism. Influenced by Western feminist theories, Chinese feminist criticism has helped elevate the position of women's writing, but has not yet made a substantial impact on the gender relationship in society. Woolf's feminist criticism is thus limited to the literary realm. The feminist critics mainly focus on androgyny theory and the female perspective. During this period, Chinese critics also have compared Woolf with a number of other Western figures like James Joyce, Jacques Derrida, and Charlotte Bronte. While stressing the study of the foreign authors, some critics compare Woolf with the Chinese woman writer Xiao Hong (1911-1942), focusing on the theme of psycho-novel and death consciousness. Some critics also compare Woolf's stream of consciousness with the Chinese writer Li Tuo (1939–), and her poetic writing with Zhang Chengzhi (1948–). In 2005 and 2006, Michael Cunningham's novel *The Hours* also received significant scholarly attention, for example, in Guo Ming's "To Whom Would They Tell Their Affliction?—Decoding the Women's Lives in the Novel *The Hours*" (2005), Wu Qinhong's "A Modern Feminist View of *The Hours*" (2006), and Song Wen's "Writing Up the Female Urban Frustration in Michael Cunningham's *The Hours*" (2006). In recent years quite a few papers examine death consciousness and the quest for life's meaning in Woolf's novels. This special area of Woolf criticism reflects the ontological quest of Chinese people in contemporary China. Around thirty years after Deng Xiaoping's open door policy, Chinese society is overwhelmed by materialism and consumerism. As some social observers have noted, Chinese people are undergoing a spiritual wasteland. Various attempts have been made to search for ontological thinking through Chinese Classics, Western philosophy, literature and different religions, hence this new wave in Chinese Woolf studies.

Other than discussion and criticism of Woolf in the Chinese academic world, contemporary China is also witnessing the teaching of Woolf in high schools and universities. "The Mark on the Wall", for example, has been collected in a standard textbook for high school students in which the focus of teaching is the "stream of consciousness" novel. "Street Haunting—A London Adventure," another important essay by Woolf, is collected in the *Advanced English Writing Course* for English majors in the university. In various textbooks on English literary history, Woolf is treated, together with Joyce, as a representative of modernist writers.

Outside the academic realm, reading and quoting Woolf has become a recent fashion, especially for the so-called "petty bourgeoisie women" in China. The term "petty bourgeoisie" was borrowed to describe the newly-emerged young Chinese intellectuals, probably at the end of the twentieth century. It is a group of young people influenced by European and American culture, normally with a university education. With stable profession and income, they are in better financial condition than the masses, but are not very wealthy either. The "petty bourgeoisie" are quite self-conscious of their identity in society and always keep some distance from the masses and popular culture. They do not have to be the leaders of high culture, but are the major consumers and pursuers of it. The translation and publication of Woolf's works in China draws the attention of not only Chinese critics' but also that of the "petty bourgeoisie." They form a major part of Woolf's common readers in China. Many articles and reviews of Woolf's works or adapted movies are produced in various forms. Woolf's female consciousness is one important aspect in these reviews. *A Room of One's Own* is also taken as a manifesto of female independence and is celebrated by "petty bourgeoisie women." Woolf's legendary life also fascinates Chinese common readers.

When Frank Chu introduced Woolf in 1989, he clearly stated that the reason why he chose Woolf was not only because of her novelistic innovation but also because there were no erotic and violent elements in her novels. Although later critics did argue for the homosexual inclinations in Woolf's novels, the intention of Chinese critics to select "pure" themes to suit their own cultural milieu is a constant theme of Woolf reception in China, which also poses a barrier to the Chinese readers' understanding of the depth and complexity of Woolf's works. When writing *Mrs. Dalloway*, Woolf famously wrote in her diary that "I dig out beautiful caves behind my characters; [...]. The idea is that the caves shall connect, & each comes to daylight at the present moment" (*A Writer's Diary* 60). This digging process can also be a metaphor for my study of Woolf's reception in China. The historical, academic and popular receptions of Woolf as represented by different textual forms are all but surface phenomena. It is the literary critic's task to dig behind these surfaces to discover the rich social and cultural environments where they are produced, because the reception of an author in a foreign land is bound to be tinged by local colors. It is also in this sense that the aim of cross-cultural literary reading can be achieved.

Works Cited

Cuddy-Keane, Melba, and Kay Li. "Passage to China: East and West and Woolf." *South Carolina Review* 29-1 (1996): 132-49.
Gao, Fen, and Yan Lu. "A Review of Woolf Studies in China in the Last Twenty Years." *Foreign Literature Studies* (2004): 5.
Laurence, Patricia. *Lily Briscoe's Chinese Eyes: Bloomsbury, Modernism and China*. Columbia: University of South Carolina Press, 2003.
—. *Woolf and the East*. London: Cecil Woolf, 1995.
Woolf, Virginia. *The Essays of Woolf, Vol. 2: 1912-1918*. Ed. Andrew McNellie. London: Hogarth, 1987.
—. *The Essays of Woolf, Vol. 3: 1919-1924*. Ed. Andrew McNellie. London: Hogarth, 1987.
—. *A Writer's Diary: Being Extracts from the Diary of Woolf*. Ed. Leonard Woolf. London: Hogarth, 1959.

On Patriotism and Angels: Virginia Woolf and Rosario Castellanos

by Andrea Reyes

The essays by Virginia Woolf (1882-1941) and the Mexican writer Rosario Castellanos (1925-1974), some forty-odd years later, have many bold threads in common. Castellanos learned from the writings of Woolf, and shared her internationalist outlook on the problems of human society. Both writers felt a need to unblinkingly depict the social contradictions around them. They demonstrate a profound concern for the interests of all humankind; a defiance of social pressures to adhere to "patriotism" and class privilege; an ability to portray complexities in the lives of women previously absent from the world of letters; and the willingness to challenge themselves and other women to rise to the highest expectations. The uniqueness and audacity of their writings placed Castellanos along with Woolf in the vanguard of feminism at an international level.

Rosario Castellanos never received the recognition of Virginia Woolf, yet her contribution to Mexican letters was significant. Because little is known of her outside of Mexico, a brief biography might be helpful. She was born to an hacienda-owning family in Chiapas in 1925, though the stagnant and feudalistic norms of society in that southernmost state of Mexico led her to say that she was raised "in the middle of the 16th century" ("Entre pedir y dar" 7A). Her life changed dramatically when President Lázaro Cárdenas (presidential term 1934-1940) extended the agrarian reform brought on by the Mexican Revolution to the isolated and largely indigenous state of Chiapas. Castellanos's family was dispossessed of much of their property, leaving no possibility of a traditional landowner's life for their daughter. They felt obliged to move to Mexico City in 1939 to allow Rosario to study for a professional career. Castellanos later wrote an essay contrasting the life that could have been hers before that agrarian reform, and the life that was hers thanks to Lázaro Cárdenas and "his belief in justice," calling his action the most important, decisive factor in her existence ("A Man of Destiny" 232). The coming decade of the 1940s was one of great urban growth and industrial development in Mexico. Cárdenas had also opened the doors to political refugees from the Spanish Civil War, and the influx of exiled intellectuals from Spain as well as many other countries in Latin America enriched Mexican cultural life and enhanced the rolls of college professors as well as students. Castellanos enrolled in the Universidad Nacional Autónoma de México (UNAM), the most important institute of higher education in the country, and was one of the first generation of females to enter universities in Mexico in significant numbers. It was a heady time.

It happened that in 1948, in the course of less than one month, first Castellanos' mother died of stomach cancer and then her father of a heart attack. She was orphaned at the age of 23, left profoundly alone (a younger brother had died in childhood, and only one uncle lived in the capital city), but with enough money in the bank to finish her college education. Sad as this was on a family level, for a young woman in Mexican society at that time it was also quite liberating, both from specific parental guidance for her career as well as the more general imposition of propriety. Upon receiving her master's degree in philosophy in 1950, she was granted a scholarship to continue her studies in Spain.

Although many in her circle of university friends could not believe that she would go to a Spain then under the dictatorship of Franco, Castellanos explained later that she was still woefully ignorant of politics in those years and just desperately wanted to see the world. The scholarship gave her enough money to travel first class on a ship to Spain; however, the same amount was sufficient to pay for two of the cheapest class of tickets, so she convinced Dolores Castro, her friend from high-school and UNAM and a fellow poet, to accompany her. The two young writers stayed in Spain for a year and a half during the years 1950-1951, learned of Franco's Spain first-hand, occasionally ventured to France during the days of public gatherings of intellectuals around Jean Paul Sartre, Simone de Beauvoir and other existentialists (despite the young Mexicans' limited knowledge of French), then travelled across Europe to many different countries for two months before returning to Mexico. Castellanos had already published poetry and literary criticism before that trip, which she continued despite a bout of tuberculosis with its corresponding convalescence. She returned to Chiapas to work in the National Indigenist Institute for a couple of years, eventually writing two novels and short stories drawing on those experiences, and going back to the capital at the end of 1957. In 1961, she accepted a position as Director of Information and Press Relations for the UNAM, and soon thereafter another post as professor of literature. In addition to her work at the university, she wrote fiction about life in the capital as well as poems, essays and a weekly column in the editorial pages of a prominent newspaper, *Excélsior*. In 1971, she was appointed ambassador of Mexico to Israel, where she died tragically in an accident at the age of 49, at the height of her maturity and happiness in life.

She is best known for the fiction of her "cycle of Chiapas" and for the outspoken feminism of her later poetry. Nevertheless, in the course of the research for my dissertation on her essays, I found so many uncollected texts by Castellanos that it is now clear it was in this genre that she was at her most prolific. These essays display her role as Mexican intellectual and thinker, and provide the sharpest comparisons to the work of Virginia Woolf.

Castellanos had examined the purported reasons why there had been limited contributions in literature and arts by women in her master's thesis, entitled *On Feminine Culture*, in 1950. Unknowingly, her study almost coincided with Simone de Beauvoir's *The Second Sex* in 1949, which she did not read until it was translated into Spanish a few years later. Yet Virginia Woolf definitely was an influence; Castellanos mentioned *Three Guineas* in the bibliography of her thesis. Though there were no direct quotations in the text of the thesis, Castellanos wrote that the study of creative writers such as Woolf, along with Sappho, Saint Teresa of Avila and Gabriela Mistral, was crucial for any analysis of women and culture. In a world in which the philosophers of the canon, whose work she had assiduously studied, had defined women as naturally inferior to men, incapable of reaching the lofty heights of cultured discourse (in which their participation was supposedly contrary to nature), Castellanos wondered, "What was it that pushed them [those creative women] so inexorably to risk themselves [...] to violate the law? These women and not the others are the point of the discussion; they, not the others, the problem" (*Sobre cultura femenina* 32). She concluded with the proposition that we will not know what women are capable of contributing to culture until many more creative feminine thinkers seek deeply within themselves for their own true image, which has only been falsified or unrecognized by tradition. They need to "make it emerge to the conscious surface, free it through expression"

(97; my translation). Castellanos dedicated her life to the realization of such a goal, and Woolf and especially *Three Guineas* were part of that inspiration.

In their respective countries and times, both Woolf and Castellanos confronted major social questions. For Woolf, the issues were world war, militarism, the growth of fascism, the Spanish Civil War, and the continued marginalization of women within society. For Castellanos, the concerns were the almost feudalistic domination of indigenous peoples by whiter Mexicans, the severe inequalities of race, class and gender in the context of a society trying to open up to "democracy" and "modernity." While the national contexts for the writers were disparate—one in the homeland of a dominant world empire, the other in a developing country only a few decades past the fall of a dictatorship subservient to foreign powers—each took a stance against nationalism, in favor of an internationalist view of mankind. The strongest links between the two authors lie in their defiance of social mores regarding both "patriotism" and the submissiveness of women.

Woolf coined the expression "unreal loyalties" for the psychological binds that trap people in the narrow thinking of the status quo. In *Three Guineas* she argued that "you must rid yourself of pride of nationality in the first place; also of religious pride, college pride, school pride, family pride, sex pride and those unreal loyalties that spring from them" (80). She challenged the basis for patriotism on the part of women who had been denied basic rights and education in their own country. For instance, at that time, if an English woman were to marry a foreigner, she would lose her citizenship. This marginalized status of women led Woolf to insist that when an educated man's daughter reflects upon the real meaning behind the call to support one's country in war, "she will bind herself to take no share in patriotic demonstrations; to assent to no form of national self-praise; [...] to absent herself from [...] all such ceremonies as encourage the desire to impose 'our' civilization or 'our' dominion upon other people" (*TG* 109). Thoughtful consideration of the bellicose habits of men in authority, and the outsider status of women in relation to those decisions, will lead her to say, "in fact, as a woman I have no country. As a woman I want no country. As a woman my country is the whole world" (*TG* 109).

It must have been different for Woolf to challenge patriotism within an empire as compared to the situation for Castellanos in Mexico, where a nationalistic fervor for a country long held in dependence was one of the outcomes of the Revolution of 1910-1920. The Mexican author's first two novels and collections of short stories depicted the abject discrimination against indigenous communities in her home state of Chiapas. While she was not attacked for the critical portrayal, the contradictions she raised were ignored by most and she was marginalized within the world of Mexican letters as an "indigenist" writer, though she never limited herself to that theme. When the rebellion of the Zapatistas in Chiapas broke out years later in 1994, many Mexicans recognized the insight of what Castellanos had been writing about decades before. In the first few years after beginning to write her weekly column in 1963, the author challenged the nationalistic responses made by a number of prominent individuals to foreigners for having made critical observations of Mexican life or culture. Castellanos denounced as "false patriotism" the outcry by authorities against a supposed "denigration of Mexico" when an anthropologist from the U.S. dared to reveal embarrassing social problems in her homeland ("Oscar Lewis" 621). When a fistfight erupted in early 1965 between Mexican artists themselves over the "Mexicanness" of their works at an art contest, Castellanos was fed up: "Because what was raised on high at the event, like a flag, was not the aesthetic merit of the works in dispute, nor the theoretical worth of the beliefs sustained by each of the trends, but rather an argument that is expected from the mouths of demagogues, but not from the mouths of artists: *el patrioterismo*" ("Cultura y violencia" 325; my translation). I leave that word in its original Spanish to point out the similarity to the term *patriotismo*. The additional syllable puts a spin on the meaning to make it ostentatious and superficial patriotism, knee-jerk nationalism, chauvinism or jingoism. It is a concept that Castellanos condemns resoundingly in a number of essays.

In the aftermath of the massacre of student protesters in 1968 during the weeks prior to the Olympics in Mexico City, and again before the World Cup in 1970, the government tried to drum up "patriotism" by paying youths to march around chanting "Me-xi-co! Me-xi-co!" Considering the mere fact of being born there insufficient to bestow importance upon a country, Castellanos demanded that someone explain to her exactly what is Mexico. The lies and cover-up of official misdeeds in '68 and beyond while keeping the population in ignorance did not speak well for such a nation: "Because this repeating of syllables of a name without knowing exactly to what one is alluding seems to me, in the short run, absurd. And later, but not much later, dangerous" ("México, México" 497; my translation). She raised her voice in favor of truthfulness and freedom of expression about all social ills in Mexico, in opposition to censorship, political repression and knee-jerk nationalism. She compared the situation in Chiapas to the civil rights struggle in the U.S., and denounced the contradiction between words and deeds of the U.S. government in the war in Vietnam. For Castellanos as for Woolf, the question was that of the entire human race—neither was ever limited to concerns about the role of women alone, even less to the borders of their own countries. In a reflection on what should be expected of a Mexican citizen, Castellanos drew on the guidance of a distinguished poet and intellectual of Mexican letters, Alfonso Reyes (1889-1959):

> This society of which we speak is called our homeland, and to be a good patriot, for don Alfonso, is no more than the preliminary step to becoming a citizen of the world who preserves, along with other nations, a harmonious relation, in which one does not get carried away by either pride or humiliation. ("El héroe" 560; my translation)

She refused any "unreal loyalty" to a demagogic government, and defined her ideal as that of becoming a citizen of the world.

It is worth noting that perhaps the year and a half spent in Europe during 1950-1951, which must have included observation of the aftermath of World War II, a result of the unbridled nationalism of Nazi Germany, may well have influenced her insistence on this point. In 1971, her first year in Israel as ambassador of Mexico, Castellanos went to the airport to receive a delegation of the Israeli Sports Club of Mexico, Mexican youths of Jewish descent, as they arrived for an international competition. She wrote of the hope they inspired in her:

> Healthy, confident, happy. Looking at them all, listening to them speak, I felt a secret pride: that my country knows how to also be the country of those who

have received its hospitality and continued their lineage in our territory. That those who establish themselves among us do not suffer from the "strangeness" of being a stranger among those who feel themselves to be equals. And I fervently desired that we strive over and over again to erase the differences that some, following Hitler, still dare to call race; or religion or language or customs so that the only thing that prevails is the brotherly sentiment of solidarity. ("Nubes de verano" 6A; my translation)

A sense of the inherent worth of all human beings infused the writings of Rosario Castellanos.

The first detailed appreciation of Woolf by Castellanos was published in 1961, entitled "Virginia Woolf or Literature as an Exercise in Freedom." It showed the influence of *The Death of the Moth and Other Essays*, *A Room of One's Own*, Woolf's biography and probably her diaries. She mentioned how Woolf's portrayal of the "Angel in the House"—the ever-present, self-sacrificing, charming and "pure" phantom of traditional femininity in Victorian England—rang a chord with the "*cabecita blanca*" or "little white-haired lady" of Mexican lore. Woolf had insisted that a writer must have a mind of one's own regarding

> human relations, morality, sex. And all these questions, according to the Angel in the House, cannot be dealt with freely and openly by women; they must charm, they must conciliate, they must—to put it bluntly—tell lies if they are to succeed. Thus whenever I felt the shadow of her wing or the radiance of her halo upon my page, I took up the inkpot and flung it at her. She died hard. Her fictitious nature was of great assistance to her. It is far harder to kill a phantom than a reality. [...] Killing the Angel in the House was part of the occupation of a woman writer. ("Professions for Women" 238)

Castellanos observed that traditional advice to be angelic, self-sacrificing and subservient was quite similar in Mexico. In 1968, when a local Catholic leader made the unusual comment that family planning should be a private matter, the author was encouraged that "motherhood is now a free act." Yet she noted that this news would not be well received by the "little white-haired ladies," because "it strips them of that halo of victimization that awakens such filial concerns, so many indissoluble attachments, so many umbilical cords that are never cut" ("Estrictamente privado" 117; my translation). The essays of Castellanos examined multiple cultural beliefs that result in "the annulment of women" ("Woman and Her Image" 242). Her challenge to traditional taboos was lucid and direct:

> We must remove that glorious halo that encircles the white gown and flowery veil. They are symbols of something quite tangible that we should know well since it is located in our own body: virginity. Why do we preserve it and how? Does free choice take part or is it only to follow the current of opinion? We should have the courage to say we are virgins because we really feel like it, because it is convenient to be so for ulterior motives, or because we have not found the way to stop being so. Or that we are not because that is what we decided and we count on appropriate support from our partner. But please, we must

not continue to disguise our responsibility in abstractions absolutely foreign to us such as what we call virtue, chastity or purity, of which we have no authentic experience. ("La participación de la mujer" 889; my translation)

Similar expositions of beliefs regarding motherhood, marriage, birth control and husbands were part of her effort to belie the counsel given by the "little white-haired lady" of Mexican tradition.

Yet the fundamental concept embodied by that phantom in both cultures was the abnegation of self for females. Castellanos' most resounding essay was her speech given to a large audience including the President of Mexico, Luis Echeverría, in February in 1971: "Self-Sacrifice is a Mad Virtue." In it, Castellanos laid out succinctly the ways in which the laws granting women equal rights in Mexico had not changed the many stultifying customs of everyday life. Her list of unacceptable and illegal practices between the two genders concluded:

> It is not just—therefore it is not legal—that one of them is master of his own body and disposes of it at will, while the other reserves her body, not to derive benefits, but to unwillingly have it acted upon.
>
> It is not just, the way men and women are treated differently in Mexico, but we allow ourselves the luxury of violating the law in order to continue circling like mules around a draw well, out of habit, even though the law exists (and we are aware of it) to correct whatever custom retains that is obsolete, defective and unjust. ("Self-Sacrifice" 262-3)

This lecture at the prestigious Museum of Anthropology in Chapultepec Park was described by Elena Urrutia as a "memorable diatribe that Rosario Castellanos pronounced before the chief executive, a diatribe that the sustained ovation of the women congregated there underscored with passion" ("La mujer y la cultura" 289; my translation). Yet Castellanos did not complete her speech with the simple recital of inequities; she expected more of her listeners. The challenge she presented was reminiscent of the commencement address by Woolf to women university students in *A Room of One's Own* in 1929. Even though the influence of British colonialism in the early twentieth century was evident, the message was sharp:

> How can I further encourage you to go about the business of life? Young women, I would say, and please attend, for the peroration is beginning, you are, in my opinion, disgracefully ignorant. You have never made a discovery of any sort of importance. You have never shaken an empire or led an army into battle. The plays of Shakespeare are not by you, and you have never introduced a barbarous race to the blessings of civilisation. What is your excuse? (*AROO* 112)

Similarly, Castellanos concluded her discourse with a challenging assessment for that enthusiastic audience:

> If injustice still affects Mexican women, they have no right to complain. That is the choice they have made. They have scorned the legal recourses they have at hand.

They refuse to accept what the legal statutes guarantee them and what the Constitution gives them: the category of human being. ("Self-Sacrifice" 263)

Both Woolf and Castellanos demanded that new generations of women take charge of their own future, in complete opposition to self-abnegation. They defied the status quo in the public sphere of politics and "patriotism" as well as in the private front in the home. In their corresponding countries and circumstances, these two thinkers forged new identities as women intellectuals of merit that made a difference in the world.

The authors exposed glaring contradictions regarding critical issues that continue today, distinguishing themselves with their internationalist outlook on the travails of humankind. Both laid bare the opportunistic manipulation of nationalism or "patriotism" to prop up corrupt and abusive governments. They called for defiance of the culturally scripted submissiveness that still hamstrings the lives of women. Each was outspoken in her writings and extraordinary in her time. Rosario Castellanos drew great inspiration from Virginia Woolf, and when she recalled the words spoken near the end of Woolf's life about not owing anything to anyone, the Mexican author responded, "We are the debtors, whom she obliges, with her example, to continue her struggle, her task, her work" ("Virginia Woolf o la literatura" 695; my translation). Castellanos shouldered that responsibility in Mexico, and challenged others to do the same.

Works Cited

Ahern, Maureen, ed. and trans. *A Rosario Castellanos Reader: An Anthology of Her Poetry, Short Fiction, Essays, and Drama*. Austin: University of Texas Press, 1988.
Beauvior, Simone de. *The Second Sex*. 1952. New York: Vintage Books, 1989.
Castellanos, Rosario. "Cultura y violencia." *Mujer de palabras: artículos rescatados de Rosario Castellanos*. Ed. Andrea Reyes. Vol. I. México: Conaculta, 2004. 325-28.
—. "Entre pedir y dar: los caminos de la providencia." *Excélsior* (27 Mar 1973): 7A, 8A.
—. "Estrictamente privado: planeación de la familia." Reyes, *Mujer de palabras*. Vol. II. 115-18.
—. "El héroe de nuestro tiempo." *Mujer de palabras: artículos rescatados de Rosario Castellanos*. Ed. Andrea Reyes. Vol. I. México: Conaculta, 2004. 558-61.
—. "A Man of Destiny." Ahern. 232-35.
—. "México, México: contagio, no comprensión." Reyes, *Mujer de palabras*. Vol. II. 494-97.
—. "Nubes de verano: exceso de influencias." *Excélsior* (22 Sep 1971): 6A, 8A, 9A.
—. "Oscar Lewis: sublevación por la injusticia." Reyes, *Mujer de palabras*.Vol. II. 619-22.
—. "La participación de la mujer en la educación formal." *Obras*. Vol. II. México: Fondo de Cultura Económica, 1998. 877-90.
—. "Self-Sacrifice is a Mad Virtue." Ahern. 259-63.
—. *Sobre cultura femenina*. México: Ediciones de América, 1950.
—. "Virginia Woolf o la literatura como ejercicio de la libertad." *Obras*. Vol. II . México: Fondo de Cultura Económica, 1998. 685-95.
—. "Woman and Her Image."Ahern. 236-44.
Reyes, Andrea, ed. *Mujer de palabras: artículos rescatados de Rosario Castellanos*. Vol. II. México: Conaculta, 2006.
—. *Privilegio y uso de la palabra: los ensayos (extra)ordinarios de Rosario Castellanos*. Diss. University of California Los Angeles, 2003. Ann Arbor: UMI, 2003. ATT 3133009.
Urrutia, Elena. "La mujer y la cultura." *Fem.: diez años de periodismo feminista*. México D.F.: Editorial Planeta, 1988. 283-89.
Woolf, Virginia. "Professions for Women." *The Death of the Moth and Other Essays*. Orlando: Harcourt Brace, 1970. 235-42.
—. *A Room of One's Own*. 1929. San Diego: Harcourt, 1989.
—. *Three Guineas*. 1938. Orlando: Harcourt, 1966.

Falling into the Stream: From Virginia Woolf's *The Waves* to Clarice Lispector's *Living Waters*

by Julie L. Smith-Hubbard

Virginia Woolf's *The Waves* appeared in 1931; Clarice Lispector, an avant-garde Brazilian writer, published *Água viva* (*The Stream of Life* or *Living Waters*) in 1973. Lispector extends Woolf's writing legacy until her death in 1977; Cixous discovers Lispector in 1978 and claims Lispector's writing best exemplifies "*écriture féminine*" (*women's writing*), which appears in Cixous's *La jeune née* (*The Newly Born Woman*) in 1975. These qualities in Lispector's writing that perform *écriture féminine*, which will be identified in *Água viva* and discussed throughout this study, are visible forty-four years earlier in Woolf's *The Waves*. Correspondences between Woolf and Lispector illustrate how both transform women's writing by challenging phallologocentrism. Woolf's alternative aesthetics drive Lispector's experimental writing and culminate in Cixous's anti-foundational thinking about writing. Distancing themselves from male discourse, challenging and dismantling systematic modes of thinking that close off and totalize, and making writing their subject, they transfigure themselves and others by "the act of writing."

Woolf has this to say about philosophy in *Moments of Being*: "And I go on to suppose that the shock receiving capacity is what makes me a writer [...]. It is or will become a revelation of some order; it is a token of some real thing behind appearances; and I make it real by putting it into words [...]. From this I reach what I might call a philosophy" (72). To understand Woolf's opposition to inherited modes of male discourse in *The Waves*, it is important to read her characters as either representatives of or alternatives to the philosophical tradition. Percival, for instance, is both patriarchy and the *Bildungsroman* literary tradition. Classical, Medieval, and Romantic aesthetics, along with British imperialism, accompany Percival to his death in India. What remains of tradition is blurred in sublime confusion.

Woolf's "shock receiving capacity" in *Moments of Being* dovetails with William Wordsworth's "spots of time," which first appeared in the 1799 Two Book version of *The Prelude*. According to Quentin Bell's *Virginia Woolf: A Biography*, Volume II, Chapter 6, "1929-1931," in a pain free moment between illnesses, Woolf writes, "then I read one book of the Prelude" (148). Does she mean Book One of the original version? If the answer is yes, then it is important to note that it is in Book One of the original Two Book version of *The Prelude* where Wordsworth both defines "spots of time" and provides examples of them. Woolf describes her thinking at the time as moving back and forth between forms and nothing. She notes her illnesses are partially mystical. Her mind, she claims, shuts down with the pain, but after the immobility something springs. This description fits perfectly with the sublime shocks of Wordsworthian "spots of time" that momentarily preclude then transform thought when it is returned in memory. Woolf says that when her mind refuses to register impressions "It becomes chrysalis" (149). It is at this time that she rechristens the *Moths* as *The Waves*.

Reading *The Prelude* while writing *The Waves*, Woolf has understood and incorporated

Wordsworthian "spots of time," formative childhood moments that return later in life as memory traces, into her text. She locates these revelatory "shocks" in six children's experiences. In this way, her project differs considerably from Wordsworth's, whose spots are the intense, solitary experiences of Wordsworth the child. This difference reveals not only her break with the male philosophical discourse but also her link to Clarice Lispector.

Where Wordsworth went wrong in his autobiographical undertaking, "The Growth of the Poet's Mind," which impeded his ever finishing his intended magnum opus *The Recluse*, is where Woolf, Lispector, and Cixous diverge from his poetic project and his final move from the external world to the world of the mind. In "the girl who bore the pitcher" "spot of time," Wordsworth writes, "And reascending the bare slope I saw / A naked pool that lay beneath the hills, / The beacon on the summit, and more near / A girl who bore a pitcher on her head / And seemed with difficult steps to force her way / Against the blowing wind / An ordinary sight, but I should need / Colours and words that are unknown to man / To paint the visionary dreariness..." (314-22). The girl stands between the gibbet mast, an historical marker testifying to crime and its punishment, and the beacon on the hill, which prefigures Wordsworth's ascent of Mount Snowdon. Moving symbolically from human to divine law, Wordsworth circumvents the reality of the girl with the water while navigating his way between symbolic signposts of the law. She is a gap in Wordsworth's experience, an aporia in his poem, an emanation of the "visionary dreariness." In Woolf's *The Waves* this girl is present in two figures: Women passing with red pitchers to the Nile, and Rhoda with her basin of flower petals.

Wordsworth continued to be baffled by his originary "spots of time," which he repositioned in every revision of *The Prelude* over the course of fifty years. He returned to them because they enabled him to progress on his philosophical journey as poet-prophet, yet his misreadings of these spots led him to the top of Snowdon and the "egotistical sublime." It is this patriarchal trajectory, the misreadings of a subject as the blind self, that *écriture féminine* counters.

Lispector's *Água viva* performs Wordsworth's "spots of time" but undermines his traditional philosophy with her focus on sensorial responses in the writer's writing experiences. She defines herself in relation to others and objects, and becomes an "other" among others. Not appropriating the other allows for freedom. Meaning does not always exist, and love, death, and life are a diaspora of "living elements." Dialogical voices free the text from a single "voice"; the speaker is and is not Lispector and exists in both literal and literary worlds. Text re-presents reality in "now instants." Epiphanies, moments always already past tense as Lispector tries to write them, are a coalescence of both Wordsworth's "spots of time" and Woolf's "Moments of Being."

Woolf's sensorial responses and subjective revisionism unfold as six children respond to a new day; elemental fibers of the opening interlude are attached to the children's sensory experiences when Bernard points out "a spider's web on the corner of the balcony [...] [with its] beads of water [and] drops of white light" (*TW* 9). Balcony is in turn connected to girls with fans sitting on verandas in the penultimate interlude. Fan, as bones of the hand, is a synechdoche for a writer's hand, and these girls are threaded to Woolf's writing legacy. Woolf's spider's web is attached to reality at all four corners (*AROO* 41).

Lispector links senses to verbs; verbal nouns are vehicles for exploring writing as sensory response. There are linguistic chains and a web-like complexity of signs. Synaesthesia is a mode of webbing. According to Earl Fitz, "Lispector's work is always fluid and open and poetically rendered, antilogocentric and a struggle with language which denies human existence [...]. [She] leads us to ask not merely what we know (or think we know) but about how we know" (Fitz 39).

Woolf examines how language reflects and constitutes the child's reality, and how literary inheritances impinge on childhood experiences. Children chained to traditional fairy tales are unchained in Woolf's retellings. As a child, Louis suffers his Australian accent and seeks refuge from shame in nature; Jinny kisses Louis as he hides in the foliage: "She found me [...]. She has kissed me. All is shattered," is Louis's response. Woolf reverses gender roles and subtracts the moral agenda in her version of "Sleeping Beauty," which is also Grimm's "Rose-Bud." Jinny's hand is like snake skin, and Louis's belt is fastened by a brass snake, but their fall predates both Lilith and Eve when it results in Susan's suffering, fuses with the primordial image of the Great Mother archetype and Nature weeping, and gives rise to Bernard's bewitching Elvedon tales. Bernard has "seen signposts at the cross-roads with one arm pointing 'To Elvedon'" (*TW* 17). In the initial interlude, which begins with the sun not yet risen, it is "as if" the arm of a woman had raised a lamp. Elvedon is beyond the wall in the garden where the lady writing sits between two long windows, privy to both reality and fiction. In Woolf's *A Room of One's Own*, Shakespeare's fictional sister Judith "lies buried at some cross-roads" (*AROO* 48). The intersection of all these references is in the writer and the "act of writing."

Leaving Neville in the tool-house to comfort Susan with his Elvedon storytelling, Bernard interrupts Neville's boat building and carries off Neville's knife, taking phallocentrism, violence, and T. S. Eliot's tradition with him. A mystical Rhoda tries to control her fleet of make-believe ships, white flower petals floating in a basin of water, but she can neither wake from dreaming, nor control the world's chaos. She links water poured over dead mackerel in a bowl to bubbles that float to the surface in a chain when heated. Bernard calls these bubbles "words," and this chain links the children to the "school of death." Ethical dimensions associated with "schools of love" are re-written as love, specifically love for Percival, is transformed into a metaphor for death.

Lispector's childhood stories surface without temporal sequences or boundaries. Her knife, she intimates, is going dull. Writing is behind thinking, behind syntax, and the word "is." The Portuguese *é*, a single phoneme for "it is," is all there is. Each sensory response redirects her writing. She listens and the hand writes as it enters realms of painting and music, and primordial and contemporary existence. She explores her world by listening, singing, tasting, smelling, touching, and writing "now instants" to avoid systems of entrapment. She is living, dying, loving, losing until gaps between them close in the writing; characters split, multiply, die or give birth. The writer's objective is to write without thought and writing the body with the bodily senses is the goal.

Woolf transitions from the many to the one voice of Bernard who learns life is in the flow of words; there is only Bernard the aging body feeling the fragility of life, writing his story in the stream, between silences broken by words bubbling to the surface. He says they are "'scarcely to be distinguished from the river [...] bodies [...] all threaded to the world and to one another, and to the woman writing'" (*TW* 235). He wonders if his own story ends as "a trickle of water to some gutter where, burbling, it dies away" (267), but he learns characters cannot finish their stories, and no matter how high they leap—they fall back into the stream, where there are no beginnings, endings, or true order. Bernard's trickle of water originates in a "spot of time," Neville's childhood story of the man found in the gutter with his throat cut. It is also Wordsworth's "drowned man" spot, the literal drowning of his childhood teacher. Although Wordsworth's own stream of consciousness parallels the Derwent stream throughout his *Prelude*, his journey's wanderings remain distinct from the stream's windings, and his project is preclusive. Woolf and Lispector, whose projects serve as interludes, content themselves with finding the source not behind or beyond but in the here and now of the girl with the pitcher standing as 'other' in the landscape.

Lispector links "words" to bubbles, but water, the source, is the bodies'. Learning for Woolf is a transition from old age to letting go, to summing up, to being in the moment, existence being simply the denial of death in the face of death. Learning for Lispector is learning the language and ethics of "othering," which is her denial of death by denying the existence of the autonomous subject. "*Écriture féminine* is the endeavor to write the other in ways which refuse to appropriate or annihilate the other's difference in order to create and glorify the self in a masculine position of mastery" (Sellers 45). Called upon to be something "other" amidst the failed writing and useless philosophy, Woolf's Bernard is coming to *écriture féminine*.

Just as Lispector anticipates Derridean deconstruction, Woolf's Bernard, in his soliloquy, deconstructs his image in the looking glass: "this is not one life [Bernard says]; nor do I always know if I am man or woman, Bernard, Neville, Louis, Susan, Jinny or Rhoda—so strange is the contact of one with another" (*TW* 281). Bernard is "all selves," and has been without a self, a dead man, and what is it to describe the world without a self? He begins to forget, asks himself, "Who am I?" and becomes the "you are." He is also Bernard in the third person, the Bernard who made phrases and kept a notebook.

Lispector, speaking of mirrors, says: "Take away frame or contours and it spreads, as water pours [...]. No, I haven't described a mirror—I've been one" (65). Her state is "a garden with running water." She cannot define what she calls being "At the Edge of Beatitude," but she has lived it. "Real freedom, as an act of perception, has no form [...]. True thought seems authorless" (74). There are no words for freedom, and freedom has to sever itself from the slavery of the word. Words imprison as well as free. As she writes she tries to free words from the law. At times there are no words, no meaning, no follow through on a thought: "It's as if life said the following: and there simply wasn't any following. Only the colon, waiting" (70). There are realities that have no correspondences in thoughts, just sensations behind thoughts. To live is more an indirect remembering. Logical discourse is part of the tragedy, so she must disrupt thinking and blind herself to see. The subject must lose its subject-ness; "There is danger of madness in the subject getting lost in things [she says], but those who are not lost cannot know freedom and do not love it" (58). Wordsworth loses his guides but never his subject-ness, nor himself in things. The flowers at his feet only bring thoughts too deep for tears (Hutchinson 462).

The stream is not learned; it is entered into by Bernard, who, like Lispector, leaves his bodies along the way, goes to meet himself, exceeds himself by abdicating himself, and becomes the "you are." After Percival's fatal accident and Rhoda's suicide, five characters remain in Bernard's story—the single rose with five petals. In their text *Veils*, Cixous and Derrida engage in a dialogue on myopia; their discussion leads to the revelation that to see is to touch. Its significance here is in Woolf's and Lispector's contributions to seeing the rose—as touching the rose. As Lispector says in *Água viva*, "hands also see" (63).

The initial interlude of *The Waves* begins with lack and in silence. Rose is present simply as potential—in the past tense verb form. Sea and sky are indistinguishable, except "the sea was slightly creased as if a cloth had wrinkles in it" (*TW* 7). The "word" of the author is absent. As the sky whitens, grey with black strokes and waves like pen marks, still beneath the surface, are following and pursuing each other in perpetual motion. Waves are writing; bars—heaped, broke, swept. The wave is "as if" the sleeper, unconscious. It is "as if the arm of a woman couched beneath the horizon had raised a lamp and flat bars of white, green and yellow, spread across the sky like blades of a fan" (7). In the act of writing, fan as hand touches. The arm is not above but within and lifting up. Air becomes fibrous—earth bursts into red and yellow fibers that fuse in one haze—the elemental scene is composed of fibrous matter and fibrin of which the original cobweb on the balcony is formed—and these are what Woolf in *Moments of Being* calls "threads of the hidden pattern in the work of art" (72). Couched "beneath the horizon," the woman draws up the physical weight of the picture. Rose, as noun, is disseminated in verb forms until light strikes the trees in the garden, rests on the tip of a fan, and leaves "a blue fingerprint of shadow under the leaf by the bedroom window" (*TW* 8). Verb is transposed to noun when on the penultimate page of the text that "leaf" becomes "the pale rose that hangs by the bedroom window" (296). Bernard the child discovers the sign points to Elvedon; the aging Bernard must enter Elvedon, the real garden where the woman sits writing *The Waves*.

Woolf's *The Waves*, as genesis according to a woman, unfolds in a single day. Lispector's *Água viva*, as letter to an ex-lover, begins with the end of love—which is also a break in the discourse, which continues on. Following the hand writing in *Água viva*, becoming a scribe of the unconscious, breaking all textual frames, touching the source and suddenly "bewitched," Lispector is now absent, and text, as other, continues on. Bernard's Elvedon bewitches and is beyond the wall where the lady sits writing. "Water witches" are implements used for finding water, or those closest to living sources of water. Writers writing *écriture féminine* do not claim to know; they simply allow us to reach the source and content ourselves with not knowing.

Between Woolf's interludes, the woman sits writing in the garden; initially, Bernard the child says that in Elvedon we touch the earth, the ground, the ladies' garden where they walk at noon and clip roses; later, Woolf's garden, like the tree that had once held red light, is a broken vessel. Perhaps as far back as Sumerian literature the word for "garden" has stood for the body of a woman, and as Anne Carson documents in her text *Men in the Off Hours*, Hericlitus, Plato and Aristotle considered a woman's body a dangerous unbounded fluidity that needed to be contained. In the shadows of the final interlude and the darkness rolling over all, there is a "mountain where the snow lodges for ever on the hard rock even when the valleys are full of running streams and yellow vine leaves, and girls sitting on verandahs look up at the snow, shading their faces with fans" (237). While writing *The Waves*, Woolf proposed writing a sequel to *A Room of One's Own*, a feminist pamphlet entitled *Professions for Women* (Bell 2:156). Although she dropped the project at that time, these girls sitting on verandas are Woolf's legacy—Shakespeare's sister(s) for the future, sitting in gardens, writing themselves in tributaries of their own writing, no longer powerless, secluded in shadows, or looking up at Wordsworth's Snowdon. The garden as "broken vessel" is now pure flow, and this garden is Clarice Lispector's inheritance.

Surveying the meaning of his life in his soliloquy, Bernard remembers—"The lady sat writing. Transfixed, stopped dead, I thought, 'I cannot interfere with a single stroke of those brooms. They sweep and they sweep. Nor with the fixity of that woman writing.' It is strange that one cannot stop gardeners sweeping nor dislodge a woman. There they have remained all my life [...]. [And then Bernard has] one of those sudden transparences through which one sees everything" (*TW* 240-41). The stream is alive and deep, flows from January to December, and they float. There are many Bernards in the "full tide of life"; life is "floating in the stream." There is the mystery of things. Day rises and there is a girl in a desert "lifting the watery fire-hearted jewels to her brow" (291). The shadow holds something and nothing and he does not know. He is dashing "like a moth from candle to candle" (293). Then the sky kindling eternal renewal, "whether of lamplight or dawn," reveals the rose (296-97).

Woolf tells us how to read the rose. Subject and verb have become entwined, entangled in threads and vines, the being and human being are one as the rose is denuded of its symbolic trappings and allowed to exist, even after the sun which had risen inch by inch throughout the textual interludes had sunk. In Lispector's story of the rose she understands relationships, hers to the rose, what exists between them, an understanding of love understood without words, behind them and veiled. It is what Lispector calls the "slanted reality" of the "obliqueness" of the rose.

Rhoda's name signifies "rose." As "nymph of the fountain always wet," she cannot complete her metamorphosis; as a child her eyes "are like those pale flowers to which moths come in the evening" (16). Rose is transfigured with the verb "rose." At the end of *The Waves*, the looking glass, that double reflection, is no longer behind the scene by the window; there is only "a redness that gathers on the roses, even on the pale rose that hangs by the bedroom window" (296). The insubstantial nymph's metamorphosis is into the substantial flesh and blood woman, rewriting creation in the garden, making it real by putting it into words, turning "the light of this observation on to real life" (*AROO* 35), which leaves only a touch of color yet to be read. It was already in Woolf's original interlude, in the "as if the arm of the woman raised the lamp," when the earth burst into flames.

To see the rose is to touch the rose is to touch the source; to touch the source is to live the other and to live the other is "being," being both noun and verb. To reach the source, Woolf and Lispector dismantle totalizing modes of thinking in order to transfigure themselves and others in "the act of writing." Living is a noun; the best is between the lines. The secret is simply—secret. Lispector's cut rose *é*. Woolf's five-petaled rose "is." Reality, Cixous comments in her introduction to *Água viva*, has no synonyms. "One has to read the very phenomena of writing, reading oneself [...]. Everything is a giving birth to, a getting back to the origins, and the reader must help in the being born" (Lispector xxiii). To find the source is to drink from the fountain, and the nymph of the fountain is Rhoda, rising and falling into Woolf's *The Waves*, which are Lispector's *Living Waters*—without beginnings or endings or true order, where roses have threadlike roots and women have roots in real and paper gardens, and gardeners sweep, and women sit silently writing with "the hand in its infinite sensibility" (*TW* 291).

Works Cited

Bell, Quentin. *Virginia Woolf: A Biography*. 2 vols. London: Hogarth Press, 1972.
Carson, Anne. *Men in the Off Hours*. New York: Random House, 2000.
—. *Glass, Irony and God*. New York: New Directions, 1995.
Cixous, Hélène. *"Coming to Writing" and Other Essays*. Cambridge: Harvard University Press, 1991.
—. *Reading with Clarice Lispector*. Minneapolis: University of Minnesota Press, 1990.
—. *The Newly Born Woman*. Minneapolis: University of Minnesota Press, 1986.
—. *Three Steps on the Ladder of Writing*. New York: Columbia University Press, 1993.
—. *Writing Difference: Reading from the Seminar of Hélène Cixous*. Stratford, U.K.: Open University Press, 1988.
Conley, Verna Andermatt. *Hélène Cixous*. Herfordshire, U.K.: Havester Wheatsheaf, 1992.
Fitz, Earl. *Clarice Lispector*. Boston: Twayne, 1985.
Grimm, Jacob and Wilhelm. *Grimms' Fairy Tales*. London: Penguin, 1994.
Hutchinson, Thomas. *Wordsworth Poetical Works*. Oxford: Oxford University Press, 1969.
Lispector, Clarice. *The Stream of Life*. Minneapolis: University of Minnesota Press, 1989.
Peixoto, Marta. *Passionate Fictions: Gender, Narrative, and Violence in Clarice Lispector*. Minneapolis: University of Minnesota Press, 1994.
Sellers, Susan. *Hélène Cixous: Authorship, Autobiography and Love.*: Cambridge, U.K.: Polity Press, 1996.
Woolf, Virginia. *A Room of One's Own*. San Diego: Harcourt, 1981.
---. *Moments of Being*. New York: Harcourt Brace, 1976.
---. *The Waves*. New York: Harcourt Brace, 1978.
Wordsworth, William. *The Prelude 1799, 1805, 1850 William Wordsworth*. Ed. Jonathan Wordsworth, M. H. Abrams, and Stephen Gill. New York: Norton, 1979.

Virginia Woolf and María Luisa Bombal

by Mónica G. Ayuso

My research on the presence of Virginia Woolf in Spanish America has yielded over the years one certainty: that the women writers who examined her work from various Latin American countries and an ocean apart from England were basically interested in two different aspects of Woolf's work ("Thinking Back"; "Remote Inscriptions"; "The Unlike[ly] Other"). One group found inspiration in her work as a feminist spokesperson with concrete ideas on how to end female oppression, how to enable women's empowerment through education, and how to make women citizens of nations in which they were disenfranchised. Writers like Rosario Ferré (not the subject of this panel but of my research elsewhere), Rosario Castellanos, and Gloria Anzaldúa fall into this group; they quote almost exclusively from her manifestoes and extend Woolf's polemic beyond the spatial boundaries of England. The second group found her modernist experiments and innovative themes particularly inspiring because they opened perspectives in the minds of women characters. As a result, these writers concentrate on narrative strategy. This panel entitled "Virginia Woolf beyond the Anglophone Tradition" was planned as a venue for discussion of these two general directions of Woolf's influence in Latin America. María Luisa Bombal belongs to the group of writers who share Woolf's aesthetic rather than her political concerns.

In this essay, I begin by reconstructing the biographical facts that justify pairing these two writers from such different backgrounds. I concentrate exclusively on the decade of 1930. I purposefully exclude Bombal's writings of later years; the specific debate over the translation and so-called amplification of "The Final Mist" that Farrar, Strauss and Company published in the U.S. in 1947 with the title *The House of Mist*; as well as the more general scholarly debate over the assessment of Bombal's skills as a writer that some critics say were lost in English translation (Nance). Then, I position María Luisa Bombal outside the tradition of South American women writers to which critics have consistently questioned she belonged. In 1982 Jorge Luis Borges, for one, said that Bombal "does not correspond to any determined 'school'" (Preface to *New Islands and Other Stories*), a comment that he meant as a compliment, and was devoid of any regionalism. Finally, I examine one work she wrote and published in Argentina in light of Virginia Woolf's explorations of feminine thought and experience as well as the thematic similarities they shared. This examination hopes to contribute to a larger understanding of Bombal's accomplishments as a fiction writer.

Bombal resided in Argentina from 1933 until 1940. Critic Isabel Velazco, who knew her, maintains that the three acclaimed works she published during those years—*La Última Niebla* ("The Final Mist") in 1934, *La Amortajada* (*The Shrouded Woman*) in 1938, and "The Tree" in 1939—are deeply inspired by the landscape—the haciendas, the wind-swept countryside—and the culture of Argentina (18). During those years, she developed also a crucial working relationship with a group of prominent Argentine intellectuals among whom Virginia Woolf was a household name. Bombal's work was almost exclusively published in *Sur*, and her liaison with the writers of the literary journal made a lasting impression on Bombal's career and future literary reputation. First and foremost was Victoria Ocampo, founder and editor of the journal. She had met Virginia Woolf in England, was pivotal in the promotion of Woolf's work in Argentina, and kept lifelong contact with her until Woolf's death in 1941. Ocampo published "Carta a Virginia Woolf"/ "Letter to Virginia Woolf" in *Revista de Occidente* in 1934. That letter was later reprinted as the preface to Ocampo's multivolume *Testimonios*. Second was Jorge Luis Borges. He was appointed by Ocampo to translate into Spanish *A Room of One's Own* in 1935-36 and *Orlando* in 1937 for *Sur*, the same year Bombal published "The Final Mist." Bombal frequented the literary meetings of the prestigious writers connected to the journal, was familiar with its mission to make European writers known in Argentina and, though not intimate, was an acquaintance of Ocampo and a very good friend of Borges. With Borges she frequented the movie theatres—she wrote screenplays for Argentina Sonofilm—and took long walks. In short, she belonged to the inner circle of writers aggressively involved in the circulation and reception of Woolf's work in Argentina and, eventually, the rest of Latin America.

Also, Bombal seems to have shared with Ocampo and Borges some idiosyncratic life experiences that made her a good fit with the writers of *Sur*. Bombal was in contact with different languages and cultures since she was quite young. Like Ocampo and Borges, she was well-traveled (Dölz-Blackburn 51). In her "Testimonio Autobiográfico," for example, she speaks of the stories her mother told her in German and of the years she spent in France after her father died, where she attended La Sorbonne and obtained a certificate in French literature. All three writers—Ocampo, Borges, and Bombal—were trilingual, had lived abroad, and had reading horizons that extended well beyond the boundaries of Latin America. Her work, like Borges's, would later be translated into many languages. It is no wonder that some critics find her literary place within the Spanish-speaking tradition simply "inexplicable," as Marjorie Agosín has indicated (9).

The late '70s—partly because Bombal settled in the U.S. and partly because of overwhelming interest in women's writing—produced renewed critical interest in María Luisa Bombal. Prominent among those critics who wrote book-length studies on her was Lucía Guerra-Cunningham, the Chilean scholar responsible for canonizing her in the U.S. academy. Guerra-Cunningham interviewed Bombal multiple times. During an interview held in 1977, Bombal admitted to having read and liked Virginia Woolf. Then in 1979, Bombal spoke again of the identification she felt with the British writer. She plainly denied, however, admiring Woolf's feminism. Rather, Bombal explained, she liked Woolf because "she was not preachy," because "she put the concepts she believed in into practice in her novels" ("Testimonio Autobiográfico" 337). The data available from this interview and the material generated in the late '70s (a decade that coincided also with renewed interest in Woolf's literary and feminist theories in the U.S.) do not answer all questions about the links between these two writers. It is still impossible to trace with any degree of certainty when or even what Bombal read or whether she read Woolf in Spanish or in the original English. Bombal left no diaries—nothing remotely similar to Ocampo's *Testimonios*—only a few interviews and letters. Besides, she tended to be evasive when the issue of influence was broached (Gálvez Lira 447).

Still, both Virginia Woolf and Maria Luisa Bombal explore areas of feminine thought and experience with great sensitivity. Also, thematic similarities between the two are the *leitmotivs* of death and water, a poetic lyrical voice, and a subjective conception of time. Like Woolf, Bombal does not link events in a causal, temporal, and sequential manner. Her imagination consistently sidesteps plots of adventure to center on psychological states. Her fiction is honed in thought processes, in a sensitive understanding of female subjectivity.

All these characteristics are present in Bombal's first story published under the auspices of *Sur.* "The Final Mist" (which Bombal called "a modern fairy tale") is not plot-driven. Rather, it seems to be a story conceived with concern for a symmetry of interior adventure as major structural device. The nameless narrator of the story is the second wife of the aggrieved Daniel. He had lost his first wife only nine months previous to the arrival of the new couple in the hacienda in which they settle in the opening scene. An ambiguous chronology bolsters the unraveling of the narrator's two parallel lives. One lingers on the increasingly sterile relationship of the narrator with Daniel; the other on the exciting relationship of the narrator with a lover, ambiguously positioned between reality and fantasy. As one relationship becomes predictable and deadening, the other becomes exciting and life-affirming. Both are conveyed with equal immediacy because both are seamlessly recounted in the present tense. Other symmetries explored are the events surrounding the subplot of a sister-in-law's attempted suicide after her own infidelity is discovered and the suicide that the narrator seriously contemplates, which Daniel aborts. In addition, Daniel's mourning of the loss of his first wife in the opening scene is reflected in the narrator's mourning of the lover in the final scene. Likewise, Virginia Woolf in "The Legacy" (1940) explores through emotional states the love triangle of the recently deceased Angela Clandon, husband Gilbert Clandon, and the mysterious "B.M." Though Angela is not herself the narrator of the story, her diary—that Gilbert finds six weeks after her death and reads for the first time—reveals Angela's double life.

Both stories center on two women emotionally defeated. None can gain self-fulfillment in the confines of a marriage to a successful but self-absorbed man—Daniel has a hacienda and Gilbert is "a successful politician" (282). Both stories reveal also the traps of marriage within a class-based society, in which the relationship to the lover offers compensation for what the marriage denies. In Bombal, the escape is motivated by Daniel's rejection. In Woolf's, Angela seeks relief from a life "so idle, so useless" (284), in which she hopes "to help others" (285). "B.M." is a socialist, ideologically opposed to the social class the Clandons represent. For both female characters, the end of the affair is an event so devastating that both seek an outlet in suicide "under the wheels of a vehicle" (Bombal 46). Angela successfully carries on with hers, as the obsessive order of her affairs suggests. Once Gilbert arrives at the painful conclusion that his wife did not die a natural death as he had assumed previous to the finding of the diary, he visualizes her suicide as clearly as Clarissa Dalloway visualizes Septimus's without witnessing it: "She was standing on the curb in Piccadilly. Her eyes stared; her fists were clenched. Here came the car [...]"(287). Though Bombal's narrator does not carry on with hers, she visualizes herself dead: "And like a blow comes the vision of my naked body lying on a slab in the morgue: wizened flesh sticking bone-tight to a rigid skeleton, between the hips a dried and sunken womb [...]" (46). And she proceeds through life, abiding by social convention, "to die, one day, correctly," as she bitterly puts it (47). Thus ends "The Final Mist." But Bombal will go on to imagine at least two more stories written in Argentina in which similarly anguished states of mind recur in characters that are exclusively female. Bombal was not interested in polemic but in rehearsing the principles of an enlightened and women-centered aesthetic, in all likelihood nuanced by Woolf's original work.

By way of conclusion, the writers covered in this panel all seem to complete the task that Woolf began with *The Voyage Out,* when she borrowed the setting for the community of Santa Marina from South America. But America was a continent that Woolf never saw in spite of at least one offer by the International P.E.N. Club inviting her to address the 1936 meeting in Buenos Aires (Meyer 123). America was a continent that, judging by scattered references in Woolf's letters, meant nothing but distance and remoteness. "A land of great butterflies and vast fields," of "wild cattle and pampas grass," as she described it in her letters (*L5* 365), provided her with the theme of tourism in the first novel. There she placed a number of English men and women in a transient hotel rather than a home. So unfamiliar and transient was the place that when E.M. Forster reviewed the novel, Forster, a world traveler, said that Woolf wrote "a strange, inspired book whose scene is a South America not found on any map and reached by a boat that would float on any sea" (104). A generation of professional writers as diverse as Anzaldúa, Castellanos, Lispector, and Bombal, who wrote later in the twentieth-century, helped her inhabit a much broader, much more stable and better defined place in the context of the analysis of women's oppression and creativity in South America. Together, these four essays attempt a definition of that place from the moment her work started circulating in Spanish America in 1931 with the founding of *Sur* and in Brazil in 1946, when the first Portuguese Brazilian translations were published (Caws and Luckhurst xii-xiii).

Works Cited

Agosín, Marjorie. "Entre el agua y la niebla: María Luisa Bombal." Agosín, Gascón-Vera, and Renjilian-Burgy. 9-13.
Agosín, Marjorie, Elena Gascón-Vera, and Joy Renjilian-Burgy, eds. *Maria Luisa Bombal. Apreciaciones Críticas.* Tempe: Bilingual Press/Editorial Bilingue, 1987.
Ayuso, Mónica. "Thinking Back through our Mothers: Virginia Woolf in the Spanish-American Female Imagination." *Selected Papers from the Eighth Annual Conference on Virginia Woolf.* Ed. Jeanette Vicker and Laura Davis. New York: Pace University Press, 1999. 97-102.
—. "Remote Inscriptions: *To the Lighthouse* and *The Waves* in Julieta Campos's Caribbean." *Selected Papers from the Ninth Annual Conference on Virginia Woolf.* Ed. Ann Ardis and Bonnie Kime Scott. New York: Pace University Press, 2000. 86-92.
—. "The Unlike[ly] Other: Borges and Woolf." *Woolf Studies Annual* 10 (2004): 241-251.
Bombal, Maria Luisa. "The Final Mist." Trans. Richard and Lucía Cunningham. *New Islands and Other Stories.* New York: Farrar, Straus, Giroux, 1982. 3-47.
—. "Testimonio Autobiográfico." *Obras Completas.* Santiago de Chile: Editorial Andrés Bello, 1977.
Borges, Jorge Luis. Preface. *New Islands and Other Stories.* By María Luisa Bombal. Trans. Richard and Lucía Cunningham. New York: Farrar, Straus, Giroux, 1982.
Caws, Mary Anne, and Nicola Luckhurst, eds. *The Reception of Virginia Woolf in Europe.* London: Continuum, 2002.
Dölz-Blackburn, Inés. "Elementos narrativos tradicionales en la obra de María Luisa Bombal y su relación con motivos folklóricos universales." Agosín, Gascón-Vera, and Renjilian-Burgy. 51-71.
Forster, E.M. *Abinger Harvest.* London: Edward Arnold and Co., 1940.
Gálvez Lira, Gloria. "Entrevista con María Luisa Bombal." *Obras Completas.* Santiago de Chile: Editorial

Andrés Bello, 1977. 457-459.
Guerra-Cunningham, Lucía. *La narrativa de María Luisa Bombal: una visión de la existencia femenina.* Madrid: Colección Nova-Scholar, 1980.
Lagos-Pope, María Inés. "Silencio y rebeldía: hacia una valoración de María Luisa Bombal dentro de la tradición de escritura femenina." Agosín, Gascón-Vera, and Renjilian-Burgy. 119-135.
Meyer, Doris. *Against the Wind and the Tide.* New York: George Braziller, 1979.
Nance, Kimberly. "Contained in Criticism, Lost in Translation: Representation of Sexuality and the Fantastic in Bombal's *La Ultima Niebla* and *The House of Mist.*" *Hispanófila* 130 (2000): 41-51.
Velasco, Isabel. "Algo sobre María Luisa Bombal." Agosín, Gascón-Vera, and Renjilian-Burgy. 17-21.
Woolf, Virginia. "The Legacy." *The Complete Shorter Fiction of Virginia Woolf.* Ed. Susan Dick. New York: Harcourt Brace Jovanovich, 1989. 281-287.

A WOOLFIAN REVERSAL:
THE DALLOWAY MYSTIQUE IN MONICA ALI'S *BRICK LANE*

by Marilyn Schwinn Smith

Monica Ali's 2003 novel *Brick Lane* charts the transformation of its principal character, Nazreen, from birth in rural Bangladesh through her slow awakening to the possibility of individual agency, after an arranged marriage and consequent transplantation to 20th-century London. Nazreen's husband, Chanu, old enough to be her father, had emigrated years before. Chanu's and Nazreen's expectations for life in the metropole are predictably dissimilar and their lives' trajectories take reverse courses. Nazreen expects to be an obedient, Muslim wife, and no more. Inculcated by a British, colonial education which he believes has rendered him more English than the English, Chanu expects to be rewarded with advancement.

Nazreen slowly makes her way beyond the walls of their flat in immigrant Brickhall into the larger world, eventually assuming full responsibility for supporting and raising her daughters within British culture. Chanu steadily descends from an initial high optimism that his knowledge of British literature and culture will earn him a promotion. The employer, whom Chanu expects to recognize his virtues, never appears in the novel. Rather, his name is invoked ever less frequently, with ever more bitterness as Chanu's frustrations multiply, till it falls completely from the text. Chanu quits his job at the district council never receiving so much as an interview, becomes a taxi driver, falls heavily into debt and comes at last to rely on his wife's income and growing ability to navigate the world—a complete reversal of roles and expectations.[1]

Prompted by the invisible employer's name, Mr. Dalloway, I set aside the numerous correspondences between *Brick Lane* and Virginia Woolf's *Mrs. Dalloway* to ask simply: does Woolf's *Mrs. Dalloway* indeed reverberate in *Brick Lane*'s London? Ali's postcolonial novel of south-Asian immigrant experience in London is an occasion to re-read the Dalloways' genesis in *The Voyage Out* and their elaboration once they assume center stage.[2]

Richard and Clarissa Dalloway famously enter the literary scene as they step aboard the merchant ship *Euphrosyne* in the coastal waters off Lisbon. Lytton Strachey responded to the high comedy of their characterization with the comment: "Oh, the Dalloways!" More recently, Chene Heady has explored Woolf's masterful comedic satire in her handling of this one-time Member of Parliament and his daughter-of-a-Peer wife. How seriously should we consider the effect of Richard on the muddled Rachel Vinrace? Seriously, indeed. The Dalloway mystique took sway, as well, over the imagination of Virginia Woolf. The Dalloways do not disappear when they debark onto the coast of colonial Africa, but continue to preoccupy Woolf uniquely among her characters. They re-appear in the 1925 novel and a cluster of short stories composed both concurrently and subsequently to work on the novel.[3]

The Voyage Out is, among other things, a meditation on Englishness. Lorna Sage writes, "[Woolf] wanted to shrink England and get English life into a new perspective" (xii). In conversation after dinner first night aboard ship, Clarissa muses:

D'you know, Dick, I can't help thinking of England [...] Being on this ship seems to make it so much more vivid—what it really means to be English. One thinks of all we've done, and our navies, and the people in India and Africa, and how we've gone on century after century, sending out boys from little country villages—and of men like you, Dick, and it makes one feel as if one couldn't bear *not* to be English! Think of the light burning over the House, Dick! When I stood on deck just now I seemed to see it. It's what one means by London. (*VO* 51)

For Woolf as well, late imperial London has become the locus of Englishness.[4] However, the contingent status of the Dalloways' England is implicit in the contrast between Clarissa's effusions and the novel's opening portrait of the city. The contrast lies between the Dalloways' abstractly but narrowly conceived England and the continuum of "Englishnesses" which abides in the opening portrait of the Ambroses' passage from the Embankment to the docks whence they boarded the *Euphrosyne*.

Of the Dalloways themselves, Sage writes: "People like the Dalloways are the ones in charge of [...] England, [...] [they] speak for England" (xxvi, xxiii). In 1925, Woolf articulates what began with the Dalloways' brief interlude aboard the *Euphrosyne*, recurs in "Mrs. Dalloway in Bond Street" and is fleshed out in *Mrs. Dalloway*. Writing in her diary, she imagines social grouping as "people secret[ing] an envelope which connects them and protects them from others, like myself, who are outside the envelope, foreign bodies" (cited by McNichol 12). While *Mrs. Dalloway* is structured on an inviolable gulf between people—the isolation of the individual consciousness within the physical body—it is also a novel of social inter-connectedness. Onto the dazzling mosaic of individual consciousnesses, a Venn diagram of group consciousnesses is superimposed. The group consciousness of "people like the Dalloways," of "men like you, Dick," constitutes the Dalloway mystique, exuded by people "in charge" and imbibed by those under their charge.

Clarissa's formulation in *The Voyage Out* of "what one means by London" is replicated in the later works. There is the affective force exercised by *symbols* of power and sovereignty, or, as Woolf later characterized the force, "in its common appeal emotional" (*MD* 18). "The light burning over the House" becomes, first, the Queen and Buckingham Palace; in *Mrs. Dalloway* this force takes root in "thought of the dead; of the flag; of Empire" (18), as well as in the symbolic power of the Palace and the royal automobile halted in traffic before the flower shop. The ruling class which *exercises* power and sovereignty, "men like you, Dick," remains Richard who makes Clarissa understand the importance of "trade with China" ("Bond Street" 27), while in *Mrs. Dalloway*, the ranks are expanded to include the Prime Minister, Hugh Whitbread and even Peter Walsh. As for the people *over whom* power and sovereignty is exercised, "the people in India and Africa," Clarissa takes heart while shopping in Bond Street, identifying this Englishness as "something inborn in the race; what Indians respected" ("Bond Street" 21). At her power lunch with Richard and Hugh, Lady Bruton casts her gaze eastward, "Ah, the news from India!" (*MD* 111).

The Voyage Out examines, primarily, the Englishness of British tourists in San Marino: the educated middle-class (and of course there's the cameo appearance of the Dalloways). Ali's portrait of foreign bodies living in the heart of Englishness, in London, focuses primarily on the contrasting experiences within Nazreen and Chanu's marriage. However, *Brick Lane* actually presents a broad spectrum of immigrant experience and wide range of responses to colonial seduction, where the opening portrait of London in *The Voyage Out* merely alludes to such a spectrum within English society itself. Much of the comparison between Woolf's *Mrs. Dalloway* and Ali's *Brick Lane* resides in Nazreen's experiences outside her marriage.

Mirroring, or reversal, is a prominent technique within Woolf's texts. For example, Sasha's view of the English in *Orlando* reverses the British view of Russians. Reversing the gaze functions to expose or illuminate the limited and ultimately false status of the view from within any socially constructed group. The reverse inter-, rather than intra-textual gaze of *Brick Lane* exposes what the Dalloways would hide. The imperial subject gazing at the colonial other sees only himself, as an object of desire. The view from the other side is spectacularly different.

The British are largely absent or invisible in Ali's novel, mirroring the condition of colonials in Woolf's texts. *Brick Lane* is filled with those foreign bodies shut out. But we focus on Chanu, who comes closest to affirming Clarissa's assertion regarding "what the Indians respect," who is subject to the Dalloway mystique. Listen to his confidence in winning the promotion over an Anglo applicant: "[Wilkie] thinks he will get the promotion because he goes to the *pub* with the boss. He is so stupid he doesn't even realize there is any other way of getting promotion. [...] No way is he going to get promoted" (20-1). Yet, Chanu recognizes the role of networking. (Didn't letters of introduction and "special arrangements" propel the Dalloways easefully through life? And wouldn't a good word from Richard or Hugh secure an appointment for even the disgraced Peter Walsh?) While Chanu eschews lunch at the pub (or perhaps is excluded), he courts a Bengali physician whom he mistakenly believes to be Mr. Dalloway's physician. If Dr. Azad will put in a good word for him, surely the promotion is in the bag.

Basic to Chanu's understanding of getting promotion is the embrace of high literary culture's trappings. "I don't have anything to fear from Wilkie. I have a degree from Dhaka University in English literature. Can Wilkie quote from Chaucer or Dickens or Hardy?" (21). Despite his growing disillusionment—Chanu will write a "speech" to read at a community meeting titled "Race and Class in the UK: A Short Thesis on the White Working Class, Race Hate, and Ways to Tackle the Issue"—he is never entirely disabused of the effects of his colonial education. Well after arriving in London, Chanu "decided it was time to see the sights" and sets off on the bus with wife and daughters in tow (210). Having paid his fare, Chanu addresses the conductor:

> "Can you tell me something? To your mind, does the British Museum rate more highly than the National Gallery? Or would you recommend gallery over Museum?" The conductor pushed his lower lip out with his tongue. He stared hard at Chanu, as if considering whether to eject him from the bus. "In my rating system," explained Chanu, "they are neck and neck. It would be good to take an opinion from a local." (211)

Chanu clings to the notion that his valuation of British cultural monuments raises him above the "locals." As it so happens, the family excursion is to stand outside Buckingham Palace, have a family snapshot taken in commemoration of the occasion, and picnic in St. James Park. Chanu's naïve swallowing whole of the mystique is equaled only by Richard Dalloway's bombast. The illusion of assimilation is the underside of the Dalloways' construction of England.[5]

Ali's novel charts Chanu's disillusionment, his progress from "being under the influence" to his rejection of the mystique. How had the mystique ever taken hold? In her Dalloway corpus, Woolf links sexuality, power, and imperialism as the internal mechanism driving the seductive force of the Dalloway mystique. Richard's encounter with Rachel Vinrace in *The Voyage Out* sets up the essential elements. Rachel retires to her cabin after dinner to think through her impressions of these truly exotic people. She is quite entranced by Clarissa. But even more so by Richard. Richard's aura, not so much of power, but of worldly experience enthralls Rachel: "And her husband!" (46). Helen Ambrose diagnoses the root of Rachel's susceptibility accurately: total lack of knowledge and experience, of the world and of sexuality. In *Mrs. Dalloway* we have the comparable phenomenon in Clarissa's response to Sally Seton. "Sally it was who made her feel, for the first time, how sheltered life at Bourton was. She knew nothing about sex—nothing about social problems" (33). The repetition of eroticism stimulated by the aura of worldliness draws an implicit analogy between the affective power of sexual attraction to over-ride any other vision of the world and the "common appeal emotional" of the Dalloway mystique to obscure vision of anything other than the Emperor's new clothes.

Like Clarissa's in *Mrs. Dalloway*, Nazreen's consciousness is opened to the larger world and its social problems with her sexual awakening. Inexperienced as she is, Nazreen rightly and readily recognizes the emptiness of her husband's expectations. Her inexperience also leaves her, like Rachel and Clarissa, vulnerable to worldly allure. Nazreen begins to take in piece-work, delivered by a young man closer to her own age than Chanu. Worldliness enters Nazreen's secluded estate flat in the person of Karim. She soon finds herself, contrary to her every belief, in a passionate liaison, initially helpless before the power of this previously unimagined sexuality.

Aside from delivering and collecting sewing jobs for his father's business, Karim leads the Bengal Tigers, a group organized to resist the growing violence against the immigrant community, most immediately perpetrated by nationalist thugs calling themselves the Lion Hearts. Attending Karim's meetings, Nazreen witnesses immigrant responses far different from Chanu's. The 9/11 attack and consequent invasion of Afghanistan galvanize the community. The extremity of choices available to Islamic immigrants is brought into sharp focus. Should the community respond with peaceful marches, demonstrating that Islam is a religion of peace? Or, does the degree of violence against innocent civilians—from bombing or starvation—necessitate violent resistance?

By the time she wrote *Mrs. Dalloway*, Woolf understood that violent enforcement invites violent resistance. This understanding is latent in Clarissa's formulation of Englishness in *The Voyage Out*: "boys [sent out] from little country villages" and "our navies." In *Mrs. Dalloway*, Woolf casts her understanding in the shape of Conversion, "even now engaged—in the heat and sands of India" (100). Underpinning "what one means by London," effectively hidden beneath the mystique's euphemisms, lies the threat of violence.

Woolf is explicit in the novel. Following Clarissa's fine thoughts "of the dead; of the flag; of Empire" is this unique statement, lying almost invisibly:

> In a public house in a back street a Colonial insulted the House of Windsor which led to words, broken beer glasses, and a general shindy, which echoed strangely across the way in the ears of girls buying white underlinen threaded with pure white ribbon for their weddings. (*MD* 18)

Ali enlists the same matrix in her multiple trajectories. Woolf's linkage of young girls going dewy-eyed into marriage, innocent of sexuality and innocent of social problems, with the sounds of immigrant resistance echoing strangely in their ears, is strangely mirrored by the post-9/11 riots in the immigrant streets of *Brick Lane*.

Notes

1. The stress placed on traditional gender roles and expectations by immigration to the "secular, western, urban center" is a continuing thread throughout the novel. Janet Maslin notes: "Feminism is as central to 'Brick Lane' as the tensions within its immigrant community." Kaiser Haq, reflecting on the novel's conclusion (Chanu's return to Dhaka and Nazreen's decision to remain and raise her daughters in London), puts it another way. "[A] significant fact about expatriate Bangladeshis: the men dream of returning but not the women, who, even as second-class citizens, enjoy rights denied them in the mother country" (23).
2. In 2003, Monica Ali found herself the "first unpublished author to be included among Granta's 'Best of Young British Novelists'" (Haq 20), on the basis of her manuscript for *Brick Lane*. On publication, the novel rose to the British bestseller list, was shortlisted for the Man Booker prize, was soon published in the U.S. and attracted considerable press attention on both sides of the Atlantic. Early reviews acclaimed Ali as the next Zadie Smith, for both the authors' biographical parallels as "women writers in England who hail from the Indian subcontinent" (Lehmann) and their books' thematic parallels: "the immigrants' unfulfilled dreams in an adopted country; the generational conflicts between parents and the children who all too easily assimilate to the new land; the yearnings for a home" (Scaggs).
3. Collected and published by Stella McNichol as the cycle *Mrs. Dalloway's Party*.
4. See Peter J. Kalliney, *Cities of Affluence and Anger*, for its treatment of literary national identity in transition from imperialism to post-imperialism, marked by the transformation of the imperial capital to a global metropolis. Woolf's *Mrs. Dalloway* is given extended attention for not only its innovative presentation of London, but its focus on the capital city as a positive locus of national identity. Kalliney's final chapter, devoted to *The Satanic Verses*, mentions *Brick Lane* in passing.
5. *Brick Lane* can fruitfully be read alongside Salman Rushdie's *The Satanic Verses*. Ali's novel reads like a miniature, domesticated and feminized meditation on the themes of assimilation and alienation in London which Salman Rushdie elaborates in the extraordinary experiences of the erstwhile, well-assimilated hero of *The Satanic Verses*, Salahuddin Chamchawalla. During his nightmarish metamorphosis into a goat, "Chamcha" takes refuge in the Bengali enclave of Brickhall, that is, within the very neighborhood where Ali's rural-born Bengali heroine is confined. In Brickhall, or Bengla-town, Rushdie's character is disabused of his fantasized success in assimilation and begins his emergence out from under "the Dalloway mystique." Chamchawalla will eventually return to his native Mumbai, as Chanu returns to Dhaka. The one exception to reviews which place *Brick Lane* in the context of British authors from the Indian subcontinent is written by Ron Charles, who remarks: "Biology aside, a better comparison would be with Anita Brookner, that non-young, blisteringly white matron of British fiction whose quiet, incisive novels scrutinize the plight of lonely people." In discussion following the papers, Susan Stanford Friedman offered a reading of Ali's Chanu from within the British canon. She reads Chanu in a line of masculine heroes, begun with James Joyce's Bloom in *Ulysses*.

Works Cited

Ali, Monica. *Brick Lane*. New York: Scribner, 2003.
Charles, Ron. "Remember Your Place." Rev. of *Brick Lane*, by Monica Ali. *Christian Science Monitor*. 18 Sept. 2003 <http://www.csmonitor.com/2003/0918/p18s01-bogn.html>.
Haq, Kaiser. "Monica Ali." *South Asian Writers in English, DNB* 323: 20-4.
Heady, Chene. "'Accidents of Political Life': Satire and Edwardian Anti-Colonial Politics in *The Voyage Out*." In

Virginia Woolf Out of Bounds: Selected Papers From the Tenth Annual Conference on Virginia Woolf, ed. Jessica Berman and Jane Goldman, 97-104. New York: Pace University Press, 2001.

Kalliney, Peter J. *Cities of Affluence and Anger: A Literary Geography of Modern Englishness*. Charlottesville: University of Virginia Press, 2006.

Lehmann, Chris. Rev. of *Brick Lane*, by Monica Ali. "A Long and Winding Road." *Washington Post*. 16 Sept. 2003 <http://www.washingtonpost.com/ac2/wp-dyn?pagename=article&node=&contentId=A15686-2003Sep15>.

Maslin, Janet. Rev. of *Brick Lane*, by Monica Ali. "The Flavor of a New Land Can Leave a Bitter Taste." *New York Times*. 8 Sept. 2003 <http://query.nytimes.com/gst/fullpage.html?res=9C07E7D8163BF93BA3575AC0A9659C8B63>.

McNichol, Stella. Introduction. In Woolf, *Mrs. Dalloway's Party*, 9-17.

Rushdie, Salman. *The Satanic Verses*. New York: Viking, 1988.

Sage, Lorna. Introduction. In Woolf, *The Voyage Out*, xii-xxix.

Scaggs, Kevin. Rev. of *Brick Lane*, by Monica Ali. "Building Bricks For a New Life." *San Francisco Chronicle*. 14 Sept. 2003 <http://www.sfgate.com/cgi-bin/article.cgi?f=/chronicle/archive/2003/09/14/RV122931.DTL>.

Woolf, Virginia. *Mrs. Dalloway*. Foreword by Maureen Howard. San Diego: Harvest-Harcourt Brace Jovanovich, 1981

—. "Mrs. Dalloway in Bond Street." In Woolf, *Mrs. Dalloway's Party*, 19-28.

—. *Mrs. Dalloway's Party: A Short Story Sequence*. Ed. with an introduction by Stella McNichol. London: Hogarth Press, 1973.

—. *The Voyage Out*. Oxford: Oxford University Press, 2001

Roots, Woolf, and an Ethics of Desire

by Lisa L. Coleman

"flowers lead...by their way of getting through the earth, with their roots, to the core of the matter." (Cixous, *Three Steps on the Ladder of Writing* 154)

At the risk of stating a platitude, Virginia Woolf is an intuitive, poetic thinker and writer. Not only does she chronicle her own writing processes in her diaries which reveal this intuitive aptitude, she also depicts the difficulty and consequences of reaching a conceptual understanding of things in *A Room of One's Own*. Make no mistake, it is not that Woolf *cannot* think conceptually, but that conceptual thought—linked as it is with the patriarchal symbolic—requires giving a name to things and thereby changes them (*TW* 81). This presentation will maintain that in a desire to keep moving, yet figuratively take a detour around the demands of the symbolic, Woolf's writing turns or tropes her readers toward an aesthetically inspired sense of their own subjectivity and their ethical desires—not by going to the concept, but by going to the root.

To explain what I mean by going to the root, I metonymically link three texts, the essay "The Patron and the Crocus" and the novels *The Waves* and *Jacob's Room*. "The Patron and the Crocus" demonstrates Woolf's penchant for letting flowers lead and provides insight into Woolf's poetically inflected rhetorical style. Succumbing to this style will prepare us for *The Waves* and *Jacob's Room* and Woolf's performative enactment and ethical commentary on the shaping of subjectivity. Following in the footsteps of Roger Poole and Pamela Caughie, who made once forbidden postmodern readings of Woolf a possibility in Woolf scholarship, I depict Woolf as precursor and complement to Lacanian psychoanalysis. *The Waves* amplifies Lacan's linguistically inspired theory of subject formation and his postmodern ethics of desire, while *Jacob's Room* demonstrates how Aristotelian inspired modernist ethics thwart desire. In my conclusion, I briefly ruminate on Woolf's ethics and the ethics of Woolf scholarship in a postmodern world.

"The Patron and the Crocus"

The final version of "The Patron and the Crocus" (1925) reveals the desire and necessity of the writer *for* a reader, an Other whose desire will inspire desire in the writer. Stating that beginning writers are encouraged "to say exactly what is in them," Woolf points out that their advisors seldom add, "'And be sure you choose your patron wisely'...since the patron is...also...the instigator and inspirer of what is written" (*CE 2* 149). Likening one's inspiration for writing to "the sight of the first crocus in Kensington Gardens" (149), Woolf asks what sort of reader or public does the writer require to amplify the beauty of the flower, to keep it from decay. She insists on the importance of the patron but dismisses the submissive patron, since no crocus will flourish without reciprocity between reader and writer (149-50). The patron must be well-read, historically and globally aware, and able to make informed judgments on issues of indecency, society, emotion, and language. He may even tell you, "[I]f you can forget your sex altogether..., so much the better; a writer has none" (151; see also *Woolf in the World*).¹

Yet Woolf's next line, "But all this is by the way—elementary and disputable" (151), deconstructs the advice just given and enables Woolf to reach the thought she has been heading for: the only way our crocus can blossom is in the "atmosphere" of a patron who is unshockable and willing "to efface himself or assert himself as his writers require" (152). She concludes by asking: "But how to choose rightly? How to write well?" (152).

Woolf's deconstructive turn prepares breathing space for the word "atmosphere," which figures the possible mood created in what Cixous calls the "*entredeux*" between writer and patron or reader. This "passage *from the one to the other*" (rendered ungrammatically by Cixous as "*de l'une à l'autre*," not *de l'un à l'autre*) creates a poetically inflected remembering of the repressed feminine (as well as the moon). Like Woolf, Cixous is "irritated" by "locutions which are not questioned and which impose their law on us" (Cixous and Calle-Gruber 10). Like Cixous, Woolf's writing takes detours around the symbolic and its laws both by urging us to repress our sex through the interested words of the patron and then, by undercutting his advice in the next line, providing us, her current community of readers and patrons, with a sense that this call to repression denegates the repressed, enabling it to return in a new form.

The issue of sex is alluded to once again with the overdetermined word, "crocus," a late draft addition (see *Woolf in the World*). Not a bulb but a corm, which, like the rhizome, is an underground root,² the crocus gets it name from a figure in Ovid's *Metamorphoses*. *Krokos*, a mortal "flower-boy" of uncertain sexual orientation, is accidentally killed by his lover Mercury, and the flower springs up from his blood (*Paghat's Garden; Theoi*; see Ovid 82, 398). Other stories tell of *Krokos's* failed love affair with the nymph, Smilax, who is herself transformed into the greenbriar (*Paghat's Garden; Theoi*).

Unlike the greenbriar, the crocus has been seen as a desirable plant since the times of the Minoans. With saffron stigmas valued for yellow dye, myth has it that Persephone was gathering purple crocus when she was abducted by Hades (*Paghat's Garden*). The crocus, whose origin is told in a story older than the myth of the seasons, is the flower of a thwarted but unending desire that transgresses boundaries of plant and animal, sex and longing, life and death. For Woolf, the crocus leads. Not a bulb but a root, the crocus lives underground, hidden, unconscious, but nonetheless alive.

Like Woolf, Cixous goes to the "School of Roots" to explain the source of her inspiration. Her "patrons" are writers who occupy a "risky country…situated somewhere near the unconscious" (114), and they speak of what is shocking or forbidden, which "is the root" (Lispector 64, qtd. in Cixous 116). As we will see in *The Waves* and *Jacob's Room*, Woolf's writing, situated like that of Cixous' patrons, performatively practices "what going to the root is, going toward the unverifiable" (Cixous 146). For good and ill, going to the root is not somewhere that we go alone: we go there with the Other, the patron who desires our desire.

Lacan and his Others

Those of you familiar with Lacan's theory of the subject as constituted by the Other will have already heard intimations of his theory in the intercreative relationship Woolf describes between writer and patron. For Lacan, sometimes referred to by *his* patrons as the great misreader of *his* patron Freud (Schneiderman 31-32), the subject is constituted by the Other. Sometimes this Other is the other of oneself as determined by one's specular image in a mirror, seen, perhaps for the first time, by a child held up by caregivers. This is the image that Lacan uses to reveal the imaginary register, which deceptively presents to the child a sense of unity and completeness. Sometimes this Other is the big or grand Other, language itself, the symbolic register or the Name of the Father, which creates subjects when humans learn to speak. This register, with its patriarchal overtones and necessary emphasis on the signifier, forever divides the subject from the sense of wholeness the specular image affords. Lacan then uses these two registers to explain the Real, the register created by the sense of emptiness or separation that arises when one becomes linked to the signifying chain. This sense of emptiness inspires the subject to create new objects to fill the gap. Lacan styles this other *le petit objet a.* These *objets a,* standing in for the sense of lost wholeness, can only be found as *found again*; thus the subject repeats behaviors that will make this refinding possible. (Freud's grandson and his *fort/da* game with the cotton reel are paradigmatic.) Lacan then integrates these registers and these "others" into the various psychoanalytic concepts provided by his patron Freud—the unconscious, repetition, transference, and the drive (see *Four*).

Woolf and *The Waves*

Eschewing concept for performance, avoiding the terminology of psychoanalysis and linguistics altogether, Woolf nonetheless offers us insight into the psychoanalytic process of subject formation in *The Waves*. If Lacan posits a subject split by the signifier, Woolf pushes the subject toward Deleuze and Guattari's multitudes and intensities with her six speaking personae. In her diary Woolf imagines "a playpoem" (*A Writer's Diary* 134) with moths coming to a candle or a flower and a "mind thinking" (140). This early configuration becomes voices speaking from direct discourse artfully interrupted by interstitial scenes depicting birds and sun, a house and waves that make us aware of a day's time inexorably passing.

We know the Hogarth Press published the writing of Freud and that Woolf met him (Hussey 93-94), but paradoxically and proleptically, what *The Waves* provides is a kind of gloss on Freud's patron, Jacques Lacan, and his rereading of Freud—Jacques Lacan, whose major works were not published till after Woolf's death. Could we more reasonably conjecture that Woolf, in her playpoem, offers a poetic gloss on Freud's theories that precedes and parallels Lacan's own?

As we listen to the speakers, who move from childhood to death and middle age during the course of the novel, we can almost imagine a session between analyst and analysand, with the personae offering up whatever comes into their minds. As Lacan tells us, "*the unconscious is structured like a language*" (*Four* 20; see also *Ethics* 32), and Woolf's intuitive sense in the presentation of her personae's enunciations brings this home. Lacan tells us that cause may be the fluttering of butterfly wings (*Four* 76),[3] and in Woolf we have the fluttering of the moths who ultimately *become* these personae (*A Writer's Diary* 140). Lacan tells us that our thoughts are unconscious, and it is only by articulating them that we can hear ourselves think (*Ethics* 48). We must put our thoughts into words to hear them, and this is the accomplishment of the speakers in *The Waves*.

In the opening chapter we see how each speaker comes into being at the behest of the other. Bernard says, "[W]e melt into each other with phrases. We make an unsubstantial territory" (*TW* 16). Jinny kisses Louis on the nape of the neck (13), and Susan and Bernard feel that kiss for the rest of their lives. Our desire is the desire of the Other.

Ultimately we learn from Lacan that it is only by owning our desire that we can avoid guilt and regret. What do we learn from the repeated patterns of these speakers?

Each of them latches on to different bits of reality (Lacan, *Ethics* 47). Bernard takes up phrases (*TW* 18), Susan sees closely. She loves; she hates (15). Jinny is of the moment. She freezes Louis with her kiss just when he has escaped the world and become a rooted stalk (12-13). She stops his metamorphosis and draws him back into the world where he is a banker's son with an Australian accent. Neville makes himself perfect, a poet; he would be different and desire differently. Rhoda lives in a world where flower petals become ships that drown in bowls, cut off from real earth where flowers might flourish (18-19). Louis, too, is cut off. After Jinny's kiss he spends his life marching to the tune of the stamping elephants that link him to global affairs and accounts that are kept.

What Woolf's repeated patterns of language provide are a way to see humans owned by their *objets a*, trapped by their own signification. Only Bernard has a chance to extricate himself, yet even he, like the others, wishes to gravitate around the unspeaking Percival, a collective *objet a* who never speaks, their fantasy of perfection, whose very existence assures them that all is right with the world—until his untimely and ignominious death.

At the end of *The Waves*, Bernard, the phrasemaker in the role of analysand, sums up, speaking to an Other, the analyst which can only be Woolf's patrons, the readers of her text. He tries to make sense of the enunciations of the others. There are more questions raised than conclusions reached, but he is certain that he must fight death and expend whatever effort it takes to vanquish it. The waves, nevertheless, beat the shore.

The Thing

Before we can see what awaits us in *Jacob's Room*, we need Lacan's last register, home to Freud's *Das Ding*. The Thing is a *petit objet a* raised to the status of a Thing, something we are willing to die for, to destroy the world for. Today the Thing might be democracy, Lacan mentions the woman in medieval courtly love (*Ethics* 125-26).

The Thing takes us to the root of the ethics of psychoanalysis and the analysand's demand for happiness, a demand, Lacan insists, that the analyst cannot grant. The job of the analyst is to offer the analysand his desire, a mature desire that asks one question: "Have you acted in conformity with the desire that is in you?" (314). Because each analysand's guilt is tied to this question (along with a concomitant reluctance to reply without the veil of good intentions), to receive a useful answer, the analyst must ask this question from the place of the Last Judgment—not on this side of life, before the first death, but on the other side, the side of the second death, the place you would ostensibly find yourself in after you die.

Lacan maintains that what traditional or modernist ethics measures, what Aristotle calls the good, is not so much the good as power. Aristotle's "morality is the morality of the master, created for the virtues of the master, and linked to the order of powers." "The morality of power, of the service of goods," Lacan tells us, "is as follows: 'As far as desires are concerned, come back later. Make them wait'" (315).

With *Jacob's Room*, told from the side of the second death, Woolf demonstrates this distinction between Aristotelian inspired modernist morality and postmodern ethical desire and shows how and why, in the end, Jacob's room and the yellow iris on his mantelpiece will persist (*JR* 38), but he will not.

Jacob's Room

From the very beginning when he seizes the sheep's skull (*JR* 10), Jacob is marked for death. He is an absent presence who becomes the Other for many, the object of their desire, but no one ever *has* him or *knows* him in any kind of permanent way. In the end, he leaves to participate in a war that fulfills the prophecy of the novel's first chapter—his mother's sadness and his brother's repeated efforts to find him—Jacob is the object always already lost.

What Woolf gives us in Jacob is the thinking man's Percival, the man who speaks and acts, who comes under the influence of his family, his friends, his lovers, and his education, Deleuze and Guattari's rhizomatic root that "ceaselessly establishes connections between semiotic chains" (7). But this semiosis, this desire, ends when Jacob studies the Greeks and then goes to Greece, where we see him confirming himself in their image, becoming the idealist who will turn an object into a Thing, who will read Plato, and, believing in the Good, will relinquish *his* desire to serve the modernist desires of the state and ultimately become a victim of its power.

Owning Your Own Desire

Lacan's seminar on *The Ethics of Psychoanalysis* culminates in a close reading of the play *Antigone* and the role played by desire. Antigone loses her brother and pays with her life to give him a proper burial. Lacan uses the play to help his students understand the difference between an Enlightenment morality like Kant's and the morality figured by Freud, who has interminably witnessed good mistaken for evil and evil mistaken for good.[4] Freud knows that a psychoanalytic ethics that sets out with standards of good and evil is always already compromised.

In *Antigone,* Creon is the representative of the state and the good of his people. Polyneices, Antigone's brother, is a traitor who attacks his uncle and the state. Thus, when he is killed, Creon decrees it is just to punish him with a second death—they will not bury him. For Antigone, her brother is her brother, and his actions—good or bad—are not at issue. Her connection to the signifier that is her brother causes her to bury him anyway.

Creon, mistaking good for evil and evil for good, decrees that Antigone, too, will die, walled up alive; he will punish her beyond the first death to the second. As a result, everyone dies, due to Creon's mistaken commitment to the service of goods.

For Lacan, Antigone provides a vision of the analyst's desire for the analysand, not to die, of course, but to own her own desire in the symbolic. Antigone is not swayed from her desire to respect her brother. She knows the price she will pay, but she acts, and when she dies, when she kills herself in her own tomb, it is not in the name of the Good.

So how do we square Antigone's acts with Woolf's life and death and my contention that Woolf, too, practices an ethics of desire?

Until the end of her life, Woolf strives to "'make something of what has been made of [her]'" (Hebdige, qtd. in Worsham 85).[5] She is a writer, a creator. She not only precedes

Lacan in her possible rereading of Freud, she makes a detour around Oedipus and castration by persistently calling the symbolic and its structurations into question, efforts to circumvent and alter the symbolic whose reverberations continue to this day.

Like Bernard, Woolf battles against death; she is the lady writing (*TW* 17; *A Writer's Diary* 142), who produces, through great discipline, some of the greatest novels and essays of the 20th century. It is not till the end that she falls back on Creon's role, the service of goods, underscored in her suicide notes that wished to spare her family further pain (Poole 255-56). I do not excuse Woolf's actions, but I understand them. As Lacan says, if you take the road of the service of goods you must know what you have given up. I think she did.

But for most of her existence, Woolf owned her own desire—scrupulously, brilliantly, artfully, and she did not compromise. She did not write for a patron; she created patrons—the coming community (Agamben 1-2)[6]—as a postmodernist would,[7] not by formulating concepts and seeking agreement, but by seducing our minds—by "put[ting] forward the unpresentable [desire] in presentation itself" (Lyotard 81).[8]

Woolf's ethics pass beyond her own untimely end. Engaging to this day with her patrons, Woolf insists that each of us must own our own desire—and champion others to do the same, not to create a homogeneous view of Woolf and her writing, but to create a productive, desiring, multiply-nuanced view that champions all the perspectives her work has inspired and engendered. Only then will we realize her vision of "One life," that is never one but always Other (*TW* 229, 276)—an invitation to a table set for whoever manages to find the turning and show up.

Notes

1. The Smith College Libraries website, *Woolf in the World*, has manuscripts of "The Patron and the Crocus" revealing Woolf's edits, including the emendation, "a writer has none."
2. This information on the crocus is gathered from the community sponsored website, *Wikipedia*, under the terms "crocus" and "corm."
3. Lacan is alluding to Freud's case "The 'Wolfman'" (288-91) in which the fluttering of butterfly wings reminds the analysand of the opening and closing of a woman's legs. Freud uses this image to lead his patient back to the primal scene and *cause* of his neuroses—witnessing his parents' copulation.
4. Kant's Enlightenment morality, based on the categorical imperative, states that one should only will that which should be universalized (willed by all others) and presupposes a rational subject able to recognize evil and good and act accordingly. Freud's experience tells him that, given human drives, good and evil can be mistaken for each other.
5. Borrowing this line from Hebdige (139) (who borrowed it from Sartre), Worsham examines *écriture féminine* like a subculture, "as a new language and a form of postmodern expression" that indirectly resists a given society's hegemonic meaning making systems (85). Analogously, I am arguing that Woolf provides her readers with a new language and a new form of expression born of her singular style, one that is not so much modern as postmodern in its effects.
6. For Agamben the coming community is composed of "whatever beings," a translation of *quodlibet ens*, which means not just any being, but "being such that it always matters" (1). This being can't be identified by its qualities or class. It is neither universal nor individual. Rather, it is being that is loved for its singularity, its "being-*such*" (2).
7. For Lyotard the modern and the postmodern are not historical time periods but artistic forces that push against the notion that what is "real" exists unproblematically and may be depicted with the correct language or image (74). Since the postmodern is always already "a part of the modern" (79), "[a] work can become modern only if it is first postmodern. Postmodernism thus understood is not modernism at its end but in the nascent state, and this state is constant" (79).

8. Lyotard maintains it is only through art that one may attempt to express the unpresentable, *to make its absence apparent* (77-78). See also McGee.

Works Cited

Agamben, Giorgio. *The Coming Community*. Trans. Michael Hardt. Minneapolis: University of Minnesota Press, 1993.
Cixous, Hélène. *Three Steps on the Ladder of Writing*. New York: Columbia University Press, 1993.
Cixous, Hélène, and Mireille Calle-Gruber. *Rootprints: Memory and Life Writing*. Trans. Eric Prinowitz. London: Routledge, 1997.
"Corm." *Wikipedia, The Free Encyclopedia*. 4 Aug. 2007, 08:55 UTC. Wikimedia Foundation, Inc. 13 Aug. 2007 <http://en.wikipedia.org/w/index.php?title=Corm&oldid=149110766>.
"Crocus." *Wikipedia, The Free Encyclopedia*. 13 Aug. 2007, 10:14 UTC. Wikimedia Foundation, Inc. 13 Aug. 2007 <http://en.wikipedia.org/w/index.php?title=Crocus&oldid=15093122>.
Deleuze, Gilles, and Felix Guattari. *A Thousand Plateaus: Capitalism and Schizophrenia*. Trans. Brian Massumi. Minneapolis: University of Minnesota Press, 1987.
Freud, Sigmund. *The "Wolfman" and Other Cases*. Trans. Louise Adey Huish. New York: Penguin, 2002.
Hebdige, Dick. *Subculture: The Meaning of Style*. London: Methuan, 1979.
Hussey, Mark. *Virginia Woolf A-Z: A Comprehensive Reference for Students, Teachers, and Common Readers to Her Life, Work, and Critical Reception*. Oxford: Oxford University Press, 1995.
Lacan, Jacques. *Ecrits: A Selection*. Trans. Alan Sheridan. New York: Norton, 1977.
—. *The Four Fundamental Concepts of Psychoanalysis*. Ed. Jacques-Alain Miller. Trans. Alan Sheridan. New York: Norton, 1978.
—. *The Seminar of Jacques Lacan: Book VII: The Ethics of Psychoanalysis, 1959-1960*. Ed. Jacques-Alain Miller. Trans. Dennis Porter. New York: Norton, 1992.
Lispector, Clarice. *The Passion According to G. H.* Trans. Ronald W. Sousa. Minneapolis: University of Minnesota Press, 1988.
Lyotard, Jean-François. *The Postmodern Condition: A Report on Knowledge*. Trans. Geoff Bennington and Brian Massumi. Minneapolis: University of Minnesota Press, 1984.
McGee, Patrick. "Woolf's Other: The University in Her Eye." *Novel* 23 (1990): 229-46.
Ovid. *Metamorphosis*. Trans. A.D. Melville. Oxford University Press, 1986.
Paghat's Garden: Saffron Mythology I. Paghat. 13 Aug 2007 <www.paghat.com/saffronmyth.html>.
Poole, Roger. *The Unknown Virginia Woolf*. 3rd ed. Atlantic Highlands, NJ: Humanities Press International, 1990.
Schneiderman, Stuart. *Jacques Lacan: The Death of an Intellectual Hero*. Cambridge: Harvard University Press, 1983.
Theoi Greek Mythology: Exploring Mythology in Classical Literature and Art. "Plants of Greek Myth." 13 Aug. 2007 <www.theoi/Flora1.html>.
Woolf in the World: A Pen and a Press of Her Own. The Common Reader. Mortimer Rare Book Room Collection. Smith College, Northhampton, MA. 13 August 2007 <w.smith.edu/libraries/libs/rarebook/exhibitions/penandpress/case71.htm>.
Woolf, Virginia. "The Patron and the Crocus." *Collected Essays*. Vol II. New York: Harcourt, 1925. 149-52.
—. *Jacob's Room*. San Diego: Harcourt, 1922.
—. *The Waves*. 1931. San Diego: Harcourt, 1959.
—. *A Writer's Diary*. Ed. Leonard Woolf. San Diego: Harcourt, 1954.
Worsham, Lynn. "Writing Against Writing: The Predicament of *Ecriture Féminine* in Composition Studies." In *Contending with Words: Composition and Rhetoric in a Postmodern Age*, ed. Patricia Harkin and John Schilb, 84-104. New York: MLA, 1991.

FLIGHTS OF IMAGINATION:
AERIAL VIEWS, NARRATIVE PERSPECTIVES, AND GLOBAL PERCEPTIONS

by Erica Delsandro

In "Flying Over London," Virginia Woolf narrates an imagined aerial experience. As brief and fantastic as the essay, so is the flight itself; Woolf concludes that "We had not flown after all" (*CDB* 210). Despite never leaving the runway, Woolf's essay unlocks the potential of the change in perspective offered by flight. Taking my cue from this flight of fancy, I explore Woolf's global perspective and how, through the experience of flight and the figure of the airplane, she suggests the power of imagination to disorient and reorient perceptions in a productive, critical, and creative manner useful both to scholars and common readers alike.

Before this presentation "takes off," I would like to say a bit about how this project came into being and potential directions that it could take. Exploratory in nature, this presentation emerged from my reading for two other projects: one interested in queer studies and queer history and the other concerned with history, historiography, and the interwar novel. At the confluence of these two inquires I found the airplane. First, views from above *queer* or make strange the familiar by mixing human, nature, and machine in a way that, in the first half of the twentieth century, disrupted the normative order, presenting a simultaneously threatening and empowering view of the world. Second, airplanes provide history with a turning point, a marker of the transition into modernity by way of technology, travel, and military means while concurrently influencing the way people thought about and experienced time and distance. This confluence of queer studies and historical perspective, in addition to recent scholarship on Woolf's essays, is the impetus for this exploratory project. Current trends, or rather questions, in feminist studies, as well as the academy's turn toward the global and transnational, suggest to me that a reevaluation of the presence and function airplanes and aerial views in Woolf's writing has the potential to provide us with new perspectives.

Valentine Cunningham, in *British Writers of the Thirties*, notes the presence and importance of airplanes and aerial perspectives by identifying the emergence of the words *airmindedness* and *airminded* that, according to the *OED*, appear in 1927 and 1928 respectively. Writing "Flying Over London" in 1928,[1] Woolf prefigures both what Cunningham characterizes as the unifying lexicon of the 1930s—airplanes, airmen, and aerial views—and Elizabeth Bowen's use of *airmindedness* in her 1932 novel *To the North* (Cunningham 167). "Flying Over London," unlike Bowen's novel, depicts an imaginative flight; because of its imaginative quality, "Flying Over London" provides the perfect starting point for a reevaluation of airplanes and aerial views, suggesting, as Woolf always does where airplanes are concerned, that there is room for interpretation.

I'd like to begin my investigation of aerial views, narrative perspectives, and global perceptions with the essay that got this all started, "Flying Over London." Following are four short sections, each of which introduces a mode of inquiry that Woolf's *airmindedness* facilitates. These sections are not intended to represent a comprehensive discussion, but rather, serve to organize my thoughts and open up categories for critical thinking and discussion. Similar to Woolf's essay, this presentation is meant to stimulate thinking, queer the familiar, and give flight to our scholarly imaginations.

"Flying Over London"

Woolf's own pen, like the thousand pens she evokes, describes the "sensation of leaving the earth": "'The earth drops from you,' they say; one sits still and the world has fallen. It is true that the earth fell, but what was stranger was the downfall of the sky" (*CDB* 203). Perhaps stranger still to the contemporary reader is Woolf's characterization of airplanes: like "a flock of grasshoppers" they are, and like the grasshopper, the plane, too, "springs high into the air" (*CDB* 203). For twenty-first-century readers, the line between air and land has almost always been permeable and airplanes are more likely to be used to describe grasshoppers than the other way around, so natural and normative airplanes have become. However, for Woolf in 1928, air travel was linked to fantasy—as the ending of *Orlando*, published the same year, suggests. Airplanes and the travel that attended them was intriguing, fascinating, and even frightening; in addition to a haunting association with death and destruction by way of World War I (characterized in the 1917 section of *The Years*), air travel and airplanes also connoted the mythology of Icarus, the power of technology, new horizons of experience, and consequently, *airmindedness* carried with it the promise of emancipation, freedom, and boundless, albeit potentially dangerous, liberty.

Thus, one intention of "Flying Over London" seems to be emancipation, of perspective as well as of the earth: "Habit has fixed the earth immovably in the centre of the imagination like a hard ball; everything is made to the scale of houses and trees" (*CDB* 203). But as "the sky pours down over one" the earth "dissolves, crumbles, loses its [...] habits, and one becomes conscious of [...] trespassing up here in a fine air" (*CDB* 203). However, habit only loosens its grip so much as imagination emerges not only as anthropocentric but also as Anglo-centric and imperialist: "Yet, though we flew through territories with never a hedge or stick to divide them, nameless, unowned, so inveterately anthropocentric is the mind that instinctively the aeroplane becomes a boat and we are sailing towards a harbour and there we shall be received by hands that lift themselves from swaying garlands; welcoming, accepting" (*CDB* 204). Even in our imaginations the presence of imperialism threatens: the sky, too, will be our domain. Tempering the implied critique, however, is Woolf's utopian turn: "Wraiths (our aspirations and imaginations) have their home here; and in spite of our vertebrae, ribs, and entrails, we are also vapours and air, and shall be united" (*CDB* 204). An echo of the airplane scene in *Mrs. Dalloway*, Woolf's imaginative flight has the power both to be divisive by constructing meaning and to be unifying by erasing difference.

Air and matter are not the only things united in "Flying Over London." Time collapses, too, as the plane begins a downward spiral and the past comes flying up. If, as Holly Henry suggests, "looking out into space" through a telescope "always marks a looking back in cosmological time" (140) then looking back onto the earth from an airplane proposes a looking back in terrestrial, historical time: "the River Thames was as the Romans saw it, as paleolithic man saw it, at dawn from a hill shaggy with wood, with the rhinoceros digging his horn into the roots of rhododendrons" (*CDB* 204). Like the aerial perspective that maps history onto the English countryside in *Between the Acts*, Woolf's 1928 flight looks back into time; but this historical mapping is interrupted as domes, spires, a factory chimney, and a gasometer emerge: in short, writes Woolf, civilization emerged (*CDB* 205).

Up and down swoops Woolf, imaginatively and rhetorically; finally, emerging from the clouds, civilization spreads out before Woolf's imaginative eye. From high above the movements of men are barely perceptible. With Zeiss glasses, however, one could "see the tops of the heads of separate men and could distinguish a bowler from a cap, and could thus be certain of social grades" (*CDB* 208). Thus, through the lens of the German binoculars, "civilized" humanity becomes discernible: Rolls Royces in London traffic, workers in the poor quarters laboring (*CDB* 209). And here, through the lens of the Zeiss glasses, "Thoughts on Peace in an Air Raid" is prefigured, an essay in which the airplanes are hornets not grasshoppers and airmen look down through their binoculars to the land illuminated by searchlights to drop bombs. In that 1940 essay, Woolf enacts what she proposes in this earlier essay: to perpetually "change air values into land values" (*CDB* 208). But even through the Zeiss glasses not all is visible; surfaces become clear, but what lies underneath? Woolf explains: "And then it was odd how one became resentful of all the flags and surfaces and of the innumerable windows symmetrical as avenues, symmetrical as forest groves, and wished for some opening, and to push indoors and be rid of surfaces" (*CDB* 209).

And it is at this moment, when Woolf's resentment is at its peak, that a woman's face appears from behind a door. Immediately, however, the promise of interiority vanishes, because, as Woolf explains, "the power that buys a mat, or sets two colors together, became perceptible" (*CDB* 210). Civilization—clearly a complex and vexed term for Woolf—overshadows individuality. Woolf's claim that "[e]verything changed its values seen from the air" is thus ambiguous: are air values empowering or threatening? Is this a lament or a promise of potential? Unlike its exhilarating beginning, the flight ends on a sober note of dissatisfaction: "Personality was outside the body, abstract. And one wished to be able to animate the heart, the legs, the arms with it, to do which it would be necessary to be there, so as to collect; so as to give up this arduous game, as one flies through the air, of assembling things that lie on the surface" (*CDB* 210).

And so she does give up this arduous game with the last line of the essay: "So we had not flown after all" (*CDB* 210).

The Hero, the Airman, and the Pacifist

Stephen Kern, writing about technological developments in the period of 1880-1918 recognizes the function and importance of time and space for conceptualizing and understanding not only literature, philosophy, science, and art, but also class structure, diplomacy, and war tactics (5). More specifically, aerial technology altered the significance of borders—geographic, national, and otherwise. Writing "Flying Over London" nearly thirty years into the twentieth century, Woolf enacts the paradox that changing conceptions of time and space bring into modernity by oscillating between a sense of unity and the desire for difference. Such oscillation is a product of technological advancements like the airplane: heightening nationalism and facilitating international cooperation while simultaneously dividing nations as they vie for imperialist supremacy. Thus, one of the greatest ironies of the twentieth century is the presence of world war only after the world had become so highly united (Kern 24).

Written in the wake of national and international political changes wrought by World War I, Woolf's "Flying Over London" is very attentive to the large and small scale alterations that developments in technology—and their attendant reorientation of time and space—initiated. Additionally, Woolf recognizes the airplane's complex symbolic potential; extrapolating from Kern's cultural observations, Gillian Beer reads Woolf's airplanes as "bearer[s] and breaker[s] of signification" (Beer 152). Thus, Beer explains in her seminal essay about Woolf and airplanes that in post-WWI Britain the airplane provided a dual connotation: individualism and heroism on one hand, internationalism on the other (162).

Cunningham, too, takes up the paradoxical nature and pervasiveness of airplanes, aerial views, and the airman. For Cunningham, *airmindedness* is inextricably connected to debates about heroism that inflected the 1930s: writers of the 1930s present "issues of heroism as a matter of size, of scale, of contrasting dimensions" (159) and suggest that "the air was the only location where it was, after the War, widely supposed that heroics had survived" (168). In this manner, airplanes and the airman represent an antidote to—as well as a dangerous symptom of—the crisis of heroism that emerged after World War I and thus, are inseparable from the politics of the interwar period. Although "Flying Over London" prefigures Cunningham's 1930s, politics find their way into Woolf's imaginative essay, even if between the lines: pervasive martial concerns are evoked through the lens of Zeiss glasses.

Henry, mentioned earlier, takes up the presence and symbolic weight of Zeiss glasses, both in "Flying Over London" and the historical climate of interwar Britain, explaining that they were "manufactured by a German optical company known for the extreme acuity and performance of its visualization instruments" (150). Henry's observation becomes all the more powerful when placed alongside the history of martial technology as represented by Paul Virilio, who makes chillingly explicit the link between instruments of perception and of war: "Thus, alongside the 'war machine' there has always existed an ocular [...] 'watching machine'" (3). Consequently, "weapons are tools not just of destruction but also of perception" (Virilio 6) and accordingly, the history of warfare is actually the history of drastically changing modalities of perception. Or, in other words, "*the function of the weapon is the function of the eye*" (Virilio 20 [emphasis in original]).

What does it mean then that Woolf, in her rather whimsical essay, inhabits the eye of the soldier by way of the Zeiss glasses? Woolf positions herself in the role of the airman, who in "Thoughts on Peace in an Air Raid" plays a much more menacing part. Henry suggests that Woolf's use of technical and rhetorical "scoping devices"[2] participates in her antiwar argument and pacifist stance. Aware of the historical and cultural connections between visual technology and the military, Woolf appropriates the aerial and telescopic view as her own, employing it as a vehicle not for war and destruction but instead for productive perceptual reorientation—a reorientation that is elucidated and amplified in *Three Guineas*.

A Queer Perspective

Scholars read *Three Guineas* as Woolf's most explicit and powerful statement on women, war, and patriarchy. The Outsider's Society is one way Woolf suggests in *Three Guineas* that women, who have no country and who want no country, can band together (*TG* 109). But, one might protest, the daughters of educated men are not outsiders; the daughters of Englishmen do have a country. Woolf, however, is not interested in inhabiting the conventional positions or looking through the normative lens of tradition. Instead, as in "Flying Over London" written a decade earlier, Woolf is interested in queering normative perceptions and their attendant conventions. Woolf's argument in *Three Guineas* is based on queering: following the *OED*, to puzzle, to put out of order; or, following Eve Kosofsky Sedgwick, to cross, transverse, twist (*Tendencies* xii). Such queering means seeing things through a "bird's eye view" (*TG* 22). According to Woolf, "our bird's eye view of the outside of things is not altogether encouraging" (*TG* 22); however, it is by way of the "bird's eye view"—the outsider's view—that Woolf is able to present "your world, then, the world of the professional, of public life seen from this angle" as "undoubtedly […] queer" (*TG* 18).

Anne Herrmann makes the link between Virginia Woolf, queering, and airplanes in her book, *Queering the Moderns*: "The point is not that Woolf is queer, but that she queers things in a way that is no longer familiar to us. What she looks at appears strange and is made strange, so much so that the relationship between women and airplanes becomes a queer one" (4). For Herrmann, like Woolf, the airplane provides the means for encounters with new spaces and new modalities of time; it provides the means for new perceptions, new unities, and new understandings of difference. Airplanes promise the experience of a radical elsewhere; however, that radical elsewhere is nearly always saturated with established conventions and prior formations (Herrmann 5). Similarly, as land values and air values vie for privilege, it is difficult to tell whether it is the earth that drops from beneath or the sky that descends from above. In this manner, air planes, air travel, and perhaps even the airman, offer as much positive potential as they promise martial danger, if, as Woolf proposes in *Three Guineas*, the outsider's view is the bird's eye view.

Woolf and the Essay

Another queer or puzzled perception, according to Beth Carole Rosenberg and Jeanne Dubino, is the critical reception of Woolf as an essayist and critic. Their collection revises the critical consensus that Woolf "was only an occasional essayist, one who wrote essays primarily to justify her fiction" (Rosenberg and Dubino 6). Although they note that this trend has and is shifting, they take on the residual normativity that desires to label Woolf as only one kind of writer. The "bird's eye view" that Woolf takes in *Three Guineas* that allows her to "queer the professions" (*TG* 50) suggests that labels of identity—authorial or otherwise—are complex and deserve to be complicated, not simplified. Thus, more recently, Kathryn N. Benzel and Ruth Hoberman propose that Woolf, more than being simultaneously a novelist, essayist, and critic, was actually one whose intention was to trespass these generic boundaries. Such trespassing suggests that generic transgression is fundamental to her view of how literature works (Benzel and Hoberman 1). Accordingly, Woolf's short fiction should be read as "ambitious and self-conscious attempts to challenge generic boundaries" (Benzel and Hoberman 2), boundaries that, like those between air and land, reality and imagination, "Flying Over London" challenges and trespasses.

For Melba Cuddy-Keane,[3] Woolf's essayistic generic trespassing emerges in that "[the essay's] form runs counter to, and thus encounters the interference of, the expectations established by linear expository prose" (118). As an example, she cites characterizations of Woolf's style as "'both/and' thinking" and as "'frank heterogeneity'" (118). Both these descriptions critically assess what Woolf enacts in "Flying Over London": London, as seen from above, is *neither* civilization *nor* primeval earth but *both* simultaneously, and flying is the epitome of modern existence *as well as* a reminder of mortality. It all depends upon perception. With the emphasis on positions of perception, it is not surprising that the journey—with its focus on movement rather than destination—appears as a trope for reading (Cuddy-Keane 120). "Flying Over London" illustrates such a trope, and following what Woolf identifies as her "'turn & turn about method'" (Cuddy Keane 135; *D2* 247), the journey itself is troped or twisted as the conclusion reveals that "we had not flown after all" (*CDB* 210).

With the emphasis on journeys, the reader's active engagement is encouraged. In this manner, Woolf's essays illustrate their social and political relevance: according to Cuddy-Keane, "they cultivate active minds in opposition to the normative and regulative influence of authoritarian discourse" (121). In "Flying Over London"—as in "Thoughts on Peace in an Air Raid"—the essay itself models active minds and engaged reading practices; as the airplane swoops and turns, so too does the reader change position and alternate perception, continuously oscillating between diverse interpretations within a unifying narrative. Consequently, Woolf's reader is invited to concomitantly occupy differing positions within a single text and to dismantle normative binary constructions of "right" and "wrong"—or, in the case of "Flying Over London," air and land values—that are not presented as exclusive but instead, as translatable. Thus, the importance of Woolf's "'turn & turn about method'" is located not simply in the fact that questions of perception are raised, but moreover, in the fact that such questions are raised by means of disorientation and reorientation. Accordingly, the powerful binary relation between knowing and not knowing dissolves into ironic tension (Cuddy-Keane 141). Such tension emerges when readers of "Flying Over London" realize that not only does the airplane never leave the ground but also that Woolf never experienced the "bird's eye view" she so gracefully and convincingly depicts.

Feminist Flights of Fancy

Perhaps one of the most subtle and complicated examples of Woolf's "'turn & turn about method'" appears in *Three Guineas*. The paradox underlying the imaginative flight in "Flying Over London" is critically performed in *Three Guineas* when Woolf, writing one of the many hypothetical letters that compose it, declares that "the word 'feminist' is destroyed" (*TG* 102). Articulated in the middle of what is arguably one of the most powerful and literary feminist polemics of the twentieth century, Woolf's declaration seems out of place. However, when read in the larger context of her letter-reader/letter-writer alternation, when read in the context of her characterization of the word "free" (*TG* 101), when read in the pervasive context of her deconstruction of the identity of the "daughters of educated men," the destruction of the word feminist emerges as just one more "turn about" in a Woolfian rhetorical strategy that seeks to queer, or make strange, the familiar—in this case, the relationship between women and war.

Just as Woolf reappropriates the aerial view in service of her pacifist aesthetics, so too does she deconstruct the concept of "feminist" in service of her own brand of feminism: one that excavates the idea of gender difference in order to reveal the economic, political, and thus, ideological differences that attend and facilitate it. My intention here is not to provide an interpretation of *Three Guineas*; rather, it is my intention to identify the manner in which the "bird's eye view" employed in *Three Guineas* provides a way to "turn & turn about" the concept of feminism so that it can be seen anew. When the old definitions no longer seem to apply Woolf has accomplished her goal of productive disorientation and critical reorientation.

Susan Stanford Friedman, in *Mappings: Feminism and Cultural Geographies of Encounter*, provides a Woolfian inflected revision and re-envisioning of feminism that emerges from what one might call a "bird's eye view" of the gendered and the global. Focusing on borders and boundaries as a way to explore gendered positionality in emergent transnational politics, Friedman, like Woolf, seeks to "'turn & turn about'" traditional notions of feminism in order to disorient and reorient feminism in line with "new ways of thinking that negotiate beyond the conventional boundaries between us and them, white and other, First World and Third World, men and women, oppressor and oppressed, fixity and fluidity" (Friedman 4). In this manner, Friedman employs a Woolfian aerial view: one that privileges neither the endless multiplicity of meaning nor the exclusivity and essentialism of difference.

Thus, Friedman's prophecy about feminism's future—that its future resides in "turning outward, an embrace of contradiction, dislocation and change"—echoes Woolf's own feminist investigation (Friedman 4). Perception and its attendant locationality are the keys to unlocking the potential of feminism's future. The horizon of feminism is marked by a "locational epistemology" that recognizes, necessitates, and incorporates changing historical and geographical perceptions which in turn produce diverse—although not incongruent—feminisms (Friedman 5). Just as the political and critical subtext of "Flying Over London" depends upon historical, cultural, and literary contexts, so too does feminism, in order to thrive productively in the twentieth-first century, depend upon a recognition and incorporation of rapidly expanding contexts: geopolitical, transnational, religious, and technological, in addition to historical, cultural, and literary.[4]

One is reminded of the woman's face that marks the end of Woolf's imaginative aerial experience: "it was a woman's face, young, perhaps, at any rate with a black cloak and a red hat that made the furniture—here a bowl, there a sideboard with apples on it, cease to be interesting" (*CDB* 209-10). And it is the woman's face, the culmination of Woolf's "bird's eye view," that motivates her wish "to be able to animate the heart, the legs, the arms with it […]; so as to give up this arduous game, as one flies through the air, of assembling things that lie on the surface" (*CDB* 210). Go deeper, Woolf seems to say, go deeper in order to fly higher.

Notes

1   Holly Henry, in "From Edwin Hubble's Telescope to Virginia Woolf's 'The Searchlight,'" dates the essay, citing the holograph version in the Berg Collection (150).
2   Henry's term describing narrative perspectives and strategies that imitate the view provided by the telescope, the searchlight, binoculars, and by extension, the airplane.
3   Cuddy-Keane's work on Woolf's essays appears in the Benzel/Hoberman collection and in expanded form in *Virginia Woolf, the Intellectual, and the Public Sphere*.
4   A big step toward recognizing and integrating such complex and vexed contexts is illustrated in the October 2006 edition of *PMLA*; in the "Theories and Methodologies" section, feminist scholars of varying ages, theoretical affinities, and positions within the academy speak on "Feminist Criticism Today" (1678-1741).

Works Cited

Beer, Gillian. *Virginia Woolf: The Common Ground*. Edinburgh: Edinburgh University Press, 1996.
Benzel, Kathryn N., and Ruth Hoberman, eds. *Trespassing Boundaries: Virginia Woolf's Short Fiction*. New York: Palgrave, 2004.
Cuddy-Keane, Melba. *Virginia Woolf, the Intellectual, and the Public Sphere*. Cambridge: Cambridge University Press, 2003.
Cunningham, Valentine. *British Writers of the Thirties*. Oxford: Oxford University Press, 1988.
Friedman, Susan Stanford. *Mappings: Feminism and Cultural Geographies of Encounter*. Princeton: Princeton University Press, 1998.
Henry, Holly. "From Edwin Hubble's Telescope to Virginia Woolf's 'Searchlight.'" *Virginia Woolf in the Age of Mechanical Reproduction*. Ed. Pamela Caughie. New York: Garland Publishing, 2000.
Herrmann, Anne. *Queering the Moderns: Poses/Portraits/Performances*. New York: Palgrave, 2000.
Kern, Stephen. *The Culture of Time and Space 1880-1918*. Cambridge, MA: Harvard University Press, 1983.
Rosenberg, Beth Carole, and Jeanne Dubino, eds. *Virginia Woolf and the Essay*. New York: St. Martin's, 1997.
Sedgwick, Eve Kosofsky. *Tendencies*. Durham: Duke University Press, 1993.
"Theories and Methodologies." *PMLA*. 121.5 (October 2006): 1678-1741.
Virilio, Paul. *War and Cinema: the Logistics of Perception*. Trans. Patrick Camiller. New York: Verso, 1989.
Woolf, Virginia. *Between the Acts*. New York: Harcourt, 1941.
—. "Flying Over London." *The Captain's Death Bed and Other Essays*. New York: Harcourt Brace Jovanovich, 1950.
—. *Mrs. Dalloway*. New York: Harcourt, 1925.
—. *Orlando*. New York: Harcourt, 1928.
—. *The Years*. New York: Harcourt, 1939.
—. "Thoughts on Peace in an Air Raid." *The Death of the Moth and Other Essays*. New York: Harcourt Brace and Jovanovich, 1942.
—. *Three Guineas*. New York: Harcourt, 1938.

Bloomsbury in Bloom:
Virginia Woolf and the History of British Gardens in *Orlando*

by Elisa Kay Sparks

What do Virginia Woolf and her works have to do with gardens and garden history? When she was born in 1882, Britain had already begun a revolutionary transition in gardening style—the shift from the geometrical formality of the elaborate annual bedding arrays favored by the Victorians (still popular today for municipal plantings) to the more natural "wild garden" arrangements, introduced by William Robinson and developed by Gertrude Jekyll and others into the Edwardian version of the "cottage garden" now accepted as the ahistorical archetype of all British gardening styles. This return to native plants, hardy exotics that could be naturalized, and informal plantings was part of a new democratic age of gardening in which middle class suburban gardens replaced the estates of aristocratic country homes as the paradigm of botanical bliss.

Woolf's Garden Knowledge and Acquaintances

Under the tutelage of Violet Dickinson, herself an avid reader about and maker of gardens, the young Virginia Stephen was introduced to some of these trends, traces of which appear in her earliest journals. We know, for instance, that on July 30, 1897, about two and a half months after Virginia had been set to gardening in the ashy back yard of 22 Hyde Park Gate and less than two weeks after Stella's death, she was reading Maria Theresa Earle's *Pot-Pourri from a Surrey Garden (PA* 118). Organized in part as a series of monthly meditations on gardening, cooking, flower-arranging, interior decoration, and other housekeeping rituals, spiced with occasional quotations from (mostly Romantic) poetry and a few proto-feminist comments on gender education, Earle's chatty semi-memoir begins by citing the work of William Robinson as one of her chief inspirations (Earle 17). Although Earle's book is a forerunner to the work of Jekyll in its abhorrence of carpet bedding, its championing of native plants such as old roses, and its careful attention to the composition of color in the garden, it is not as modern in its attitude towards gender roles. Open-minded enough in 1895 to think that "Marriage should not be a woman's only profession," Earle still believed "it should be her best and highest hope" (331) and argued against formal schooling for most upper class girls because she feared it would "destroy...her adaptability for a woman's highest vocation...marriage and motherhood" (328). Perhaps it is this advice on raising daughters that caused Virginia to object to Violet's staying with Mrs. Earle in March 1904, when she claimed that "I never read such positive nonsense as her books are" (*L1* 133). And it is certainly plausible to think that Earle's advice on not over-educating girls is one of the targets of Virginia's sarcasm in her 1907 fantasy biography of her friend Violet, *Friendships Gallery*, in which she notes that parents and guardians must control exactly the "number of drops" of education which "benefit the system of a maiden" because "a teaspoonful in excess has been known to ruin the constitution for life" (*Friendships Gallery* 278).

As Virginia's friendship with Violet deepened in the years following Stella's death (it was at its height according to Quentin Bell from 1902-1907 [Bell I, 84]), there is evidence that Virginia had at least heard of the leading fashionable gardeners. In April 1903 the Stephen family stayed at Blatchfield in Chilworth, Surrey. Sonya Rudicoff points out that the house was near several Jekyll gardens (131); a brief look at a map shows it was only about four miles from Munstead Wood, the home and garden Jekyll had begun developing in 1883, the year after Virginia's birth. Virginia spent the summer of 1904—the next year—with Violet in her Arts and Crafts-style house and garden at Burnham Wood in Hertfordshire north of London, where she probably heard much about Jeykll and her predecessor and friend, William Robinson. On January 28, 1905, Virginia notes in her diary that she actually met Mr. Robinson—"the gardener and designer of grates, an interesting man"—while visiting Violet's house in London (*PA* 228), and on February 1, she and Violet rendezvoused at Robinson's shop in Lincolns Inn Fields to look at iron grates, one of which she intended to buy (*PA* 231).

Both Jeykll and Robinson owed a good deal of inspiration to the Arts and Crafts movement, especially to William Morris's love of old fashioned flowers and kitchen gardens, and the predominance of William Morris in Virginia's reading list of 1905—she read Mackail's biography as well as some of Morris's early works (*PA* 274)—flowered a year later in her attempt to imagine the life of a woman in medieval times: "The Journal of Mistress Joan Martyn" set in 1480 (*CSF* 33-62). By 1907, Virginia was familiar enough with gardening personalities to tease Violet about her preoccupation with her "Jeyklls, [her] new puppies, and [her]budding trees" (*L1* 291), and one wonders if her claim at the end of the sentence that she [Virginia] has "melted into an indistinguishable mass: pearl grey and vaporous," is a clever reference to Jeykll's habit of framing the far ends of her flower borders in grey foliage, to accentuate the intensity of the red and yellow colors in the center (see "The Main Hardy Flower Border" in Jeykll's *Colour Schemes for the Flower Garden,* p. 54).

Violet was not the only source of information about Gertrude Jekyll available to Woolf. Although the garden designer was almost 40 years older than the author (Gertrude Jekyll lived 1843-1932), they moved in contiguous circles. At the age of seventeen (in 1861) Gertrude began a two-year course of study at the School of Art in South Kensington, located in the Stephen neighborhood on the present site of the V&A (Brown, *Golden Afternoon* 21), and by the age of 30 had become a master of a number of decorative arts, especially silverwork and wood-inlaying (Francis Jekyll, qtd. by Brown, *Golden Afternoon* 23). Edward Burne-Jones became one of her clients, and she became good friends with the Blumenthals, living for a while at their London home, 43 Hyde Park Gate, next door to Leslie Stephen's birthplace and just down the block from 22 Hyde Park Gate. And Jekyll continued to orbit in and out of Woolf's adult life. In 1910 Roger Fry hired her to design the garden for Durbins, (see Spaulding 110; listed as a commission for 1910 in Brown, *Golden Afternoon,* 189). In the summer of 1923, Dame Ethyl Smythe was one of a trio of musicians invited to perform for Jekyll at Munstead Wood (Festing 238). And in 1933, Logan Pearsall Smith wrote an essay about his long friendship with Jekyll, dating back to his college years at Oxford in the 1890s, collected in his *Reperusals and Recollections.*

Garden History in *Orlando*

All of these gardening connections did NOT, however, necessarily mean that Virginia Woolf had more than a superficial awareness of contemporary garden fashion. Woolf's knowledge of plants and garden history is at best sketchy and is often conflated with her much more detailed knowledge of the history of English prose style so that her description of the gardens of a particular period are often metaphorical expressions of her sense of the literary spirit of the age. This is particularly true of the panorama of history offered in *Orlando*, her extended biographical fantasy about the life and lineage of one of Britain's greatest gardeners, Vita Sackville-West. In terms of garden history *Orlando* is rife with the kinds of careless but witty anachronism that pervades other aspects of the novel, the chronological extension of Orlando's character over some 350 years of history making for a few temporally confused but symbolically apt vegetable metaphors.

In *Orlando* as in many of Woolf's works including *To the Lighthouse*, individual characters are sometimes identified with particular plants (see Zeiss 100), and here Woolf shows herself to be, like her husband, more of a plantsman than a designer, more interested in individual varieties than overall effects. For example, when Orlando first meets Queen Elizabeth, who according to the internal chronology of Orlando visited Knole in 1573, he wears shoes with "rosettes on them as big as double dahlias" (*O* 21).[1] However, as Ray Desmond points out in his history of Kew Gardens, dahlias only reached Europe two centuries later, in 1798, when they were first sent from Mexico to the Botanic Garden in Madrid (16). One would, of course, not expect Woolf to know such details of plant provenance, except for the fact, also noted by Desmond, that dahlias were first grown in England at Holland House (n. to plate 16). Also, dahlias were among her husband Leonard's favorite flowers, and as an obsessive plantsman, he was likely to have known their heritage.

Not quite so anachronistic is Orlando's comparison of Sasha to a pineapple. He meets her sometime around 1603/4—James I was crowned in July of 1603; *Othello* was first performed in 1604—but, as Jane Brown notes, pineapples were not grown in Europe until the 1650s, so the date of the actual Great Frost (1683, 80 years later than in *Orlando*) might be more horticulturally accurate (Brown, *Pursuit of Pleasure* 243). At any rate, the exotic fruit is an adequate emblem of Sasha's rarity and preciousness; a new book on the history of pineapple cultivation estimates that during the 1700s the cost to produce one pineapple was about £5000 in today's money (Beauman 85).

An interesting number of the plants cited in *Orlando* are of Greek, Persian, or Middle Eastern origin, perhaps in recognition of Vita's widespread travels in the Middle East. The novel begins with an apparent dichotomy between the foreign flowers—such as the Greek asphodel, seen by Orlando's paternal ancestors who were traveling soldiers—and the native flowers in his mother's garden (*O*13). Classically associated with the flower fields of Hades (Ward 50), in *Orlando* the asphodel is also associated with the imaginative enchantment of literature. It is the pollen of the asphodel which fatally "substitutes[s] a phantom for reality," so that Orlando completely ignores his house and heritage to lose himself in reading (74). Near the end of the book, an exotic-looking purple flower native to Britain, *Fritillaria melagris* (Snake's head) seems to take on a similar inspirational role when the Lady Orlando begins to write poetry and produces a passage from Vita's poem *The Land* about fritillaries: "the snaky flower / Scarfed in dark purple" (*O* 265). Its more spectacular cousin *Fritillaria imperial* is also known as "Persian lily" (Heilmeyer 40).[2]

Another English complement to the exotic asphodel seems to be the rose, the flower mentioned most frequently in *Orlando*. Like the asphodel, it is associated with death. There are numerous evocations of roses à la Herrick as emblems of the evanescence of beauty; for instance, life is said to be "briefer than the fall of a rose leaf to the ground" (*O* 99). But along with the elkhound, the rose is also an emblem of the stability of life at Knole: "Two things alone remained to him in which he now put any trust; dogs and nature; an elkhound and a rose bush" (*O* 97).

One other main character is identified through flower associations—Lady Orlando's husband, Marmaduke Bonthrop Shelmerdine. As she walks across Hyde Park, Orlando's vision of her husband's possible death is associated with the view of a fine bed of red, blue, and purple hyacinths, which so remind her of him that she calls him "my hyacinth, husband I mean" (*O* 287). The autumn crocus, Colchicum, which she also associates with her husband's name Shelmerdine, is similarly purple, but its purported origin on the shores of the Black Sea in Russia may be a hidden link between Shelmerdin and Sasha (*O* 260; 309).[3]

While Woolf's knowledge of plant history and provenance can be surprisingly accurate, her account of garden design in *Orlando* is whimsical and fairly hazy. Elizabeth Pomeroy points out that Woolf typically associates Elizabeth prose and gardens with the expansive fertility of Shakespeare's imagination: "language then in its green time" (Pomeroy 500). But Orlando's "natural" love of "solitary places, vast views" (*O* 18) seems more characteristic of eighteenth century gardening's evocation of the natural and the picturesque than the Elizabethan park and garden, typically more geometrical in their organization. In fact, in creating the oak tree mount from which Orlando views the land, Woolf was violating even the known chronology of her model, Knole, itself. In the chapter on The Garden and The Park in her history of *Knole and the Sackvilles*, Vita notes that on November 11, 1723, three shillings and ten pence was spent on "cutting and leveling a new walk in ye Wilderness and making ye mount round ye Oak tree" so in actual fact, Orlando's mount was created about 200 years later than he initially climbed it (Sackville-West 22-3).

Orlando misses the rest of the 17th century in England, as he is carrying out his Ambassadorial duties in Constantinople and she is adventuring with the Turkish gypsies. Woolf's horticultural comments on the 18th century are confined mostly to gentle satire of Addison, Pope, and Swift, who "liked arbours...collected little bits of coloured glass, [and]...adored grottos" (*O* 208). And she seems to know enough about Pope's horticultural preferences to sit down and meditate under a willow tree during the century of his prominence (*O* 215).

The full force of Woolf's botanical critique, however, is visited upon the excesses of the Victorian age. Her descriptions of horticultural fashion in the nineteenth century seem rather off the historical mark, subordinated to her desire to dramatize the dullness, dampness, lack of form, and over-expansive fertility of her predecessors, literary and political style. The "great cloud" which hangs over the century, dulling the colors of gardens, replacing the "more positive landscapes of the eighteenth century" with "purples, oranges and reds of a dull sort" seems an inaccurate account of the Victorian penchant for brightly colored carpet bedding, but could be a plausible comment on Jekyll's habit towards the end of the century of mixing greys in with complimentary colors (*O* 227). Woolf emphasizes the repressive, disorganized profusion of Victorian plant growth: houses are "smothered in greenery. No garden, however formal its original design, lacked a shrubbery, a wilderness, a maze" (*O* 229). Here she seems to be mixing up features like mazes that are typical of much earlier gardens with the woodland gardens popularized at the end of the century by Robinson and Jeykll, extending the combined sexual repression and license of the Victorian household to a description of its plantings.

But of course it is her evocation of the tumescence of Victorian Britain's vegetable empire that most hilariously caricatures the many-volumed tomes of Victorian and Georgian fiction:

> Wherever he looked, vegetation was rampant. Cucumbers 'came scrolloping across the grass to his feet'. Giant cauliflowers towered deck above deck till they rivalled, to his disordered imagination, the elm trees themselves. (*O* 230)

Here Woolf collapses, or rather inflates, the expansion of the British Empire and the increased fertility of women, into the profusion of literature: "sentences swelled, adjectives multiplied, lyrics became epics" (*O* 229).

In the end, in the present moment, in fact, Orlando abjures all the magic of period garden styles and returns to the generic tradition of timeless gardens. She buys flowering trees (*O* 312), taking them back to the courtyard where "the same flowering trees that let their leaves drop for so many hundred years are shedding their leaves again" (*O* 315). Her final vision on the oak tree mound is one which annihilates all the differences she's made into a green and purple continuity of country and city, past and present; "the ferny path up the hill along which she strides" becomes "not entirely a path but partly the Serpentine" in London; the white hawthorne bushes turn into the powdered hair and laces of "ladies and gentlemen sitting with card cases and gold-mounted canes" (*O* 323). As she answers "the old crooning song of the woods…and the fields…, and the gardens blowing irises and fritiallaries" (*O* 325) she welcomes the shade of the dead queen, declaring "The house is at your service, Ma'am…Nothing has been changed" (*O* 328).

Notes

1 This is the date given by Maria DiBattista in her annotations to the new edition of *Orlando* (258). But according to the history provided by Sackville-West, because Knole was "both let and sub-let," it was not until 1603 that the first of the Sackvilles was able to take possession and move in (39). No visit from Queen Elizabeth to Knole is recorded in Vita's history. Queen Elizabeth did visit Sissinghurst in 1573, but Vita did not purchase it until 1930, two years after the publication of *Orlando* (Nicolson 9, 7).
2 Vita writes about both species in her later work, *Some Flowers*. She describes *melagris* as a "sinister little flower" (36) and confirms the identification of its larger cousin with Persia by recounting a sighting of it on its native ground on one of her trips (30).
3 Woolf may have learned about this Russian association from reading Horace or Erasmus Darwin, among others (Ward 91). Colchicum were also among Leonard's favorite flowers; according to his garden account book, he bought 100 of them the year after *Orlando* was published.

Works Cited

Bell, Quentin. *Virginia Woolf: A Biography*. New York: Harcourt Brace Jovanovich, 1972.
Beauman, Francesca. *Pineapple: The King of Fruits*. London: Chatto & Windus, 2005.
Brown, Jane. *Gardens of a Golden Afternoon: The Story of a Partnership: Edward Lutyens and Gertrude Jekyll*. New

York City: Viking/Penguin, 1985.
—. *The Pursuit of Paradise: A Social History of Gardens and Gardening*. London: Harper Collins, 1999.
Clark, Timothy. "Mrs. C. W. Earle (1836-1925), a Reappraisal of Her Work." *Garden History* 8.2 (Summer, 1980): 75-83.
Desmond, Ray. *Kew: The History of the Royal Botanic Gardens*. London: The Harvill Press with the Royal Botanic Gardens, Kew, 1995.
Earle, Mrs. C.W. *Pot-Pourri from a Surrey Garden*. 1895; rpt. and enl. London: Thomas Nelson & Sons, n.d.
Festing, Sally. *Gertrude Jekyll*. New York City: Viking/Penguin, 1999.
Heilmeyer, Marina. *The Language of Flowers: Symbols and Myths*. London: Preste Verlag, 2001.
Jekyll, Gertrude. *Colour Schemes for the Flower Garden*. 1908. Intro and rev. Graham Stuart Thomas. Salem, NH: The Ayer Company, 1983.
Jennings, Anne. *Victorian Gardens*. London: English Heritage [Museum of Garden History], 2005.
Nicolson, Nigel. *Sissinghurst Castle Garden*. The National Trust, 1994.
Pomeroy, Elizabeth W. "Garden and Wilderness: Virginia Woolf Reads the Elizabethans." *Modern Fiction Studies* 24 (1978-79): 497-508.
Rudikoff, Sonya. *Ancestral Houses: Virginia Woolf and the Aristocracy*. Palo Alto: The Society for the Promotion of Science and Scholarship, 1999.
Sackville-West, V. *Knole and the Sackvilles*. 1922. London: Lindsay, Drummond, 1948.
—. *Some Flowers*. 1937. New York: Harry N. Abrams, 1993.
Smith, Logan Pearsall. *Reperusals and Recollections*. London: Constable & Co., 1936. [1933. "Gertrude Jekyll." 49-66]
Spalding, Frances. *Roger Fry: Art and Life*. 1980. Black Dog Books, 1999.
Ward, Boby J. *A Contemplation Upon Flowers: Garden Plants in Myth and Literature*. Portland: Timber Press, 1999.
Woolf, Leonard. *Garden Diary* and *Account Books*. University of Sussex Library, Special Collections, Leonard Woolf Papers. Box II, item 3i.
Woolf, Virginia. *The Complete Shorter Fiction of Virginia Woolf*. Ed. Susan Dick. New York: Harcourt, 1985.
—. "Friendship's Gallery." 1907. Ed. Ellen Hawkes. *Twentieth Century Literature* 25 (1979): 270-302.
—. *The Letters of Virginia Woolf*. Vol. 1. 1915-1919. Ed. Nigel Nicolson and Joanne Trautmann. New York: Harcourt, 1977.
—. *Orlando; A Biography*. 1928. New York: Harcourt, 1956.
—. *Orlando: A Biography*. Ed. Mark Hussey. Introduction and annotations by Maria DiBattista. New York: Harcourt, 2006.
—. *A Passionate Apprentice: The Early Journals 1897-1909*. Ed. Mitchell A. Leaska. New York: Harcourt, 1990.
Zeiss, McKenzie L. "The Political Legacy of the Garden: (Anti)Pastoral Images and National Identity in Virginia Woolf and Vita Sackville-West." *Virginia Woolf in the Real World: Selected Papers from the Thirteenth International Conference on Virginia Woolf*. Ed. Karen V. Kukil. Clemson: Clemson University Digital Press, 2005. 100-04.

TEXTUAL ARCHAEOLOGY AND THE DEATH OF THE WRITER

by Suzanne Bellamy

This essay presents new critical and historical material about the 180,000 word MA thesis on Virginia Woolf that was completed at the University of Sydney, Australia, in 1942 by the young scholar Nuri Mass (1918-1993). Having presented a broad field survey of the thesis recovery, context, structure and themes (Bellamy 2007), now we approach a moment of dramatic shift, and focus upon the point where international news of Virginia Woolf's death in early 1941 impacts upon Mass's almost completed colonial study. Recently, Mass's actual collection of Woolf first edition texts became available to me through the Horwitz family, adding new dimensions to the possibilities for research. Some of these treasures have additional news clippings, reviews and other markings of interest. In particular this essay focuses on Mass's own signed edition of *Between the Acts*, acquired by her with luck just in time to add its analysis to her thesis, thus making her work a complete study of Woolf's major novels, possibly the first in the world, and attracting the publishing interest of Leonard Woolf.

The experimental concept of "textual archaeology" continues to be a useful one in finding ways to interrogate the thesis as an historical artefact, to which I am now adding Mass's collection of working texts, examples of material culture. I define the overall study as a site where no prior biographical material or related contextual work was available to influence the scholar other than the texts. Artefacts like words shift their meanings from one time to another, becoming lost or hidden, then re-emerging as examples of a reading based on the full body of work, textual responses with no supporting biographical, diary or other critical material. This literary/historical example is remote by distance from the centre of critical discourse of the time, a colonial hybrid Oxbridge-type campus during wartime.

The sudden and unexpected news of Woolf's drowning (see *Sydney Morning Herald* News Report) came upon Nuri Mass at a creatively charged time, in the last stages of her thesis writing. She knew almost nothing about her subject's real life, except this, death by drowning. The news impacted the English Department and the local literary scene, in a country by now at war, and Mass's supervisor R.G. Howarth published an obituary/essay.

"Fear Death By Water!" It is strange to read that the author of *The Voyage Out, To The Lighthouse* and *The Waves* is presumed drowned in the River Ouse—and pitiful.

Yet, like James Joyce, whom she so closely followed to death, Virginia Woolf had probably done all the work she was endowed to do, for there has been no new novel from her hand since 1937, when she published *The Years*, which may be said to bring her methods to a climax. (Howarth, "A Prose Poet")

The death news here creates a retro-reading, and Woolf moves from being a living writer to a completed body of work and life, filled with ironies of interpretation. The historical roots of the problematic teaching of Virginia Woolf's work beyond the United Kingdom, and beyond her death, are here encapsulated. Unknown to Howarth at that point, a new posthumous Woolf novel was about to appear, and so the death acquired new meanings in the process of its arrival. In a classic "town and gown" scenario, Nuri Mass had a non-academic mentor, W.G. Cousins, a trade publisher/editor for the pioneering Australian book firm of Angus and Robertson. Their letters began when she was only 19, sending him her first novel manuscript, and their correspondence lasted from 1937 to 1955. She talked about ideas, writing and problems about her thesis, with delightful precocity, all of which was generously encouraged by Cousins. He then played a major role in the next step in the story of the thesis by sending her news of the U.S. and U.K. publication dates of *Between the Acts*, and a crucial U.S. review essay by Hudson Strode which strengthened her independent reading of the last novel. On 8 November 1941, Cousins wrote, "Enclosed announcement and review of a new V.W. novel—Copies will not reach us until the end of Dec." (See Cousins/Mass Letters).

> I am working for my thesis, you know, and that takes a lot of time, as there are certain books in the Library (Fisher) which must be read for it and yet which are in fair demand among the lecturers and other students. I have to read them just whenever I can get them, and I'm writing another novel. (Mass to Cousins, 10 July 1940, letter 361)

> Re the book itself (*Between the Acts*), I was extremely fortunate. My guiding fairy conducted me whirling into A&R's about 6 weeks ago, just in time to purchase the last copy in stock, and ever since I've been simply marvelling at my good fortune, for the value of the thesis would, I feel, have been considerably impaired by a lack of first-hand acquaintance with this last, extremely important book—then, having read it and written an 11,000 word long analysis of it, there remained one thing concerning it that I desired more than all others: that I might be able to know someone else's opinion of it. I devoured the article you sent. Its [sic] been a splendid moral support for the book itself contained a number of complexities of which I was most anxious that my interpretations should be entirely sound. Thanks to you and the reviewer, Prof Strode, my mind is now completely at ease. The thesis is progressing well, though its [sic] really an enormous work—several times larger than anything of its kind I've ever attempted before." (Mass to Cousins, 10 Nov. 1941, letter 369)

Mass's own signed copy of *Between the Acts* now becomes an artefact, with its pasted clippings. When combined with the W.G. Cousins' correspondence, it confirms and corroborates the time sequences for the completion of the thesis and its shifting significance by framing for us the news of the death of Woolf, the gap in time before the awareness of the existence of *Between the Acts*, the acquiring of the U.K. edition, the Strode review/ obituary, the earlier Howarth obituary, and the add for the U.S. Harcourt edition. The newsclippings are glued into the endpapers of Nuri Mass's signed copy, which can be described as a First Edition of *Between the Acts*, stamped "Colonial Cloth," first published 1941, The Hogarth Press London, distributed in Canada by their exclusive agent The

Macmillan Company Toronto, original jacket, intact, designed by Vanessa Bell. An advertising galley for *Between the Acts,* billed as "The new novel by Virginia Woolf" with review comments by Hudson Strode, Mary Ross and David Cecil, includes comments by Mary Ross (*New York Herald Tribune Books*): "*Between the Acts* is a beautiful curtain, rung down too soon on one of the most distinguished literary careers of our times."

Hudson Strode's essay acts as a combined obituary and a review of the Harcourt Brace edition of *Between the Acts*. While Nuri Mass read this American view, she did not have access to the Harcourt edition but the original Hogarth edition via Canada, as part of the restrictive British publishing agreements with the former colonies. Strode's essay is written a month before the events of Pearl Harbour and the entry of the U.S.A. into the Second World War. An academic from the University of Alabama, a novelist and memoirist, Strode had travelled in Europe, met Stein and other modernist writers, and taught literature at the University of Alabama. A book of Memoirs, *The Eleventh House*, published in 1975, explores his teaching ideas, travels and life among writers and artists, and he quotes from a letter to him from Virginia Woolf (Strode 226). His review/obituary goes straight to the death, imagines the scene, and asks about its reasons. The death is the central big news and lens, and clearly remained so, from this time on.

> When Virginia Woolf quietly wrote a farewell note to her husband, took her stick—so fixed is habit—and went on her favorite walk across the summery meadows down to the Ouse to slip under the water, it was a sad hour for English letters. Why did she do it? No one knows precisely. It may well have been a combination of four factors—sorrow over the war with its breeding hatreds; the demolishment of her Bloomsbury apartment ("They are destroying all the beautiful things!" she cried); the revising of her book, which always caused her pain; and the fear of "an old madness" coming over her. (Strode, "The Genius")

Mass's reading of the new novel is initially a struggle, as she tells Cousins (16 Nov. 1941, letter 373): "I have a serious bone to pick with most critics of modern literature. To write about *Between the Acts* and omit any consideration of its unpalatable bitterness of tone and inartistic predominance of personal grievances seems a curiously one-sided method of approach."

She finished her thesis with the additional work on the new novel, and finally submitted it in February 1942, hearing of her results in April 1942. The degree of MA (the PhD degree not being statuted at the University of Sydney until 1947) was conferred at the ceremony "Conferring of Degrees" on Saturday 6 June 1942, to Nuri Heather Celeste Mass, English - Class 1 and University Medal (Howarth, Letters).

In a letter from R.G. Howarth, dated April 1942, he writes :

> Dear Miss Mass,
> Professor Waldock has told you of the success of your thesis[...]. It was a remarkable piece of work, you completely understood Virginia Woolf, and you are the first to accomplish that. Will you address the Australian English Association on Virginia Woolf? [...] You might also consider publication of part of your work in *Southerly*.

After the thesis was finished, Mass's life was about earning money, correspondence with Leonard Woolf (Woolf, Letters), preparing a lecture and essays for journals. The offer to her of a tutorship was not taken up and she went into the world of trade publishing, after some tough decision-making (Mass, *Unpublished Autobiographical Notes* 120).

> Since practically the very day of the completion of my MA thesis, I have been working in the publishing department of Angus and Robertson, where I am Junior Editor, and busy revising my book *The Little Grammar People*. My after-business time of late has been about the preparation of an hour's address on [...] Virginia Woolf's last novel, for the Australian English Association. (Mass to Iredale, 3 July 1942)

A number of articles appeared over the course of 1942 by both Mass and Howarth, debating the merits and status of Woolf's legacy and the "last novel." Howarth maintained an attitude of critical comparison between Woolf and Joyce (Howarth, "Dayspring"), about hope and hopelessness, and the restorative role of the modern novel in the post-war world (WWI) to restore beauty and consequence, but he never embraced *Between the Acts* as a work of radical departure in relation to a new war, unlike Mass, who came to that view.

A Folder of Drafts, some hand-written, among the Mass Papers are interesting additions to her thought processes as she attempts to respond to increased interest in Woolf's work and newsworthy death (Drafts, ML 289/94 Box 10B). Initial hope that Leonard Woolf might be able to publish her thesis (Woolf, Letters) dissolved in the realisation she could not face revising it and reducing the length. It is still something of a puzzle to me that this became such a final loss, and awaits more research.

In Notes called "Virginia Woolf: A Writer and a Woman" (July 1942), Mass wrote:

> Mrs Woolf has done more valuable and permanent work than has even James Joyce or D.H. Lawrence, since she has never (as have these other two) dissected the human heart so clumsily and brutally that it has ceased to beat [...]. She was a woman. And she was a feminist in her own right [...]. She asserted the importance and necessity of woman's intellectual freedom. Literature she said had been man-made. The time had come for a new society and a new literature.
>
> The very nature of the sentence will probably undergo a change [...]. She was a women's woman.

In three hand-written pages, she continues this theme: "Her influence has done much towards re-establishing in literature some measure of the balance, sanity, and kindliness of spirit largely ejected from it by contemporaries such as Joyce, Eliot, Aldous Huxley and D.H. Lawrence" (Mass, "Virginia Woolf").

In draft notes for an article on Virginia Woolf's philosophy, Mass assumes the suicide was related to some feeling of failure in the life philosophy and work ideas, and then defends that notion. Like other writers, she moves into an analysis of the death in the context of the life about which she knows nothing really, but has nonetheless been deeply affected.

> The pursuit of truth, she maintains with an unflagging zeal that is often actually painful. And we can follow the course of this search throughout her novels, from Rachel's perplexed enquiry in her first, "What's the truth of it all?"—to the far more tormented (because more hopeless) note struck in her last, "From cow after cow came the same bellow. The whole world is filled with dumb yearning." Yes, it was the search for truth that inspired Mrs Woolf's highest achievements in life—and it was her failure to find it that killed her in the end. Her books are books of silence [...] they deal with those subconscious urges and instincts which defy articulate expression, a pattern of complete spiritual unity. But this unity is also technical. The main principle on which the novels are constructed is pattern rather than plot [...]. So according to the standards of conventional fiction, nothing ever actually "happens" in V.W. She is too honest, too conscientious, to allow for that. Life is not a sharply defined black and white, but a fluctuating, indeterminate grey; moreover, its essence is fluidity and constant renewal, [...] the whole of time and space may be contained within one moment [...]. The same searching passion is seen in her technique. Craving the licences of poetry minus its conventional limitations, she craved also the supreme abstraction of music, the picturesqueness of painting—and the logicality of prose. The result is something entirely new in English prose fiction. (Mass, "Virginia Woolf's Philosophy")

Mass's reading of *Between the Acts*, both in her thesis and in her article in *Southerly* (1942), is complex and layered. Her critique has gone through a change, though concern lingers about the novel's bitter language. Clearly affected by an over-reading of the life ending, absorbing critical assessment from Strode, biographical and other mental health speculation about Woolf, her reading is still robust, innovative and generous.

> *Between the Acts*, Virginia Woolf's last novel, published posthumously in July 1941, is a book not of fulfilment but of preparation, ending with "The curtain rose. They spoke." It is one of the most sorrowful books ever to come from Virginia Woolf, fraught with an agonising sense of incompleteness and frustration. (Mass, *Virginia Woolf the Novelist* 483)

Mass considers the question of the suitability of the decision to publish the novel at all, knowing Virginia Woolf had not made final revisions. Leonard Woolf stated in a preliminary note that it was improbable that Virginia would have made "any large or material alterations to it," but, as the book itself stands, Mass feels "it is surely one of the most remarkable if disappointing of all her works" (*Virginia Woolf the Novelist* 483).

For the first time in her thesis Mass is engaging in discussion of a text in the larger context of the writer's life story, the critical shift moment, the death of the author, the decision to posthumously publish an unfinished work, and her husband's role in deciding that matter. There is recently a new focus on whether the book should have been published at all, the effect on Woolf's legacy, the role of John Lehmann in wanting a successful book as part of his role with the Hogarth Press, the evidence of changes made (Hussey), and how it should now be regarded within the whole oeuvre (as a late draft). Mass's critique stands well within that debate.

While considering the text was indeed not ready to publish, Mass still grasps its newness. However, she curiously does not seem to see the humour which is now more clearly present to readers, perhaps as the text has itself morphed to a new period and audience. Nevertheless she responds to a wholly new art coming into play, a new form emerging in this last novel, being the "last" only because of the death of the writer but by no means reflecting a writer who has stopped developing.

Between the Acts as a posthumous work is charged with these paradoxes, and what might have come, had Woolf survived. Mass finds that "the general tone is one of extreme complexity" (*Virginia Woolf the Novelist* 488), "the hopelessness of self-expression. Practically every character is striving for something out of reach" (491). "The snake was unable to swallow; the toad was unable to die" (492).

Mass also feels that an abiding sense of beauty remains, in the obscure depths of the lily-pond, the almost Arcadian nature of the open-air setting. "Nebulous uncertainty lies brooding over human relationships and over the nature of man's position in the universe" (*Virginia Woolf the Novelist* 493). "A June day in 1939, the recent coronation, scraps of gossip about the Duke of Windsor and bodings of war. We have, as it were, arrived safely in the present moment. And Mrs Swithin replies: "The Victorians, I don't believe that there ever were such people. Only you and me and William dressed differently" (496).

"There is a new prose rhythm, thoughts flow in rhythmic streams .. For Isa, "The play keeps running in my head"' (502) Indeed the play keeps running in everybody's head. "Was it an old play? Was it a new play?" (502).

"There is a waltz, and the prose following it could be divided off into perfect ¾ time [...]" (504), "and later when there is a change to a foxtrot, it is thus that the prose responds: 'So abrupt. And corrupt,' and of course the rhymes beat out the stresses with marvellous effect" (504). Mass here is aware of new experimental versification, repetition, sounds and echoes, as well as subject matter. "Miss La Trobe in the end glimpses another pageant [...] the curtain would rise" (514).

The face of war in 1942 in Australia, air-raid shelters on campus, Japanese bombing of Darwin, the Pacific war, was now impacting all perception.

> This then is Mrs Woolf's vision just as it is Miss La Trobe's. But life is infinitely complex, and in its material manifestations is perpetuated only with and through the bitterest of conflicts and contradictions[...]. perpetual combat [...] enmity and love. First they must fight [...] there is at once the greatest possibility of union and the greatest danger of disruption. The music strives to keep the scattering audience together [...]. During that one long interim [...] all is kept still and restrained [...] but then repressed powers will soar upward, volcanoes will erupt [...]. Ultimately the curtain will rise, and of what will the Act consist? What will the first words be?" (Thesis 515)

Life choices were made in that extended moment of war. Nuri Mass made hers, she put her thesis in a box and moved on. "Why that choice?" she asked later, "an inverted sort of cowardice. Leaving the University was one of the most significant departures in my life, a whole other world, learning about the commerce of books" (Mass, *Unpublished*

Autobiographical Notes 107).

> I remember the protracted laser-like mental concentration in one direction excluding all other interests, during those last six months of the thesis, followed by an extreme reaction, as often happens in Nature and in history. I remember the completeness of my identification with Virginia Woolf, followed by an exorcism—using perhaps too strong a word, but a graphic one. And together with this, I remember the feeling that never, as long as I lived, would I be able to look at that thesis again, let alone rework it." (*Unpublished Autobiographical Notes* 120)

Gillian Beer, in a resonant lecture at Newnham College in June 2003 entitled *Virginia Woolf Abroad* (recollection based on my own hand-written notes), identified the trajectory of Virginia Woolf's influence abroad as multidirectional, transformed by the lens of the cultures and generations over time and space. In this remote Australian wartime example we see how the complex forces of post-colonialism, time lag, publishing empires, teaching and campus circumstances, luck, loss of resources as a result of war, intervention and mentoring, allow us to glean interesting information from a lost moment in Woolf scholarship. In applying archaeological tropes, we re-visit moments of lost textual consciousness, like messages in a bottle. Further work on the Mass thesis will follow more specifically the context of Australian modernism and comparative texts, while an annotated edited version of the thesis is prepared for publication.

Copyright Permission

I have been granted exclusive rights for publication from the copyright holders, the Horwitz family, to the Nuri Mass papers, to prepare, edit and research the MA thesis on Virginia Woolf, and related unpublished autobiographical materials deposited in the Mitchell Library, Sydney, Australia.

Works Cited

Bellamy, Suzanne. "Textual Archaeology: An Australian Study of Virginia Woolf in 1942." *Woolfian Boundaries: Selected Papers from the 16th Annual International Conference on Virginia Woolf.* Ed. Anna Burrells, Steve Ellis, Deborah Parsons and Kathryn Simpson. Clemson: Clemson University Digital Press, 2007. 1-7.
Cousins, W.G. Letters To/From Nuri Mass. 1937-1955. Angus and Robertson Publishers, Sydney. Folder ML MSS 3269/459.
Howarth, R.G. "A Prose Poet. Virginia Woolf." *Sydney Morning Herald* 10 Apr. 1941.
—. Letters to Nuri Mass from R.G.Howarth. 4 Apr. 1942, 1st July 1942. Nuri Mass Papers ML 289/94. Box 1.
—. "Dayspring of Virginia Woolf." *Southerly* (The Magazine of the English Association) Apr. 1942.
—. *Union Recorder* 9 July 1942: 102. Rev. of *Between the Acts*, report of Nuri Mass Lecture by R.G.Howarth, Fisher Library Archives of The University of Sydney.
Hussey, Mark. "Should *Between the Acts* Have Been Published?" Unpublished Conference Paper. 17th Annual International Conference on Virginia Woolf. Miami University, June 2007.
Iredale, Tom. Letters File. Letters from Nuri Mass. 1942-46, 1955. ML MSS 7546.
Mass, Nuri. Material deposited in the Nuri Mass Papers, Mitchell Library, Sydney. 10 boxes ML 289/94.
—. *Virginia Woolf the Novelist.* MA Thesis, University of Sydney. University Medal 1942. Archives of Nuri Mass, Mitchell Library, Sydney.
—. *Unpublished Autobiographical Notes* (1988-92), bound as "Passing Through." Box 2B ML 289/94.
—. "Virginia Woolf : *Between the Acts.*" *Southerly.* Sept. 1942: 34-35.
—. "Virginia Woolf's Last Novel." *Union Recorder.* University of Sydney Union, 9 July 1942: 101-102.
—. "Virginia Woolf: A Writer and a Woman." Typed draft, n.d., approx. July 1942. Box 10B, ML 289/94.

—. Draft for obituary and article, 3 hand-written pages, Draft, Box 10B ML 289/94.
—. "Virginia Woolf's Philosophy," typed sheets, 6 pages, draft for article. Box 10B ML 289/94.
News Report. AAP source quoting *The Times* London UK. *Sydney Morning Herald* 3 Apr. 1941.
Strode, Hudson. "The Genius of Virginia Woolf. In Her Last Book the English Novelist Again Says the Unsayable." *The New York Times Book Review* 46.40 5 Oct. 1941. Front Page.
—. *The Eleventh House. Memoirs.* New York: Harcourt Brace Jovanovich, 1975.
Waldock, C.J. Letter/Reference for Nuri Mass. 17 Jan. 1946. Nuri Mass Papers ML 289/94 Box 1.
Woolf, Leonard. Two Letters from Leonard Woolf to Nuri Mass. 8 Aug. 1941, 3 July 1942. Nuri Mass Papers ML 289/94 Box 1.
Woolf, Virginia. *Between the Acts.* Ex-Libris, Nuri Mass, signed copy. London: Hogarth Press, 1941. Colonial Cloth Edition (stamped in purple ink). Distributed in Canada by The Macmillan Company of Canada. First Edition. Includes newscuttings, death notice and related newspaper advertising, glued into endpapers by Nuri Mass. Original dust jacket, design by Vanessa Bell. Book artefact now in possession of Mass's daughter, Tess Horwitz.

Virginia Woolf, Metamorphoses, and Flights from Nation

by Jane de Gay

This paper will contribute to the theme of Virginia Woolf and internationalism from the perspective of Woolf's scepticism towards the concepts of nation and nationalism. As her cogent argument in *Three Guineas* demonstrates, Woolf saw the concept of nation as intimately bound up with constructions of gender and power, not least because full participation in the institutions that constituted the national establishment—parliament, the universities, the legal profession, the medical profession, the church—was restricted to males of a certain class. The "nation," then, consisted of a relatively small but powerful interest group who sought to control everyone else. As we know, the solution proposed by Woolf was a flight from the concept of nation: "as a woman, I have no country. As a woman I want no country. As a woman my country is the whole world" (*TG* 125). Nationalist affiliations are clearly rejected in favour of affinities that could be both international and cross-cultural.

Woolf's rejection of "nation" as an ideological construct went alongside a quest for a cultural identity that could breach national boundaries: this quest involved journeying outwards but also backwards into literary, cultural and archaeological pasts where the geography of nations was very different. This dynamic may be seen in the essay "On Not Knowing Greek," where Woolf seeks to forge intimate connections between classical culture and English literature. Woolf starts by acknowledging an acute awareness of the foreignness or otherness of classical literature: "between this foreign people and ourselves there is not only difference of race and tongue but a tremendous breach of tradition" (*CR1* 23), but she moves on to deny cultural differences by asserting a form of essentialism: "the stable, the permanent, the original human being is to be found there" (*CR1* 27). Furthermore, Woolf goes on to bridge the divide by identifying in classical Greek literature the prototype of what later writing would become: "Here we listen to the nightingale whose song echoes through English literature singing in her own Greek tongue" (*CR1* 28). Eliding the countries of England and Greece, Woolf embraces the classics as part of her own cultural past. The nightingale becomes an important point of reference for this idea, as we will see.

While Woolf saw classical Greek culture as a point of origin in this essay from 1925, her later writings betray a desire to drill down even deeper into the past: to ancient Egypt, a culture that preceded the Greek one, which is the subject of a series of allusions in *The Waves*, as David Bradshaw has pointed out, and in *Between the Acts*, as shown by Mitchell Leaska; thence to prehistory and the dinosaurs, which Gillian Beer has identified as a preoccupation in *Between the Acts*. As we will see, Woolf demonstrates that the further we reach into the past, the more untenable the concept of nation becomes.

This paper will demonstrate that the trope of metamorphosis plays a key role in Woolf's rejection of nation, her embracing of transnational cultures, and her archaeological journeying down into the past. I am going to pass over Woolf's most famous metamorphosis, Orlando's sex change, which has been discussed by Theodore Ziolkowski (91-7) and Sarah Annes Brown (201-16). For this paper, I want to concentrate on a set of metamorphoses in which people are transformed into birds, animals, trees and even stones. The trope is found in several of Woolf's writings, but to offer some brief examples, it is seen in the opening sequence of *Mrs. Dalloway*, where Clarissa's neighbour likens her to a jay: "A charming woman, Scrope Purvis thought her...a touch of the bird about her, of the jay, blue-green, light, vivacious...There she perched, never seeing him, waiting to cross, very upright" (*MD* 4). This description becomes more than a simile, because the verb "perched" and Clarissa's upright bearing attribute bird-like qualities to her. In *The Waves* the six characters are in constant flux, transforming into natural phenomena as well as flowing in and out of one another. Bernard in his summing-up remembers his childhood companions as a flock of birds, "that sudden rush of wings, that exclamation, carol and confusion...from among them rise one or two distinct figures, birds who sang with the rapt egotism of youth by the window...Jinny, Susan, Rhoda" (*TW* 206-7). The girls then quickly metamorphose from birds into horses: "they had grown long pigtails and acquired the look of startled foals, which is the mark of adolescence" (*TW* 207). Bernard continues by describing Jinny and Rhoda in equestrian metaphors that are hard to translate into human qualities: "Jinny was the first to come sidling up to the gate to eat sugar...but her ears were laid back as if she might bite. Rhoda was wild—Rhoda one never could catch" (*TW* 207).

Metamorphosis is an apt focus for internationalism because it is cross-cultural, found in legends from the Graeco-Roman and Celtic worlds to parts of North and South America. Metamorphoses can happen for a variety of reasons: escape from danger; compensation, punishment or reward; and even reincarnation—the epitome of a past that adapts and survives into the present. The Latin poet Ovid is an important point of reference for this concept because of his epic poem, *Metamorphoses*, written from around 2-8 CE, but I want to stress that although he popularised the concept, he did not invent it. As E.J. Kenney has noted, Ovid excelled at "invention" which, in classical terms, was "not the faculty of making things up, but that of finding them," and "the resources of material at Ovid's disposal for this undertaking were immense—the whole field of Greek and (what there was of it) Roman myth and legend." Ovid uses metamorphosis to convey an ancient idea, found in the writings of philosophers such as Pythagoras, Heracleitus, Epicurus and Lucretius, that the universe is in a state of flux (Kenney xiii-xv).

Woolf herself took the trope of metamorphosis from a wide range of cultural sources. Metamorphosis was something of a keynote in modernist culture: as Theodore Ziolkowski has argued, "through such thinkers as Bachofen, Burckhardt, Jung and Schuler, theories of transformation and metamorphosis, quite independently of Ovid, made their way into the consciousness of the twentieth century" (78). Alongside the acute awareness of flux in the modernist era, metamorphosis also facilitated the spread and acceptance of the ideas of Darwin and Jung. Pound and Eliot also took up the idea in their work, as is best exemplified by Eliot's inclusion of Tiresias in *The Waste Land*. Against this general background, Woolf also found her own route into this material. In her studies of Latin and Greek with George Warr, Clara Pater, and Janet Case, she would have learned of metamorphoses through a study of Greek myths and through reading Ovid, and we know that she owned two volumes of Ovid's works, inherited from her mother's first husband Herbert Duckworth.[1] Furthermore, she encountered metamorphoses through English literature: she absorbed Ovid's work through sources in the English tradition, for she also owned a copy of his tales as translated by Dryden.[2] Woolf was familiar with the works of Shakespeare (who drew on

Ovid) and also with Milton's *Comus*, where the villain can turn people into animals: amid a series of quotations from *Comus* in *The Voyage Out*, we find the transformation of Rachel Vinrace's doctor into an animalistic man with an "unintelligent, hairy face" (*VO* 393). The following discussion will point to some particular Ovidian traces in Woolf's work, while acknowledging that she derived her metamorphoses from a much wider range of sources.

The first novel I will consider is *Mrs. Dalloway*, which, as we know, is set against the backdrop of the aftermath of World War I, when traditional national power-structures were reasserting themselves—the king and queen are back at the palace and Clarissa is planning her society party—while victims of the war, and the system, like Septimus struggle for survival. Woolf uses metamorphosis to critique the relationship of disenfranchised individuals to an establishment that is rapidly regaining power. She offers the trope as an escape from danger in the scene where Septimus and Rezia Warren-Smith wait for the doctors to come and take him away to a nursing home. As Septimus dreads having his freedom taken from him by the authorities, Rezia recovers a more positive and powerful memory of Septimus, recalling her first impressions of him: how with his "beautiful fresh colour," his "big nose, his bright eyes, his way of sitting a little hunched" he often reminded her of "a young hawk" (*MD* 191). The way this sentence builds follows a particularly Ovidian pattern of transformation, where first attributes accrue, and then the person is pronounced to be an animal or bird. Specifically, it evokes the story of Daedalion's transformation into a hawk:

> And there Apollo, pitying him and ruing his mishap,
> Whenas Daedalion from the cliff himself had headlong flung,
> Transformed him to a bird and on the sudden as he hung
> Did give him wings and bowing beak and hookèd talons keen
> And eke a courage full as fierce as ever it had been....
> And now in shape of goshawk he to none indifferent is....
> (*Metamorphoses* XI: 392–9)

The allusion is fitting: when Rezia first meets Septimus, he is a soldier like the warrior Daedalion. Both characters suffer breakdowns. Daedalion, in grief for the death of his daughter, attempts suicide by leaping from a cliff and is transformed into a bird. It is ironic that Septimus's transformation into a bird is only fleeting, and that no miracle occurs to break his death-plunge. Woolf does not offer metamorphosis as an achieved escape; the sudden return to reality reminds us that real change in the real world would be needed if the likes of Septimus are to be saved from ruin.

Rezia undergoes a series of brief metamorphoses in this scene, too, each one suggesting (but not actually delivering) escape from the situation. First, Septimus sees her mind as a bird:

> he could feel her mind, like a bird, falling from branch to branch, and always alighting, quite rightly; he could follow her mind, as she sat there in one of those loose lax poses that came to her naturally, and if he should say anything, at once she smiled, like a bird alighting with all its claws firm upon the bough. (*MD* 192)

Next, Rezia metamorphoses into a tree, and this time Woolf uses a metaphor rather than a simile: "she was a flowering tree; and through her branches looked out the face of a lawgiver" (*MD* 193). Septimus imagines here that Rezia, as a tree, has the power to protect him from the doctor he sees as such a threat: there are shades here of Daphne, transformed into a laurel tree to escape from the sexual predations of Apollo. A final metamorphosis occurs as Dr. Holmes climbs the stairs and Septimus "could see her, like a little hen, with her wings spread barring his passage" (*MD* 194). This incarnation too sees Rezia as a protector, but now in such a small and fragile form that she cannot stand up to the powers that be. The image of the hen is less grand than the others: it is not an allusion to Ovid (where hens are scarcely mentioned); the frame of reference here is more likely to be folk tradition, in which the hen is a hard-working, often maternal bird (as in the nursery-rhyme "I had a little hen" and the children's story "The Little Red Hen"). This sequence, in its twists and turns, offers a series of images that seek to release Septimus and Rezia from the clutches of authority, suggesting a fundamental freedom of spirit, even though in the material world they both fall victim: Septimus in his suicide and Rezia in her bereavement.

Woolf offers a more powerful challenge to the establishment at the very end of the novel, where Clarissa briefly becomes a mermaid:

> And now Clarissa escorted her Prime Minister down the room, prancing, sparkling, with the stateliness of her grey hair. She wore ear-rings, and a silver-green mermaid's dress. Lolloping on the waves and braiding her tresses she seemed, having that gift still; to be; to exist; to sum it all up in the moment as she passed. (*MD* 227-28)

Here, metamorphosis happens when an analogy suddenly becomes literal: Clarissa's dress is described as being similar in colour to a mermaid, then immediately she is "lolloping on the waves." This image offers great potential for escape from patriarchal configurations, for a mermaid is alluring, but unattainable; it operates as a critique of national pride and power, for Clarissa is not with *the* Prime Minister, simply her Prime Minister. The choice of phrase, of course, conveys the focalizer Peter Walsh's expatriate scepticism for the establishment, but it suggests that here, at least, Clarissa is in control.

These metamorphoses happen against a wider backdrop of a vision of the ancient world in the present. The first is the "ancient song" of the street singer, which assumes the sound of gushing water, as the woman metamorphoses into an underground stream, her mouth eliding in Woolf's elastic syntax into "a mere hole in the earth, muddy too, matted with root fibres and tangled grasses" (*MD* 106). This image invokes a natural world with rich archaeological layers, free from the artificial boundaries of national borders.

This idea becomes clearer in the second image: Septimus's delusion of hearing sparrows singing in Greek, an incident based on an experience of Woolf's own. The sparrows sing that "there is no death" (*MD* 31), recalling classical myths of heroes enjoying an afterlife in Elysium and myths of the reincarnation of heroes as birds, such as the myth of Er, as retold by Plato. These birds are analogous to Woolf's description of Greek choruses as "the undifferenciated voices who sing like birds in the pauses of the wind" (*CR*1 29) in her 1925 essay. Birds therefore function as an echo of the classical world in the present and as a sign that the voices of the nameless, insignificant chorus members (which included women) continue to be heard. Birds are of course capable of crossing national boundaries at will and so here we have the nation and culture of the present interpenetrated by a classical past that speaks of a different culture with different power structures. In both of these important images, Woolf establishes a view of ancient culture as part and parcel of the natural environment: man-made structures of nation or empire give way to the long-established territories of birds and nature.

This pattern of individual metamorphoses set against the backdrop of an ancient past represented by birdsong is repeated in *The Waves*. Birdsong features prominently in the interludes, of course, but the characters also frequently hear birds singing. For example, Rhoda asks, "What song do we hear—the owl's, the nightingale's, the wren's?" (*TW* 191). Of these, the nightingale emerges as a prominent image. Louis hears it frequently and he associates it with political turmoil: "I have yet heard rumours of wars; and the nightingale" (*TW* 77); "Listen…to the nightingale, who sings among the trampling feet; the conquests and migrations" (*TW* 182); "the nightingale who sings among conquests and migrations" (*TW* 236). This bird recalls Philomela of Greek myth, who is turned into a nightingale to escape the wrath of her brother-in-law Tereus, who has raped and maimed her. In the myth, the metamorphoses of Philomela and her sister Procne represent an escape from a background of war, because Procne was married to Tereus in the first place by her father Pandion, King of Athens, to cement an allegiance that would afford his kingdom protection against attacks by the barbarians. Louis's visions speak of a nightingale who sings and survives all shifts in power, "conquests and migrations," and even "rumours of wars" that in Christian terminology are harbingers of the apocalypse and the fall of all kings and kingdoms (Matthew 24: 6). The marginalized female figure survives the nation that has excluded her, to sing through the years.

In *The Waves*, the nightingale is also set within a nexus of allusions that show how this excluded voice continues to sing in English literature, "the nightingale whose song echoes through English literature" that Woolf referred to in "On Not Knowing Greek." This is seen in a sequence where Jinny leaves a party for a sexual encounter with a man she has just met. The hide-and-seek of their erotic adventure is compared with a chase in the forest; Jinny's luring of the man is first described as the flight of a dragon-fly and then as the song of the nightingale, "Jug, jug, jug" (*TW* 146). This refrain (well-known to twentieth-century readers through *The Waste Land*) comes from a tradition of Elizabethan songs. The encounter ends in sexual intercourse, which Jinny hints at in two images of penetration: a reversed image of the hunt, where deer pierce her with their antlers, and the nightingale, who in the Elizabethan lyrics leans its breast against a thorn. Jinny's monologue entwines classical and English cultural references to suggest a versatile, shape-shifting female who remains in control.

Woolf offers the trope of metamorphosis as an escape from the establishment in the figure of Louis, an Australian who feels alienated by British culture. Louis's metamorphosis, firstly into a stalk and then a tree, is a cross-gendered version of the myth of Daphne. His transformation follows the pattern of Ovid's account of Daphne's metamorphosis: "Her hair was turnèd into leaves, her arms in boughs did grow; / Her feet that were erewhile so swift now rooted were as slow" (*Metamorphoses* I: 673-4). The leaves and roots respectively become symbols of Louis's present-day life as a young boy and his past life in ancient Egypt:

I am the stalk. My roots go down to the depths of the world... Up here my eyes are green leaves, unseeing... Down there my eyes are the lidless eyes of a stone figure in a desert by the Nile.... I see camels swaying and men in turbans. I hear tramplings, tremblings, stirrings round me. (*TW* 7)

Here we also have hints at a second metamorphosis, this time into stone. The present, natural landscape of England is pictured as a top layer, intimately connected with a distant past that lies in a different, subterranean country. The journey back to Egypt is significant because it hints at a pre-classical history, and the "tramplings, tremblings, stirrings" Louis hears indicate how all empires and nations are subject to change. Louis repeats his transformation later in the novel, when, feeling acutely aware of being patronized because of his colonial background, he becomes a tree to escape the overbearing authority of his headmaster. In this metamorphosis of escape, Louis discovers that his "roots... wrap themselves around some hardness at the centre. I recover my continuity" (*TW* 26). This continuity with the ancient past goes beyond the limits of the British Empire (past the commercial exploitation of Egypt described by David Bradshaw), and indeed reminds us that all empires fall.

The pattern we have seen in *Mrs. Dalloway* and *The Waves* is repeated in *Between the Acts*. The theme of metamorphosis is established in the opening sequence where transformation hangs around the incipient love-triangle between Isa Oliver and Mr. and Mrs. Haines. The latter is described as a "goosefaced woman with eyes protruding as if they saw something to gobble in the gutter" (*BTA* 3). Isa and Mr. Haines, on the other hand, become swans. Isa enters the room "like a swan swimming its way" (*BTA* 4). Isa's bird-like qualities emphasize her detachment from her kinsfolk: she is late for the gathering; she seems surprised to find people there at all; and she is introduced by the distancing epithet of Bart's son's wife. The image soon develops into a dream of flight from this community altogether, as in her imagination she and Haynes float "like two swans down stream. But his snow-white breast was circled with a tangle of dirty duckweed; and she too, in her webbed feet was entangled, by her husband the stockbroker" (*BTA* 5). Here, Woolf rewrites the story of the seduction of Leda by Jupiter, who is disguised as a swan: by offering *two* swans, she suggests that both Isa and Mr. Haines have a part to play in a potential affair. Unlike Leda (and like Clarissa and Jinny), Isa has a measure of sexual power, although the mention of entanglement shows that it is impossible fully to escape from society's conventions and expectations.

As a backdrop to this situation, Woolf questions nation by establishing a picture of a landscape in flux, as Bart Oliver gives Mrs. Haines a lecture on the local topology: "From an aeroplane, he said, you could still see, plainly marked, the scars made by the Britons; by the Romans; by the Elizabethan manor house; and by the plough, when they ploughed the hill to grow wheat in the Napoleonic wars" (*BTA* 3-4). The change in landscape is created by changes in political power: Great Britain is not a fixed political unit, but it is a territory once ruled by the Britons, then the Romans, and then in Napoleonic times faced the prospect of being invaded by the French. At the time when the novel was written and set, Great Britain was threatened with invasion by Germany. The shifting nature of political power becomes a theme of Miss La Trobe's pageant, seen in the villagers' song: "Palaces tumble down... Babylon, Ninevah, Troy... And Caesar's great house... all fallen they lie" (*BTA* 125).

This sequence, towards the end of Woolf's last novel, echoes Ovid's reflection, towards the end of *Metamorphoses*, that all nations are subject to flux. He recounts the fall of various powers (like Woolf, he includes Troy, but adds Sparta and Thebes), and infers that Rome, too, could succumb to change: "So we see all things changeable. One nation gathereth strength; / Another waxeth weak; and both do make exchange at length" (*Metamorphoses* XV: 463-64). In Woolf, as in Ovid, nations are clearly subject to metamorphosis.

Bart's view of topography provides a more archaeologically sound version of Woolf's imaginative perception of the coexistence of past and present in *Mrs. Dalloway*, or her vision of a subterranean past in *The Waves*. The idea is developed by Lucy Swithin's reading of H.G. Wells' *Outline of History* and her vision of a prehistoric age when London was a forest, the earth was inhabited by dinosaurs and the British Isles did not exist because they were physically attached to the European landmass. Lucy's archaeological vision embraces evolution by recognizing human descent from the earlier earth creatures: "the iguanodon, the mammoth, and the mastodon; from whom presumably...we descend" (*BTA* 8).

As in *Mrs. Dalloway* and *The Waves*, birds and birdsong form part of the backdrop to *Between the Acts*, pointing to a continuation of the past in the present and a re-envisioning of territory. This, too, is established in the opening sequence where the company in the drawing-room hear birdsong, which Mrs. Haines thinks is that of a nightingale. Although she is corrected by the others—nightingales do not come so far north—nonetheless, here we have a significant, if gratuitous mention of the bird that Woolf associated with the continuity of classical literature. As if to demonstrate how the Greek nightingale has its echoes throughout English literature, Woolf weaves quotations into the novel from two English poems which involve this bird: Keats's "Ode to a Nightingale" and Swinburne's "Itylus," the latter poem being a retelling of the story of Procne and Philomela.

The myth of Procne and Philomela becomes part of the fabric of *Between the Acts* because alongside the nightingale, the novel is dominated by swallows which fly about the barn. Lucy comments on the swallows several times. For her, they represent continuity: she remarks that "the same birds" come every year (*BTA* 91). Mrs. Manresa is tempted to correct her by pointing out that these would not be the same birds, but the pedantry of this thought lends greater weight to Lucy's remark. Swallows are an integral part of Lucy's vision of prehistory, for she imagines that they have flown here from Africa "when the Barn was a swamp" (*BTA* 93), "before there was a channel, when the earth...was a riot of rhododendrons, and humming birds" (*BTA* 98). Lucy's affinity with swallows leads to her own metamorphosis where she becomes a swallow, for we see her "perched on the edge of a chair like a bird on a telegraph wire before starting for Africa" (*BTA* 105). Lucy's metamorphosis into a swallow chimes with her brother's recitation and modulation of Swinburne's Itylus: "What's the use, what's the use...O sister swallow, O sister swallow, of singing your song?" (*BTA* 104). In this image, Lucy briefly takes flight from the confines of her family and her nation.

National boundaries mean nothing to birds; they represent continuity with a time before Great Britain existed, and long before the British Empire. Birds were there before human habitation, and before all the regimes that have come and gone—and they will remain after these have passed. As the villagers sing: "Where the plover nests was the arch... through which the Romans trod" (*BTA* 125). Procne's voice, then, survives alongside that of Philomela, rising above oppression and outliving the nation that sought to subjugate them both.

These examples all bear out Woolf's idea that "as a woman, I have no country...my country is the whole world." Female characters—and male characters marginalized by disability, such as Septimus, and colonial status, such as Louis—though excluded from the power-structures that constitute the nation, are able to transcend such structures, albeit briefly, by becoming plants, stones, animals or birds. Furthermore, the whole natural world is imbued with ancient culture: the land is a cipher for a wide-ranging cultural past, the sedimentation of years of culture too wide-ranging to be captured by any particular regime. The three novels we have looked at explore this quite differently: *Mrs. Dalloway* critiques the establishment and *The Waves*, a novel imbued with critique of colonialism, as Jane Marcus has shown, points us beyond the British Empire and indeed speaks of the mutability of all empires. *Between the Acts* is more troubled, for it is set in a community living under the shadow of invasion: here, the sedimentary layers show that, while political powers come and go, traces of a wider and deeper culture remain as integral parts of the natural world.

Notes

1. Ovid. P. *Ovidi Nasonis Tristivm liber secondvs*. Ed. and Trans. S. G. Owen. Oxford: Clarendon Press, 1924. Ovid, P. *Ovidii Nasonis Opera: Ad fidem editionis Burmannianae expressa*. London: Rodwell and Martin, 1815. 3 vols. Vol. 1 only. Herbert Duckworth—signer, bookplate (King and Miletic-Vejzovic).
2. Dryden, John. *Fables Ancient and Modern: Translated into Verse from Homer, Ovid, Boccace, and Chaucer, with Original Poems*. London: J. Tonson, 1721 (King and Miletic-Vejzovic).

Works Cited

Beer, Gillian. "Virginia Woolf and Pre-History." *Virginia Woolf: The Common Ground*. Edinburgh: Edinburgh University Press, 1996. 6–28.

Bradshaw, David. "Beneath *The Waves*." Unpublished Conference Paper. 14th Annual International Conference on Virginia Woolf. University of London, June 2004.

Brown, Sarah Annes. *The Metamorphosis of Ovid: From Chaucer to Ted Hughes*. London: Duckworth, 1999.

Kenney, E.J. "Introduction." Ovid. *Metamorphoses*. Trans. A. D. Melville. Oxford: Oxford UniversityPress, 1986.

King, Julia, and Laila Miletic-Vejzovic, eds. *The Library of Leonard and Virginia Woolf: A Short-Title Catalog*. Pullman: Washington State University Press. May 2007 <http://www.wsulibs.wsu.edu/holland/masc/OnlineBooks/woolflibrary/woolflibraryonline.htm>.

Leaska, Mitchell A., ed. *Pointz Hall: The Earlier and Later Typescripts of Between the Acts*. New York: University Publications, 1983.

Marcus, Jane. "Britannia Rules *The Waves*?" *Decolonizing Tradition: New Views of Twentieth-Century "British" Literary Canons*. Ed. Karen Lawrence. Urbana: University of Illinois Press, 1992. 136-62.

Ovid. *Metamorphosis*. Trans. Arthur Golding. Ed. Madeleine Forey. 1565-67. London: Penguin, 2002.

Woolf, Virginia. *The Voyage Out*. Ed. Lorna Sage. 1915. Oxford: Oxford University Press, 1992.

—. *Mrs. Dalloway*. Ed. Claire Tomalin. 1925. Oxford: Oxford University Press, 1992.

—. *The Common Reader, First Series*. Ed. and intro. Andrew McNeillie. 1925. Orlando FL: Harcourt, Brace, 1984.

—. *The Waves*. Ed. Gillian Beer. 1931. Oxford: Oxford University Press, 1992.

—. *Three Guineas*. Intro. Hermione Lee. 1938. London: Hogarth Press, 1986.

—. *Between the Acts*. Ed. Frank Kermode. 1941. Oxford: Oxford University Press, 1992.

Ziolkowski, Theodore. *Ovid and the Moderns*. Ithaca: Cornell University Press, 2005.

Notes on Contributors

Natasha Allen is a graduate student at Miami University of Oxford, specializing in Black feminist and queer theories and literatures. She is currently completing her MA. This essay reflects her interests in resistance and dissident identities in literature.

Judith Allen is associated with the Kelly Writers House at the University of Pennsylvania and has published articles on Virginia Woolf, Michel de Montaigne, and James Joyce. Her book on Virginia Woolf and politics will be published by Edinburgh University Press in 2009.

Charles Andrews is Assistant Professor of English at Whitworth University. His current project is *Modernism's National Scriptures*, which examines the interaction between nationalism and religion in novels by Joyce, Lawrence, Woolf, and Wyndham Lewis.

Mónica Ayuso is Associate Professor of English at California State University, Bakersfield. She has published several essays on Woolf, including "The Unlike[ly]Other: Borges and Woolf," in *Woolf Studies Annual* (10); "Thinking Back Through Our Mothers: Virginia Woolf in the Spanish-American Female Imagination," in *Virginia Woolf and Communities: Selected Papers from the 8th Annual Conference on Virginia Woolf*; and "Virginia Woolf in Mexico and Puerto Rico," in *Woolf Studies Annual* (14).

Suzanne Bellamy is an Australian artist and writer, working in text/image fusions and exhibiting internationally. She is currently also doing a PhD in Australian Studies at the University of Sydney on the rediscovered Woolf artifact, the 1942 thesis by Nuri Mass, a lost piece of Woolf scholarship and early Australian modernism.

Xiaoqin Cao has taught in the Foreign Languages Department, North China Institute of Technology. Having been awarded an MPhil in European Modernisms at the University of Birmingham, UK in 2006, she is currently doing independent research on Virginia Woolf and China. A member of the International Virginia Woolf Society, she has a bilingual website on Virginia Woolf (http://globe.eworkway.com).

Kimberly Engdahl Coates is Assistant Professor of Literature at Bowling Green State University in Bowling Green, Ohio. She is currently working on a comparative study of contemporary feminists' responses to our current wars and the work of British and American women who were writing between World War I and World War II.

Lisa L. Coleman is Professor of English and Honors Program Director at Southeastern Oklahoma State University. She co-edited a special double issue of the online journal, *Enculturation*, entitled "Rhetoric/Composition: Intersections/Impasses/Differends" (2003-2004) and is currently developing a manuscript entitled *Woolf, Writing, and an Ethics of Desire*. Her co-edited monograph on diversity in honors education, *Setting the Table for Diversity*, is forthcoming (2008) from the National Collegiate Honors Council.

Jane de Gay is Senior Lecturer in English and Director of MA Programmes in Humanities at Leeds Trinity and All Saints, UK. She is the author of *Virginia Woolf's Novels and* *the Literary Past* (Edinburgh University Press, 2006) and, with Marion Dell, she is rescuer and guest-editor of *Voyages Out/Voyages Home: Selected Papers from the Eleventh Annual International Conference on Virginia Woolf.* She has been invited to deliver the Virginia Woolf Birthday Lecture in London in 2009.

Erica Delsandro is a PhD candidate in English Literature at Washington University in St. Louis where she studies 20th-century British literature; her interests include modernism, the interwar novel, women, gender and sexuality studies, and Virginia Woolf. Her current project focuses on the interwar novel.

Madelyn Detloff is Associate Professor of English and Women's Studies at Miami University, Oxford, OH. Her book, *The Persistence of Modernism: Loss and Mourning in the Twentieth Century*, is forthcoming from Cambridge University Press. She has published articles on Woolf in *Women's Studies, Approaches to Teaching Woolf's* Mrs. Dalloway, and *Modernism and Mourning*. She is currently Vice President of the International Virginia Woolf Society.

Sara Gerend is an Assistant Professor of English at Purdue University North Central. Her teaching and research interests include twentieth-century British and Anglophone literature, British and American modernism, and gender studies. She is currently working on a book project, *Spectral Modernity: Ghosts of Empire in the Early Twentieth Century*, involving a study of the figure of the ghost in British and American modernist fiction.

Diane F. Gillespie, Professor Emerita of English at Washington State University, is author of *The Sisters' Arts: The Writing and Painting of Virginia Woolf and Vanessa Bell* and of numerous book chapters and articles. She is editor of Woolf's *Roger Fry: A Biography* and of *The Multiple Muses of Virginia Woolf* as well as co-editor of Julia Stephen's writings, *Virginia Woolf and the Arts*, and Cicely Hamilton's *Diana of Dobson's*.

Patricia Laurence teaches in the City University of New York and is critic, reviewer, oral historian and writer. She is the author of *The Reading of Silence: Virginia Woolf in the English Tradition*, and the Chinese translation of her book, *Lily Briscoe's Chinese Eyes: Bloomsbury, Modernism and China*, will be published by the Shanghai Bookstore Publishing House in May. She is presently working on contemporary Chinese women writers and a critical biography of Elizabeth Bowen.

Benjamin O'Dell is a Master's Student at Miami University. He has recently presented papers at the Louisville Conference on Literature and Culture Since 1900, and regional graduate conferences. His research interests include gender studies and performative identities in nineteenth century literature. This is his second published work.

Andrea Reyes, Ph.D., is currently a Visiting Professor at Scripps College in Claremont, CA. Her dissertation is a study of the central themes in the essays of the Mexican writer, Rosario Castellanos. She edited a collection of previously uncollected essays by Castellanos, the third and final volume of which was published in December of 2007.

Notes on Contributors

Diana Royer is Professor and Coordinator of English on Miami University's Hamilton Campus. She is co-author (with Carl Royer) of *The Spectacle of Isolation in Horror Films: Dark Parades* (Haworth 2005) and author of *A Critical Study of the Works of Nawal El Saadawi, Egyptian Author and Activist* (Edwin Mellen 2001).

Tracy Savoie is currently a Master's student in English Literature at Miami University, Oxford, Ohio. Her research interests include modernism, cosmopolitanism, and postcolonial theory.

Marilyn Schwinn Smith is an Associate with Five Colleges, Inc. in Amherst, MA. As an independent scholar, she has presented and published internationally in the fields of British and Russian Modernism, and ethnic diasporic festivals. Her current projects include a book-length study of Jane Ellen Harrison and Russia, and a cross-disciplinary symposium on the theatre of Isaac Babel.

Julie Smith-Hubbard, Assistant Professor of English at Cardinal Stritch University, has recently published an article on Virginia Woolf and is presently teaching Woolf's fiction. She is currently working on a book entitled *Spots of Time*.

Elisa Kay Sparks, Associate Professor of English and Director of Women's Studies at Clemson University in South Carolina, has published articles about Woolf's connections to gardens and garden history, to the visual arts, and to the American painter, Georgia O'Keeffe—topics she also explores in the visual medium of printmaking. She co-edited the *Selected Papers* from the 2005 International Woolf Conference at Lewis and Clark College with Helen Southworth.

Diana L. Swanson is Associate Professor of English and Women's Studies at Northern Illinois University. She has published numerous essays on Woolf, including an essay on "Lesbian Approaches," in *The Palgrave Companion to Woolf Studies*; "Safe Space or Danger Zone? Incest and the Paradox of Writing in Woolf's Life," in *Creating Safe Space: Violence and Women's Writing*; and "'My Boldness Terrifies Me': Sexual Abuse and Female Subjectivity in *The Voyage Out*," in *Twentieth Century Literature*.

Erika Yoshida teaches English at the Tokyo University of Science and Nippon Institute of Technology. She is currently completing her PhD. Her research interests focus on Woolf's essays in their contexts, such as publication, her lectures, and audiences. Her article, "Virginia Woolf's 'Craftsmanship' in Context: The BBC, the Mass Audience and Woolf" appeared in *English Literature* at Waseda University in 2007.

Richard Zumkhawala-Cook is an Associate Professor of English at Shippensburg University, where he teaches British literature and postcolonial studies. His book, *Scottish Culture and National Identity*, will be forthcoming in 2009.

www.ingramcontent.com/pod-product-compliance
Lightning Source LLC
Chambersburg PA
CBHW031458160426
43195CB00010BB/1021